In Defense of Politic

Politicians are reviled. From jokes on late-night TV talk shows to radio show rants, and from public opinion polls to ubiquitous conventional wisdom—politicians are among the most despised professional class in modern society. Drawing on seminal work in political science, Stephen K. Medvic convincingly argues to the masses that this blanket condemnation of politicians is both unfair and unwarranted. While some individual politicians certainly deserve scorn for misjudgments, moral failings, or even criminal acts, the assumption that all of them should be cast in a similar light is unjustified. More importantly, that deeply cynical assumption is dangerous to the legitimacy of a democratic system of government. Politicians, as a class, deserve respect, not out of blind obedience to authority but because democratic deliberation requires it.

Medvic explains how cognitive biases in the way people reason often lead us to draw unjustified conclusions of politicians in general based on the malfeasance of some. Scandals involving politicians are likely to be remembered and to serve as "evidence" of the belief that "they all do it." Most politicians, in fact, care deeply about their cities, states, and nation. But they face a trap of unrealistic and contradictory expectations from the public about how politicians should behave. Medvic, in turn, demonstrates the necessity of ambition, the utility of politics for resolving conflicts peacefully, and the value of ideology in framing political choices. In the end, citizens must learn to tolerate the inherent messiness of politics as the only viable alternative to violent conflict. In the process, we must embrace our role in the political system as well.

Stephen K. Medvic is Associate Professor of Government at Franklin & Marshall College in Lancaster, Pennsylvania.

Controversies in Electoral Democracy and Representation

Matthew J. Streb, Series Editor

The Routledge series *Controversies in Electoral Democracy and Representation* presents cutting edge scholarship and innovative thinking on a broad range of issues relating to democratic practice and theory. An electoral democracy, to be effective, must show a strong relationship between representation and a fair open election process. Designed to foster debate and challenge assumptions about how elections and democratic representation *should* work, titles in the series present a strong but fair argument on topics related to elections, voting behavior, party and media involvement, representation, and democratic theory.

Titles in the series:

In Defense of Politicians

The Expectations Trap and Its Threat to Democracy

Stephen K. Medvic

Routledge
Taylor & Francis Group

NEW YORK AND LONDON

First published 2013
by Routledge
711 Third Avenue, New York, NY 10017

Simultaneously published in the UK
by Routledge
2 Park Square, Milton Park, Abingdon, Oxon OX14 4RN

*Routledge is an imprint of the Taylor & Francis Group, an
informa business*

© 2013 Taylor & Francis

Library of Congress Cataloging in Publication Data
Medvic, Stephen K.
In defense of politicians : the expectations trap and its threat
to democracy / Stephen K. Medvic.
    pages cm. — (Controversies in electoral democracy and
representation)
1. Reputation—United States. 2. Politicians—United States.
  3. Political corruption—United States. I. Title.
HM1236.M44 2012
364.1'323—dc23

                                                      2012026312

ISBN: 978-0-415-88044-2 (hbk)
ISBN: 978-0-415-88045-9 (pbk)
ISBN: 978-0-203-84972-9 (ebk)

Typeset in Goudy
by RefineCatch Limited, Bungay, Suffolk

Printed and bound in the United States of America
by Edwards Brothers, Inc.

Contents

Much of the strength & efficiency of any Government in procuring and securing happiness to the people, depends, on opinion, on the general opinion of the goodness of the Government, as well as of the wisdom and integrity of its Governors.

Benjamin Franklin, to the Constitutional Convention,
September 17, 1787

Politics means slow, strong drilling through hard boards, with a combination of passion and a sense of judgement. It is of course entirely correct, and a fact confirmed by all historical experience, that what is possible would never have been achieved if, in this world, people had not repeatedly reached for the impossible. But the person who can do this must be a leader; not only that, he must, in a very simple sense of the word, be a hero. And even those who are neither of these things must, even now, put on the armour of that steadfastness of heart which can withstand even the defeat of all hopes, for otherwise they will not even be capable of achieving what is possible today. Only someone who is certain that he will not be broken when the world, seen from his point of view, is too stupid or too base for what he wants to offer it, and who is certain that he will be able to say "Nevertheless" in spite of everything – only someone like this has a "vocation" for politics.

Max Weber, "The Profession and Vocation of Politics," 1919

Preface

A television commercial convinced me to write this book. A Sprint Nextel ad, called "What If Firefighters Ran the World?" begins with a seasoned fireman banging a gavel and speaking to an assembly of his colleagues through a cell phone using the company's Direct Connect service.[1] "How 'bout the budget?" he asks. "Balance it!" the parliament of firefighters responds in unison. The assembly proceeds to unanimously decide that the tax code should be kept to "one page or less" and that we should have "better roads." After flipping through a stack of pages, presumably an environmental bill, the speaker of this House of Firefighters says, dismissively, "A lot of paper to tell us we need clean water. Need clean water, guys?" To which the firefighters respond, "Aye!" Looking at his colleagues, the leader of the assembly concludes, "This is the easiest job I've ever had."

Though I can appreciate the humor in the ad, it is only a slight exaggeration to say that I hate it. But I imagine millions of television viewers nodding their heads and knowingly smiling as they watch the ad. Indeed, it plays on a sentiment that runs deep in American political culture—namely, that politicians are pathetic, if not despicable, creatures who waste time and money, talk too much and deliver too little, bicker over trivial matters for partisan reasons, and fail to solve problems that should be easily solved.

But the problems of a nation of over 300 million people cannot be easily solved. In a free society, interests clash and politics is the site of the battle. It is the job of politicians to both represent a given set of interests and find ways to resolve conflict. That cannot be done by waving a magic wand (or using a push-to-talk cell phone).

This book is an attempt to help Americans atone for the sin of what the writer Thomas Mallon has referred to as "democratic pride." In explaining the lack of a great novel about Washington, D.C., Mallon noted, "A serious novelist must take his characters seriously, regard them as three-dimensional creatures with inner lives and authentic moral crises; and that's just what, out of a certain democratic pride, Americans refuse to do with their politicians."[2] Democracy, apparently, creates a political superiority complex in the people. Something about either this form of government, or the unique history and political culture of the United States, encourages citizens to think that they are better than politicians. But to do so, as Mallon suggests, they have to treat politicians as cardboard cutouts rather than real human beings.

In his final statement to the House of Commons, on June 27, 2007, British Prime Minister Tony Blair defended politics and those who make it their profession. "Some may belittle politics," acknowledged the Prime Minister as he said his farewell, "but we who are engaged in it know that it is where people stand tall. Although I know that it has many harsh contentions, it is still the arena that sets the heart beating a little faster. If it is, on occasions, the place of low skullduggery, it is more often the place for the pursuit of noble causes."[3] Imagine—politics as an arena where noble causes are not just occasionally pursued, but are pursued *more often* than is low skullduggery. I dare say most Americans (not to mention Brits) cannot imagine it.

One might reasonably ask, what else would we expect Blair to say about the field to which he devoted most of his adult life? Flattering comments about one's chosen profession may sound self-serving, but that does not make them any less accurate. Indeed, I wrote this book because I believe that what former Prime Minister Blair said in his farewell statement is as true about American politics as he says it is of politics in Britain. Politics is a noble affair and those who make it their vocation ought to be afforded more respect than they get.

Bernard Crick's *In Defense of Politics*, to which the title of the present book is an obvious homage, confirmed this belief when I first read it many years ago.[4] It is a brilliant argument about the value of politics as a process for reconciling a plurality of competing interests without coercion. Indeed, for Crick, no other way of managing society protects freedom as well as politics. The argument is every bit as relevant today, and in some ways more relevant, than when it was first published half a century ago. It is a book that should be read by every citizen.

My (limited) experiences in practical politics have also influenced my view of politicians. While in college, I was asked to manage— unsuccessfully, as it turned out—a campaign for the Texas state legislature. In graduate school in Indiana, I managed another (unsuccessful) campaign for the state legislature and also worked for a marvelous public servant in the Mayor's Office in West Lafayette. Those opportunities taught me that politicians of all stripes care deeply about their cities and states and our nation. The countless politicians I have met in my time as a political scientist have further validated this conclusion.

Most are like Maggie Lauterer, a candidate brilliantly profiled in a PBS documentary from the mid 1990s called "Vote For Me."[5] Lauterer's journey from a formerly beloved local television reporter to a congressional candidate despised by about half the electorate is revealing. She began the campaign with universal goodwill and was well liked and trusted. But as she took positions on controversial issues, and as the partisan rhetoric heated up, she was transformed into a caricature; she was "just another politician" saying whatever it takes to get elected. In truth, she was the same Maggie Lauterer whom television viewers had adored when she was reporting human-interest stories.

All politicians face a similar transformation. And they face unrealistic expectations for how they are to behave on the campaign trail and in office. I consider this a trap set by the public and I'll discuss it throughout the book. Undoubtedly, some politicians are questionable characters and would be so whether or not they entered politics. But I firmly believe that most are decent, honest people who commit themselves to public life (at great personal sacrifice—far greater than most of us give them credit for) in order to improve the lives of those they represent. This belief, perhaps thought to be naive by many readers, is what motivates the argument in this book.

It may seem an odd time to defend politicians. A host of political scandals erupted, or were in full swing, while I wrote this book. Some were of a personal nature; others were the result of improper public behavior. Even the normal course of politics has often appeared scandalous in recent years. How else to describe the showdown—and near meltdown—over the nation's debt ceiling in the summer of 2011?

I would describe it, without hyperbole, as the democratic process at work. It was frustrating, no doubt, but that is a consequence of the way disparate viewpoints get expressed, and different interests protected, in a democracy. What we often take to be the product of absurd behavior on the part of politicians is more often than not the result of a very complex, and in certain ways contradictory, system of government that produces a particular kind of politics.

As for the actual scandals, they are certainly lamentable. But the politicians entangled in them are the exception, not the rule. As I will try to make clear later in this book, politicians are no worse, on the whole, than the population at large. There may even be reason to believe that they are better in certain respects.

Ultimately, the argument of this book is that a general dislike and distrust of all politicians creates a deep cynicism in the American public. That cynicism, in turn, is a threat to democracy because it can undermine the legitimacy of our government. The antidote to this poison is a more realistic understanding of politics, more reasonable expectations for politicians, and a citizenry more active in both politics and governing. My hope for the book is that it will encourage its readers to rethink their attitudes toward politics and politicians and, in so doing, that it might begin to help rebuild trust in our government and elected officials.

I am extremely fortunate to teach at an institution—Franklin & Marshall College—with a long history of encouraging students to enter public service. I suppose we could hardly do otherwise given our namesakes (Ben and John, as we like to call them). But the faculty of the Government Department at F&M, from the founding members of the modern department—Sidney Wise, John Vanderzell, and Richard Schier—through Stanley Michalak and the current members of the department, have taken practical politics and civic engagement seriously and it shows in the countless alumni who have entered politics, government, law, and related fields. Among my colleagues, Joe Karlesky patiently provided me with a perspective that served as a valuable check on my own views as I developed them for the book. G. Terry Madonna and Berwood Yost, who run one of the best polls in the United States—the Franklin & Marshall College Poll—generously added several of my questions to their surveys. And a special word of thanks is due to Bob Friedrich and Matt Schousen. Both have obligingly listened to my argument for years and both have contributed significantly to my thinking about this and many other subjects. They are not only great colleagues; they are dear friends.

Other friends and colleagues have also been tremendously helpful to me in writing this book. John Campbell, professor of psychology at F&M, convinced me early in the project that the "fundamental attribution error" was relevant to understanding Americans' attitudes about politicians. Dale Miller, chair of the Department of Philosophy and Religious Studies at Old Dominion University, was a trusted sounding board for many of the ideas in this book. His wise, and gentle, criticism is always an invaluable benefit to me and I am exceedingly grateful for his willingness to help.

At Routledge, Michael Kerns has been supportive and encouraging from the moment I proposed the idea for this book. His patience, as I missed deadline after deadline, made life considerably less stressful and his editorial insights have made the book better than it would otherwise have been. Emma Håkonsen, the book's production editor, and Gail Welsh, its copy-editor, were efficient and effective and were a delight to work with. Thanks also to Kate Legon, who compiled the index. Matt Streb has assembled a wonderful collection of books as series editor for *Controversies in Electoral Democracy and Representation*. I am thankful for his willingness to include mine on that impressive list.

As always, my largest debt of gratitude is owed to my family for their love and support. My wife, Laura, makes it possible for me to find time in our busy schedules to write and I cannot express how much I cherish her and appreciate all she does. My kids, Colin and Abigail, and my stepsons, George and Ross, kindly tolerate all the time I spend secluded in my office. They are wonderful children and my greatest source of pride.

S.K.M.
Lancaster, PA
June 2012

Chapter 1

The Problem

What are we to make of the following, rather obscure, anecdote from the life of Abraham Lincoln? In 1854, a Whig Party activist loyal to Lincoln placed a declaration of the budding politician's candidacy for state legislature in the local newspaper. However, Lincoln did not want to run for the legislature because he had his eye on a U.S. Senate seat and sitting legislators could not, under Illinois law, be considered by the legislature for a Senate seat. Lincoln was extremely unhappy about this public declaration of his candidacy. One observer described him as "the saddest man I Ever Saw—the gloomiest: he walked up and down . . . almost crying."[1] But he now faced a choice. He could either bow out of the state legislative race and appear disloyal to his party (which he would need if he were to have a shot at becoming a U.S. senator) or he could run for the legislature knowing full well that he would not take office if he won. Can we guess which option "Honest Abe" chose? Perhaps surprisingly, he chose the latter course and refused to take his seat after the election. Doing so, according to Lincoln biographer Richard Carwardine, was "an action which appeared to put self before cause and did his reputation some harm amongst radical antislavery men."[2]

The moral of the story might be that even our greatest political heroes are human beings who were forced at various points in their careers to make difficult decisions and who sometimes behaved in less than admirable ways. Or we could conclude that behind every great statesman is a great politician. Indeed, as Chester Maxey noted of Lincoln in his 1948 essay "A Plea for the Politician":

> Lincoln is all statesman now; it is almost a sacrilege to suggest the contrary. The scheming, contriving, manipulating frontier politician who outsmarted the best of them has faded into oblivion, and

we have instead an alabaster saint who never could have done what Lincoln did because he would not have played politics with Lincoln's calculating cleverness.[3]

I suspect, however, that what most Americans will take from such a story is that all politicians are the same, whether we build monuments to them or not. They are opportunistic and overly ambitious. And, in the end, all politicians are in it only for themselves.

This book seeks to understand why Americans dislike politicians so intensely—and argues that they're wrong to do so. Ultimately, no form of democracy can function without trust in others. In a direct democracy, the populace would have to trust their fellow citizens to be informed enough to contribute meaningfully to a collective consideration of public policy and to balance their own interests against the public interest. But in a representative democracy, citizens must trust politicians to not only represent their constituents' interests, but to do what they think is best for their districts, their states, and the nation. Unfortunately, as we'll soon see, Americans have very little trust in politicians, and a great deal of disdain for them.

This chapter establishes the problem to be addressed in the book, namely, the widespread anti-politician sentiment that exists in the United States today. I begin by exploring the ample evidence of the public's contempt for politicians. I then examine a set of contradictory expectations we hold of our politicians—or what I'll call the "expectations trap"—that will help structure the rest of the book. Finally, I introduce the argument that our disregard for politicians is not only unfair, but has the potential to damage our democracy.

The Evidence

The claim that Americans dislike politicians seems self-evident and, as such, hardly needs empirical evidence to confirm it. Nevertheless, the evidence is abundant; and it is instructive. For instance, Gallup has asked about the honesty and ethical standards of those in different occupations since 1976. In 2007, Gallup asked respondents about 22 professions. Nurses ranked first, with 83 percent of the respondents saying that their honesty and ethical standards were "very high" or "high." State office holders and Members of Congress, however, ranked near the bottom of the list, with only 12 and 9 percent, respectively, saying that they had very high or high levels of honesty and ethical standards. Only advertising practitioners (6 percent), car salesmen (5 percent), and lobbyists (5 percent) ranked lower.[4]

On a fairly regular basis since 1958, the American National Election Study has asked respondents whether quite a few, not very many, or hardly any of those running the government are "crooked." In 2008, more people than ever (53.9 percent) believed that quite a few government officials were crooked and fewer than ever (6.7 percent) thought hardly any were.[5] These numbers are similar to the results Gallup found in January 2008 when that organization asked the same question. However, in addition to the 52 percent of Gallup respondents who said quite a few of those running government are crooked, another 5 percent volunteered (that is, without being offered such a choice) that *all* of them are crooked.[6] Figure 1.1 shows the trends over time in the NES survey. Obviously, the number of people who believe that government is being run, in large measure, by crooks has increased dramatically over the last 50 years.

John Hibbing and Elizabeth Theiss-Morse have studied the public's attitudes toward American political institutions more than any other

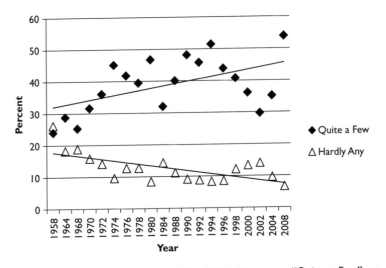

Figure 1.1 Percent of Respondents Who Think There are "Quite a Few" or "Hardly Any" Crooks Running the Government, 1958–2008.

Source: American National Election Study 1948–2004 – Cumulative and American National Election Study 2008; Survey Documentation and Analysis, University of California, Berkeley, http://sda.berkeley.edu/archive.htm (accessed July 25, 2010).

political scientists. In the mid 1990s, they conducted a series of surveys and focus groups to probe people's perceptions of various aspects of the political system. "Focus-group participants," according to Hibbing and Theiss-Morse, "were obviously highly dissatisfied with politicians in general and quickly drew upon their 'politician' stereotype—politicians are dishonest and self-centered."[7] Some participants considered all politicians liars and many believed that politicians live by a double standard; while they make laws for the rest of us, they act as though they are above the law.

In a subsequent study, Hibbing and Theiss-Morse found that Americans are highly distrustful of politicians and find them "fractious and greedy."[8] At the same time, the public found elected officials to be more intelligent and far more informed than ordinary Americans. In fact, when Hibbing and Theiss-Morse scratched the surface of survey results by conducting additional focus groups, they found the participants to "believe that [ordinary] people aren't very bright, they don't care, they are lazy, they are selfish, they want to be left alone, and they don't want to be informed."[9] The disdain for politicians is so great, however, that despite the public's unflattering view of itself, people would prefer "to shift power from institutions and elected officials toward ordinary Americans."[10]

Of course, many people can point to particular politicians they are fond of and even admire. It has long been recognized, for example, that Americans tend to like their own member of Congress but dislike the rest of Congress. Far from challenging the claim that people hate politicians, this fact bolsters it. As Hibbing and Theiss-Morse have shown, when people think about Congress, they think of the *members* of Congress and not an abstract institution.[11] Since members of Congress are politicians, people consistently give "Congress" low marks. The fact that people may like their own member more then the rest of them means only that they are able to view their own representative as an actual person.[12] In general, however, people treat politicians as caricatures.

Less quantifiable than public opinion, but every bit as damning, is the evidence from popular culture. Anti-politician sentiment is ubiquitous on late-night television talk shows like *The Tonight Show with Jay Leno* or *The Late Show with David Letterman*, satirical news programs such as *The Daily Show with Jon Stewart* and *The Colbert Report*, and sketch comedy shows like *Saturday Night Live*. Politicians regularly serve as fodder for comics, who exploit their foibles for audiences that seem never to tire of what is essentially the same routine night after night—a politician says or does something foolish and the comedian is there with a clever punchline to expose the stupidity. Though the jokes may be targeted at individual politicians, the steady drumbeat of ridicule marks them all as ignorant, hypocritical, manipulative, and/or dishonest.

Indeed, scholars have shown that the topical comedy of late-night shows generates negative attitudes about politicians, not to mention the political system generally. Political scientists Jody Baumgartner and Jonathan Morris designed an experiment in which subjects watched video taken from either *The Daily Show with Jon Stewart* or the *CBS Evening News* (a control group watched no video). The video clips reflected each show's treatment of the major party presidential candidates in 2004 (i.e., George W. Bush and John F. Kerry). The results of the experiment revealed that *The Daily Show* significantly lowered its viewers' evaluations of the candidates while watching the news had no effect on the subjects' evaluations. *Daily Show* viewers also reported significantly less faith in the electoral system, less trust in the news media's ability to report fairly and accurately, and a lower overall evaluation of the media's coverage of politics after watching the program; there was no significant change in the responses to these items by those who watched the news.[13]

Baumgartner and Morris's experiment is, of course, just one study. But their findings give empirical weight to the speculative conclusions of many observers of late-night comedy. Roderick Hart and Johanna Hartelius, for instance, accuse Jon Stewart of engaging in "unbridled political cynicism," arguing that he "does not stimulate a polis to have new and productive thoughts; like his ancient predecessors [the Cynics], he merely produces inertia."[14] The same could be said of all late-night comics. "Late-night's anti-political jokes," writes Russell Peterson, "declare the entire system—from voting to legislating to governing—an irredeemable sham." These jokes are, in other words, "implicitly anti-democratic."[15]

To be fair, some movies and television dramas take a nuanced view of politicians. *The West Wing*, for example, depicted fictional President Jed Bartlett as an honest and dedicated public servant. But for every President Bartlett, there are dozens of corrupt or buffoonish fictional politicians who serve as one-dimensional symbols of a profession that everyone recognizes as sleazy.

Slogans and humorous sayings that express contempt for politicians are routinely on display on t-shirts and bumper stickers. On one relatively popular bumper sticker, politicians are said to be like diapers—"they have to be changed, regularly and for the same reason." The disdain for politicians is also conveyed in the very use of the term itself. "Politician" is never a title that carries a positive connotation. If you doubt this, ask friends or co-workers to describe what they think of when they hear the term "politician." You are not likely to hear one positive word in one hundred. In common parlance, "politician" is inevitably used as a synonym for "liar," "cheater," or "schemer."

Perhaps the problem, then, is simply one of semantics. "Politician" may have become so freighted with negative symbolism that the word itself, and not the people it is used to describe, generates bad feelings. To test whether an alternative label would illicit more positive attitudes, I designed a split ballot experiment for a national survey conducted by the Center for Opinion Research at Franklin & Marshall College in February 2010. Half the sample was asked to choose between contrary descriptions of "elected officials" and the other half was asked about "politicians."

The responses to our questions, reported in Table 1.1, clearly indicate that people have as much contempt for "elected officials" as they do for "politicians." For example, 60 percent of the respondents think elected officials are dishonest but only slightly more (65 percent) chose the same descriptor for politicians. When asked whether elected officials/politicians are more interested in solving public problems or winning elections, 84 percent said winning elections is more important to elected officials while 86 percent said the same of politicians. And while 75 percent think elected officials do what's popular, as opposed to what's right, 77 percent think politicians do the same. There is, then, little difference between "elected officials" and "politicians" from the public's perspective.[16]

Of course, politicians themselves contribute to the dismal view of politicians. Leave aside the intensely negative campaigns that nearly all candidates engage in and that undoubtedly take a toll on the reputations of all politicians (since most of them are the targets of negative attacks at one time or another). Think of how often candidates proclaim, "I am not a politician," as if that were the best qualification for office. Is there another professional occupation in which the practitioners deny their membership in the profession?

The anti-politician sentiment I have summarized here is not particularly new. There was, however, a time when the feelings were not as vituperative as they appear to be nowadays. Stephen Earl Bennett, in reviewing studies from the middle of the twentieth century on Americans' attitudes about politics and politicians, suggests that those attitudes were ambivalent in the post-World War II era. At that time, trust in government was relatively high. Bennett is quick to point out

Table 1.1 Americans' Perceptions of "Politicians" versus "Elected Officials"

Generally speaking do you think [politicians/elected officials] tend to ...	Politicians n = 448	Elected officials n = 472
Be honest or dishonest		
Honest	25%	31%
Dishonest	65%	60%
Don't know	10%	9%
Be more interested in solving public problems or more interested in winning elections		
In solving problems	9%	11%
In winning elections	86%	84%
Don't know	5%	5%
Be more concerned about what is best for the public or more concerned with what is best for their political party		
Best for the public	8%	10%
Best for their party	87%	85%
Don't know	5%	5%
Do what they think is popular or do what they think is right		
Popular	77%	75%
Right	16%	15%
Don't know	7%	10%
Be ethical or unethical		
Ethical	27%	34%
Unethical	62%	56%
Don't know	11%	10%
Have moderate views or extreme views		
Moderate views	41%	45%
Extreme views	48%	47%
Don't know	11%	8%

Source: Franklin & Marshall College National Poll, February 2010, http://edisk.fandm.edu/FLI/keystone/pdf/keynfe10_1.pdf (accessed July 27, 2010).

that the levels of trust were actually lower than we often think and there were many more cynics, even in the 1950s, than we like to remember. Compared to the period following the 1960s, however, the levels of trust in government in the 1950s and early 1960s "look positively rosy."[17] In addition, Bennett cites research indicating that at least some positions in government carried a certain level of prestige in the 1940s. According to William Mitchell, a 1946 survey ranked several government occupations—including elected positions such as "Member of Congress" and "governor"—as quite prestigious. "Mayor of a large city" even outranked "college professor!"[18] Taken as a group, "government officials" (which includes some non-elected posts like "Supreme Court justice" and "cabinet member") ranked higher than any other occupational type.[19]

Nevertheless, Mitchell also notes that a 1944 survey revealed that only 18 percent of respondents would have liked their sons to enter politics. Though some of them appear to have wanted to shield their children from the harsh realities of a career in politics, most feared that politics would make their kids dishonest. Indeed, 48 percent agreed that "it is almost impossible for a man [sic] to stay honest if he goes into politics"; 42 percent disagreed.[20] One respondent who disagreed with the statement offered this backhanded defense of politicians' honesty—"We have more dumbbells than crooks in politics."[21] In the end, Mitchell concluded, "Americans hold ambivalent attitudes toward politics and those who make it an occupation."[22]

At a time when trust in government is at an all-time low, as it is today, we should not be surprised by the depth of the public's disregard for politicians. The point of citing evidence from the 1940s, however, is to note that even in a period of relatively high trust in government, when many office-holders were respected, politicians as a class were suspect. Thus, it seems as though politicians, at least in the United States, are condemned to be disliked.

The Expectations Trap

Politicians are a fact of public life. Representative government, by definition, is impossible without them. As such, citizens ought to give considerable thought to the role they'd like politicians to play in the political system. They should contemplate how they want elected officials to do their jobs. And they should decide what kinds of people they want to be involved in politics.

Unfortunately, American citizens would prefer to disparage politicians out of hand, rather than think seriously about what to expect from them. This lack of reflection about politicians and their role in our system of government leads to a great deal of inconsistency with respect to the public's expectations for politicians. Indeed, Americans maintain unrealistic and contradictory expectations. Collectively, I call this the "expectations trap," because it ensnares politicians in countless situations in which they're damned if they do and damned if they don't.

There are at least three specific traps that politicians face. Two of these—the leader-and-follower trap and the principled-and-pragmatic trap—have to do with the way politicians are expected to fulfill their roles as elected officials or candidates for public office. The third—the ordinary-and-exceptional trap—is about the kinds of people politicians are expected to be. These traps are a springboard into a broader discussion of what politicians do and who they are.

The Leader-and-Follower Trap

Perhaps the most obvious trap the public lays for politicians is the "leader-and-follower trap." On the one hand, the public wants politicians to be leaders. It is commonplace to hear laments about the lack of leadership in Washington or in some state capital. For example, a column in a trade magazine recently proclaimed, "There seems to be an unprecedented leadership vacuum in Washington, D.C., today, and it cuts equally across party lines."[23] Similarly, in a 2008 speech, Retired Army General Tommy Franks called for politicians to offer "ideas and leadership to move this country where it needs to go . . . I don't care which side of the aisle they're on. I'm interested in people who will lead this country."[24]

Demands for leadership are often directed at those in executive offices. Clearly the president is expected to be a leader. He or she is the commander-in-chief and head of state. Governors and mayors are also expected to be leaders as they head the executive branch of their states and cities.

However, leadership is not expected of executives exclusively; legislators are also supposed to be leaders. A column in *The Huffington Post* exemplifies this view perfectly. "[T]he problem," suggests Robert Guttman, Director of the Center on Politics and Foreign Relations at Johns Hopkins University,

> is not really the system but the lack of strong and capable leaders at the present time. We are always lamenting how bad and unworkable our political and government system is when we do not have strong leaders from the White House to the Senate to the Congress and to cities and state legislatures.[25]

Can there be 536 leaders at the national level,[26] plus hundreds more at the state and local levels? Perhaps, in a nation of over 300 million people, the answer is yes. But that is by no means certain because it isn't clear what, precisely, people mean when they call on politicians to "lead."

All too often, what "leadership" appears to mean is that the person using the term wants elected officials to do as he or she wishes, advocating policy positions in line with the critic's. Indeed, when the House of Representatives initially failed to pass a bailout package for banks in September 2008, MSNBC reported that the over 3,000 readers who commented on msnbc.com's "Gut Check America" that day disagreed over the wisdom of the plan. However, they "agreed on one thing: The vote clearly demonstrated a lack of leadership in the Capitol."[27] That is, whether readers supported the bailout or not, they accused members of Congress of failing to lead.

This is a curious meaning of the term "leadership." In practical terms, it suggests that a failure to lead is a failure to move in the direction a particular follower wants to go. It brings to mind the remark, attributed to the nineteenth-century French politician Alexandre Auguste Ledru-Rollin, "There go the people. I must follow them, for I am their leader."[28]

Ultimately, it might not be leadership that the public wants at all. Nearly three-quarters of respondents in a 2005 Gallup poll believed that the country would be better off "If the leaders of our nation followed the views of the public more closely."[29] Following the public's views more closely, of course, does not necessarily preclude leading (particularly if elected officials are not presently following those views *at all*). But, as we'll see in Chapter 3, there is considerable evidence that Americans want elected officials to not only give the public's wishes serious consideration, but to hew to their constituents' preferences. In other words, leaders should be followers.

This paradox is one part of the expectations trap. Politicians are expected to lead, until they begin to lead in a direction that citizens don't like. One might argue that this is perfectly acceptable in a democracy. Unfortunately, it puts politicians in an untenable situation. It would be far better for the public to decide whether it wanted politicians to lead or to follow and then hold them to account. Or, perhaps, the public could clarify when it wants politicians to lead and when it wants them to follow. But expecting them to lead and to follow, simultaneously, is as unproductive as it is unfair.

The Principled-and-Pragmatic Trap

In addition to expecting politicians to fulfill their duties as both leaders and followers, the public wants them to stand firm in their beliefs and, at the same time, to compromise to solve problems. In other words, Americans expect politicians to be principled and pragmatic. Perhaps these qualities are not necessarily antithetical. In practice, however, politicians have to sacrifice one to realize the other.

That the public wants politicians to be principled is perfectly reasonable. Standing for principle, in the minds of most Americans, is a sign of reliability. Principle anchors a politician's positions so that you can assume he or she will have the same positions in the future. Without principle as a foundation, a politician's positions can shift with the political winds. Indeed, one of the pejorative ways in which the term politician" is commonly used is as a synonym for "opportunist." Politicians are disliked, in part, because they are thought to be too eager to sell out for political expediency. A politician who is truly principled, however, would be willing to sacrifice political gain, perhaps even his or her entire career, for the sake of deeply held values.

A 2007 Pew Research Center poll confirms the public's desire for politicians who are committed to their beliefs. Fully two-thirds (67 percent) of the respondents said that they like political leaders who "stick to their positions" even if those positions are unpopular.[30] That result is likely to understate support for politicians who stand on principle because the question refers to "positions" rather than the more lofty "principles." Would any respondent have said that he or she does not like political leaders who "stick to their principles"?

As we'll see in the next chapter, part of the explanation for why Americans dislike politics and politicians is that people incorrectly believe there is consensus, at least within the public, about how to handle the nation's business. All the squabbling that politicians do, therefore, must be based on something other than a genuine desire to solve problems. If the public thinks there is a consensus on public policy, it is not much of a leap to infer that they also believe there is a consensus with respect to basic political principles. There isn't, of course, at least beyond the vague commitment to "democracy" itself.[31] When political principles are actually applied to concrete situations, what appeared to be widespread agreement over our most fundamental values dissolves. Nevertheless, Americans are undoubtedly convinced that, whatever our political principles are, we *all* share them. Thus, when they think of politicians sticking to their principles, people are likely to assume that those principles are the same as their own.

But what happens when people disagree with the principle behind a politician's principled stand? In that case, principle becomes far less admirable. Respondents in the 2007 Pew poll were asked if they liked politicians who take conservative or liberal positions on "nearly all issues." Only 38 percent said they like politicians who are consistently conservative in their views and another 32 percent like reliable liberals.[32]

By using the terms "conservative" and "liberal," Pew complicated matters for many respondents. If *that* is what is meant by principles, then maybe principles aren't all they're cracked up to be. But ideology is precisely what principles beget. However one defines "ideology," and there are countless definitions in the literature on the concept, it inevitably includes reference to a set of principles. As Kathleen Knight concluded after examining the use of the term "ideology" in political science scholarship, there exists a "core definition of ideology as a *coherent and relatively stable set of beliefs or values*."[33] Thus, if the public wants politicians to be principled, they will have to accept the fact that those politicians are going to be, to a greater or lesser extent, ideologues.

And, yet, Americans don't like ideologues. In fact, 60 percent of respondents in the Pew poll said they like politicians who "take a mix of liberal and conservative positions."[34] So maybe the public doesn't really want politicians to be principled after all. Or perhaps they think it's possible to mix liberal and conservative positions in a principled way. In theory, that is possible. Libertarians, for instance, take what we might describe as liberal positions on social issues and conservative positions on economic issues. But this is not what respondents have in mind when they say they admire politicians who take positions across the ideological spectrum. What they mean is that they don't want elected officials to follow one ideology dogmatically. Indeed, 75 percent of the respondents in the Pew poll said they like politicians who "are willing to compromise."[35] And when asked which they admired *most*, a political leader who sticks to his or her positions or one who compromises, 51 percent chose the more conciliatory politician (while only 40 percent chose the principled one).[36]

Following the Republicans' capture of the House of Representatives in the 2010 midterm elections, a McClatchy-Marist poll asked respondents which of the following statements came closest to their view: "The Republicans should compromise with the Democrats and President Obama to get things done"; or "The Republicans should stand firm on their positions even if it means things don't get done." Seventy-two percent of all respondents favored compromise.[37] Thus, somewhere around three-quarters of all Americans want politicians to compromise. And, yet, as we've seen, two-thirds want politicians to stick to their principles. Once again, the public's express wishes put politicians in a bind. Should they stand on principle, or should they compromise?

I've only scratched the surface of the public's confusion about its own desires in this regard. For instance, a more recent Pew poll, from September 2010, once again asked respondents whether they *most* admired a compromising politician or a principled one. This time, a plurality (49 percent) favored the principled political leader.[38] In a little over three years, the number saying they most admired a politician who was willing to compromise dropped from 51 percent to 42 percent.

Furthermore, in the same 2007 Pew poll in which 75 percent of the respondents claimed, generally, to like politicians who compromise, respondents were given a list of contentious issues and asked if the party they most agree with on those issues "should compromise on this issue, so that the two parties could reach some agreement," or whether the sympathetic party "should stick to its position on this issue even if it means no progress is made."[39] On illegal immigration and federal taxes, exactly half the public (50 percent) thought their party should compromise. There was even less appetite for compromise on the war in Iraq (45 percent) and very little on abortion (25 percent). Only on the environment did a clear majority (54 percent) of the respondents think their party should compromise and even there the majority was a slim one.[40] Compromise, it turns out, is less attractive when politicians who represent your views are the ones who are being asked to compromise.

Politicians who look to the public for guidance about whether to stand their ground or work with the other side will not get much help. Americans appear to want politicians to do both, just as they want politicians to be both leaders and followers. And, as with the leader-and-follower trap, the principled-and-pragmatic trap betrays a rather self-centered perspective on the part of citizens. They seem to be saying, "I want politicians to be principled when they share my principles; when they don't, I want them to be pragmatic and to compromise."

The Ordinary-and-Exceptional Trap

The first two traps concern how politicians are expected to do their jobs as elected officials. The third is about the kind of people we want running for office. On the one hand, we want politicians to be just like us, or at least just like what we perceive to be the typical American. And, yet, in the qualities they must possess, not to mention the standards to which they are held, politicians are expected to be far above average. The result is that we want politicians to be both ordinary and exceptional.

It would be nearly impossible to observe an American political campaign and not conclude that voters prefer candidates who seem ordinary to those who come across as distinguished in some way. Candidate behavior certainly suggests this is the case. Philip Tetlock found, for example, that statements by twentieth-century presidents were significantly more complex in office then they had been on the campaign trail. "Not only did presidents' statements rapidly increase in complexity from the pre- to post-election periods," wrote Tetlock, "they sharply decreased in complexity as the time for running for reelection approached."[41] For some reason, presidents feel the need to dumb down their statements when they run for office.

It's not just their verbal acuity that candidates feel compelled to alter when they interact with voters. They also display the symbols of the ordinary American (defined however a particular constituency conceives of the "ordinary"). In his campaign to fill Ted Kennedy's Senate seat, for example, Massachusetts Republican Scott Brown "crisscrossed the state in his 2005 GMC Canyon pick-up truck, with almost 200,000 miles . . . on the odometer, and pressed the flesh at rallies in jeans and brown work-jacket."[42] A former male model (who had once posed nude as "America's Sexiest Man" for *Cosmopolitan*), Brown is an attorney who had spent nearly 20 years in public office before running for the Senate. That's probably not the biography of the typical Bay Stater. But Brown campaigned as one nonetheless. "Pickup drivers are the everyday heroes who pull you out of a ditch, haul sandbags to a buckling levee, and bring the wood and bricks to build a family a new home," explained Joseph White on the *Wall Street Journal*'s "Washington Wire" blog. "Driving a pickup says you aren't too snooty to haul your own junk to the dump or too rich to understand the worries of people who punch a clock at work."[43]

Driving around Massachusetts in a pick-up truck is hardly demeaning. But many candidates put themselves through every manner of indignity to prove to voters that they are average Joes and Janes. They go bowling, even when they can't bowl; they go hunting, even when they barely know how to hold a rifle. They eat local delicacies with smiles on their faces even though they'd most certainly turn up their noses if offered such dishes in private. They talk about popular culture as if they really care about who wins *American Idol*. They do all of this, and much more, because they think it's important to convey to voters that they're normal human beings.

But politicians don't operate in a vacuum. The media encourage them to demonstrate their bona fides as ordinary people. As much as any other force in American politics, the media has encouraged what has come to be known as the "personalization of politics."[44] The personalization of politics is a phenomenon whereby the focus of public affairs has shifted to politicians and away from the groups (e.g., political parties; interest groups) they represent.[45] As such, an inordinate amount of attention is paid to politicians' personalities and to "getting to know them."[46] This is why the media often ask candidates seemingly irrelevant questions about their likes and dislikes. At a 2011 New Hampshire debate between Republican presidential candidates, for example, moderator John King asked the candidates a series of "this or that" questions "just to show a little bit of the personal sides of our candidate [sic]."[47] These questions included "Leno or Conan?" "Elvis or Johnny Cash?" "BlackBerry or iPhone?" "Deep dish or thin crust?" and "Coke or Pepsi?" Questions such as these are now commonplace in forums with politicians but they've been around for quite some time. At a 1994 MTV town hall-style event, for example, President Clinton was famously asked whether he wore "boxers or briefs." The question was posed by an audience member, but was part of a series of "rapid-fire" questions that MTV producers encouraged attendees to ask in order "to lighten the mood and personalize their meeting with the president."[48]

Perhaps candidates, and the media, are wrong to assume that voters want politicians to engage in bogus displays of normalcy. Maybe these spectacles are designed to satisfy a presumed desire on the part of the voters that simply doesn't exist. That's possible, but a considerable amount of anecdotal and more systematic evidence suggests that voters are in on the act. Candidates may go a bit overboard in their attempts to appear ordinary, but voters do want to see signs that a politician is at least familiar with the typical person's life.

Consider the question voters inevitably ask candidates on the campaign trail: "What's the price of _____ [fill in any basic necessity]?" That question may not reveal a great deal about a candidate's governing capabilities. But it is useful as an information shortcut for exposing politicians who are out of touch with the daily lives of voters. Knowing the price of a gallon of milk or a loaf of bread suggests that a candidate understands the world as the voters face it. And that's at least part of what voters want in a candidate. Summing up his decision in the Massachusetts race to fill Ted Kennedy's Senate seat, one voter declared, "I support Scott Brown because he understands what I'm worried about."[49]

In addition, voters have been shown to place a great deal of emphasis on the personal characteristics of candidates.[50] Indeed, in their stated assessments of candidates, voters tend to focus more on personality than on issue positions or party affiliations.[51] In his classic exploration of voting behavior, *The Reasoning Voter*, Samuel Popkin argues that voters approach the voting decision by asking what the candidates have done for them lately. However, "when they are short of both information and understanding of government, as they often are, they may ask instead, as a second-best question, How has he [sic] looked to me lately?" "Thus on many occasions," according to Popkin, "a voter falls back on a general assessment of a congressman's cultural style and personal character as a second-best alternative to figuring out what the congressman has actually done for him lately."[52] This explains why symbolic politics is so important on the campaign trail and why candidates feel pressure to bend over backwards to demonstrate their positive personal traits.

Thus, it is not just the media or the candidates themselves who have personalized politics. Of course, just because voters closely examine a candidate's personal characteristics doesn't necessarily mean that they want those characteristics to be ordinary. But to the extent that the personalization of politics does compel candidates to appear as regular folks, voters are every bit as responsible for the absurdities we so often see on the campaign trail.

Some of the best evidence that voters prefer candidates to be ordinary is provided by Roderick Hart's study of the rhetorical style of presidential candidates from 1948 to 1996. Hart analyzed candidate speeches, statements, and advertisements (among other texts) using a dictionary-based computer program (called DICTION) to determine how often each candidate differed from other candidates based on numerous variables the program tracks.[53] The result of his analysis was that candidates with the most ordinary way of communicating were the most successful. As Hart concluded, "normalcy seems best in American politics."[54]

Studies of leadership and intelligence also support the conclusion that people are uncomfortable with politicians who are outside the norm. "One of the most interesting results emerging from studies of the relation between intelligence and leading," wrote the Australian psychologist Cecil Gibb in 1969, "is the suggestion that leaders may not exceed the nonleaders by too large a margin . . . The evidence suggests that every increment of intelligence means wiser government, but that the crowd prefers to be ill-governed by people it can understand."[55] Though Gibb's summary of the research at the time is over 40 years old, there's no reason to think that voters now embrace highly intelligent leaders. Indeed,

Dean Simonton, who has studied the link between personality traits and successful leadership as much as any other scholar, has more recently surmised that "intellectual brilliance . . . may enable a president to go down in history as a great chief executive, yet such incumbents are not necessarily very popular with the American people."[56]

If the only expectation of those who would enter politics was that they be ordinary Americans, politicians would still find themselves in a difficult spot. It takes a considerable commitment to public service, not to mention substantial ambition, to voluntarily face the slings and arrows of a political campaign in exchange for the relatively modest reward of public office. That level of commitment and ambition is obviously not common. So the person who runs for office, by virtue of his or her willingness to do so, is already an uncommon person. And yet he or she must suppress any sign of the extraordinary.

However, the would-be public servant should be wary; the people have set another trap. The public insists that politicians appear ordinary (and what better way to appear ordinary, than to actually be ordinary), but they also want them to possess exceptional traits and skills. A candidate who is of average ability is not likely to get very far in a system that scrutinizes every word a politician says (or has ever said) and every move he or she makes (or has ever made). The average person could not tolerate being on guard and watching what they say, 24 hours a day, seven days a week. Given the demands placed on them by the public (as well as the media), successful politicians need to have groomed themselves for office from the earliest days of adulthood. That level of preparation for one's vocation is not ordinary; it is exceptional.

Indeed, there is one simple test to determine just how committed we are to being represented by average Americans: ask yourself if you'd like public officials to be chosen by random selection of individuals from the public at large (i.e., selection by lot). My bet is that few of us, if any, would prefer this method to the current system. That's because we realize that, as Judge Richard Posner explains,

> filling political offices by popular election rather than by lot conduces to *aristocratic* (in the Aristotelian sense) rather than democratic government. Conduces, in other words, to government by "the best" rather than by the average (as in a system of filling offices by lot) or by "the people" as a whole.[57]

In other words, we get better representatives under the current system than we would by selecting them randomly from the population. Our politicians are by no means perfect. But they are better suited to govern than the average American. "The aristocratic character of representative democracy is rooted in the fact," Judge Posner continues,

> that . . . voters will tend to pick the best candidate for each office. The best candidate—which is to say the candidate most likely to occupy the office with distinction—is likely to be a superior person, not at all typical of the voters . . . Of course voters may often be deceived about who is the best candidate; even so, an average Joe is unlikely to prevail in electoral competition, just as an average Joe is unlikely to win the world boxing title. The glib, the clever, the shrewd, the handsome, and the charismatic are likely to dominate the electoral competition, occupy the principal offices and constitute, in short, a political aristocracy.[58]

Why are the superior, as Posner calls them, more likely to "dominate the electoral competition"? In part it's because those who decide to enter politics are self-selected. As just noted, deciding to run for office requires extraordinary commitment and ambition. While we may be skeptical of those with ambition, we must admit that without it, not much of any significance would get accomplished (though, admittedly, the ambitious do not pursue only beneficial ends). Without people who possess inordinate amounts of ambition, I doubt we'd find enough volunteers to fill up a legislature.

The fact that we have a political aristocracy (in the sense in which Posner uses the term) is the result not only of self-selection by those who have what it takes to be successful in politics. It's also the result of the voters' decisions to reward certain types of people with their votes. Earlier I noted that voters rely heavily on personal characteristics in evaluating candidates. The specific traits they look for don't tell us whether or not they want candidates to exhibit higher than average levels of those traits, but they do suggest that not just anyone can be a successful politician. The three trait dimensions most commonly found to be in use are competence, integrity (or trustworthiness), and warmth (or empathy).[59] It is, I suppose, possible that voters expect politicians to be of average competence, integrity, and warmth. But that is doubtful.

Take, for example, integrity. Polls consistently show that a majority of the American public distrusts other citizens. In a 2010 Pew poll, only 31 percent of all respondents agreed that "most people can be trusted."[60] If most people can't be trusted, surely the voters expect politicians to be atypical in this regard.

The only study to attempt to directly assess whether voters are seeking "everyman" or "superman" is a study by John Sullivan and colleagues using survey data from the 1984 presidential election. The researchers asked respondents to rate "most people," as well as the two major party presidential candidates, on three dimensions of human nature (using a seven-point scale): selfishness, willpower, and trustworthiness. The key finding from this analysis was that voters' affective evaluations of the candidates were more responsive to a measure of which candidate *exceeded* the respondents' ratings of "most people" (i.e., the superman model) than to a measure of which candidate was *closer* to "most people" (i.e., the everyman model). In other words, "people want their presidents to be as trustworthy, unselfish, and in control as possible."[61]

There are several reasons to question the generalizability of this result. First, it's a study of only one election cycle. Second, it's an examination of attitudes about presidential candidates. Perhaps the same desire for the superhuman candidate doesn't exist in races for lower level offices. Nevertheless, this study, by very well-respected political scientists, offers qualified support for the claim that voters prefer exceptional, rather than ordinary, candidates.

However, the Sullivan et al. study revealed something else about voters. It turns out that

> while the superman model is the dominant one, asymmetry in evaluations of Reagan and Mondale lends support to an argument that voters applied a modified everyman standard to the incumbent, but not to the challenger. Mondale, instead, was held to a strong version of the superman standard.[62]

This suggests that voters may have different standards for different candidates. Indeed, some research on voters' use of personal traits in assessing candidates has found "that specific trait dimensions have greater and lesser influence on candidate evaluations depending on the candidate and campaign context."[63] Thus, while voters may expect candidates, generally, to be exceptional, they may also expect certain candidates to be ordinary. This is the epitome of an expectations trap.

Why This Matters

I will argue in the final chapter of the book that the expectations trap we set for politicians leads to a deep cynicism that is dangerous for representative democracy. Politicians cannot escape the trap because it contains contradictory demands. As a result, *all* politicians are subject to the criticism that they fail to be what the public wishes them to be. They fail, in other words, to be all things to all people. This failure, from the public's perspective, is not the result of the trap that they themselves have set for politicians (with significant help from the media). Nor is it a by-product of a system of government designed to encourage political conflict and gridlock. It is, instead, a failure inherent in the nature of politicians. By not meeting the standards established by the public, politicians cannot, by definition, be public servants. Their motivations must, therefore, be self-serving.

This conclusion is corrosive to political trust, which is absolutely necessary for a representative democracy to function properly. If we are to have others stand for us in government, and act on our behalf, we have to trust that what they do is in our best interest. Defining our best interest—is it only what is good for me or does the common good factor into my interests somehow—is extremely difficult and any determination of what constitutes it will be contestable. Without trust in those who represent us, all such determinations—that is, all actions a government takes—will be viewed as illegitimate. Needless to say, a government that does not govern legitimately is not much of a government at all.

Before getting to the closing argument in Chapter 8, however, I explore anti-politician attitudes in much more detail. In Chapter 2, I explore the source of these attitudes and chart their historical origins. Part of the source can be found in the nature of democratic sentiment itself. But another portion is simply the result of the way democracy functions. Chapters 3 and 4 pick up on the "operation of democracy" explanation by further examining what politicians do in office. That is, they put politicians' public activities under the spotlight. Chapter 5 offers a case study of the debt ceiling debate that took place in the summer of 2011. At first glance, the behavior of elected officials during that debate appears to have been highly dysfunctional. Upon reflection, however, their behavior was perfectly understandable given certain incentives in the system. Chapters 6 and 7 delve further into the kind of people who run for office; there the focus is on the "inner lives" of politicians. A concluding chapter appeals to Americans for a more nuanced, and less cynical, assessment of politicians. Ultimately, the goal of this book is to complicate our picture of who politicians are and what they do. Put quite simply, I aim to humanize politicians.

Chapter 2

The Sources of Anti-Politician Sentiment

The previous chapter offered evidence of the depth of Americans' disregard for politicians and introduced the notion of an expectations trap that the public sets for politicians. This chapter explores the sources of anti-politician attitudes. There are at least two possible explanations for why these attitudes seem so deeply ingrained in American political culture.

The first is a general tendency in democracies to maintain an equality of status between those with authority and those without. The "leveling spirit," as it has been called, means that no one, no matter how powerful, is to be treated as more eminent than others. The result is that politicians are to be constantly cut down to size. If such a tendency isn't universal among democracies, it may be that the United States is uniquely committed to the leveling spirit.

The second possibility is that the messiness of democracy turns people against politicians. There is a long history of political conflict in the United States. But the American people (and some reformers) mistakenly believe there is, or should be, a consensus among the public about how to govern the country. If people dislike the give-and-take of politics and, indeed, don't understand what all the bickering is about, they are bound to dislike anyone engaged in politics.

These explanations may not exhaust the possible reasons for the widespread disdain for politicians in the United States, but they hold the most promise for helping us understand this mindset. Nevertheless, the two explanations differ considerably in terms of the impulse behind them and their normative implications. The chapter will conclude, therefore, with a consideration of those implications.

The Leveling Spirit

It is possible that the values inherent in democracy encourage people to cast a suspicious eye upon those who seek, and exercise, power in a political system in which all citizens are supposed to be equal. There may, in other words, be something about the psychology of democracy that fosters anti-politician sentiment. Indeed, the democratic temperament has long been thought to contain what James Madison, among others, called a "leveling spirit," an impulse to equalize social and political status within a polity.[1]

For Alexis de Tocqueville, the early nineteenth-century French historian and keen observer of the young United States of America, the desire for equality appears to be rooted in human nature. As he wrote in his classic work, *Democracy in America*:

> There is in fact a manly and legitimate passion for equality that incites men to want all to be strong and esteemed. This passion tends to elevate the small to the rank of the great; but one also encounters a depraved taste for equality in the human heart that brings the weak to want to draw the strong to their level and that reduces men to preferring equality in servitude to inequality in freedom.[2]

In reality, such an aspiration is not likely to be a "natural" desire. Instead, its existence can be traced to the emergence of the modern age of democracy. "Throughout much of recorded history," writes the eminent political scientist Robert Dahl,

> an assertion that adult human beings are entitled to be treated as political equals would have been widely viewed by many as self-evident non-sense, and by rulers as a dangerous and subversive claim that they must suppress. The expansion of democratic ideas and beliefs since the eighteenth century has all but converted that subversive claim into a commonplace.[3]

Political equality thus becomes the "one elementary principle" upon which democracy is based.[4] Given that it is an essential ingredient of democracy, this principle is likely to shape citizens' perceptions of those who appear to violate it.

In fact, it could be argued that the principle of political equality has been distorted in contemporary liberal democracies. According to the late Spanish diplomat and writer Salvador de Madariaga, the political theorists who envisioned a system based on equality did so as a reaction to undeserved privileges that political authorities enjoyed at that time. For these theorists, "equality ultimately meant absence of privilege not justified by some reason which all citizens can approve and understand."[5] Once popularized, however, this idea came to mean opposition to *all* privileges, including those that can be justified and those that are natural. It was a short step from there to the belief that "men [sic] are interchangeable, at any rate in public life."[6] "In our liberal democracies," de Madariaga continues, "every Tom, Dick, or Harry is assumed to be apt to perform any public function . . . and we take pride in the open-mindedness wherewith we admit to the most delicate functions of government the roughest diamonds—or pebbles—which universal suffrage may throw up."[7]

It's not entirely clear what de Madariaga means when he refers to "justified social privilege."[8] And I believe we are correct to view claims of "natural" difference warily. But his point is well taken. In contemporary democracy, any suggestion that politicians ought to be held in high esteem is viewed as elitist claptrap.

Our disdain for politicians, then, may simply be a by-product, however warped, of democracy itself.[9] The contempt emerges from a democratic desire to afford all members of a political community equal respect. Politicians are no better than ordinary citizens. Pre-emptive efforts must be taken, therefore, to keep them off the pedestals they seek to mount. As a result, democratic politicians are ridiculed and mocked in ways that attack them personally; it is politicians, individually and collectively, and not the failings of "the system" that are the butt of jokes.[10] In non-democracies, however, the political *system* is the object of derision.[11] A classic joke from the Soviet Union of the 1970s has Muscovites standing in an endless line for vodka. After nearly an entire day of waiting, one man exclaims, "That's it! I can't take it any longer! I'm going to kill Brezhnev!" A few hours later he returns to his place in line and his comrades ask how it went. "I couldn't kill him . . . You should have seen the line over there!" That's not a condemnation of the leader; it's an indictment of the system. In a democracy, or at least in American democracy, jokes focus on the foibles of individual politicians—George W. Bush's presumed lack of intelligence, Bill Clinton's infidelity, or (going back almost four decades now) Gerald Ford's clumsiness—because they, not the system, are the problem.

If democracy, generally, entails such status leveling, then disregard for politicians should be found in every democratic country. In fact, when we examine comparative data on citizens' attitudes toward politicians, we find relatively low levels of trust in politicians in most contemporary democracies. However, we cannot necessarily attribute this fact to democratic sentiment and its leveling spirit. To begin with, there has been a significant decline in confidence in politicians in most (though not all) democracies over the last four decades, the time period for which we have comprehensive data.[12] If anti-politician attitudes were endemic to democracy, levels of trust in politicians should have been consistently low, especially over such a short period of time. The fact that levels of trust have fallen relatively rapidly suggests that something other than natural democratic sentiment is responsible for low levels of faith in politicians today.[13] Moreover, we cannot say what levels of trust were like in most countries in the years before we had reliable data. Indeed, levels of trust in those years could have been quite high.

Furthermore, though confidence in politicians is low in almost all democracies, the current level of mistrust and the slope of the decline in support for politicians vary from country to country. This suggests that a democracy's particular history and its political culture have some influence on attitudes toward politicians in that country. Indeed, the United States seems to be unusual in the depth of its contempt for politicians. As the editors of an academic volume exploring the widespread deterioration of democratic confidence explain, "The onset and depth of this disillusionment vary from country to country, but the downtrend is longest and clearest in the United States."[14]

Anthony King has identified two long-term factors that explain this form of American exceptionalism, only the first of which concerns us here. It is a suspicion of government that seems to have been bred in American political culture from its inception. Key to this explanation is the fact that "the peoples of the United States did not inherit their government; they invented it."[15] Of course, all governments are invented in the sense that they come into being at some historical point or another. But the United States, according to the late political sociologist Seymour Martin Lipset, "may properly claim the title of the first new nation" based on its status as "the first major colony successfully to break away from colonial rule through revolution."[16] King notes that this fact had two consequences. One is that "the government," as a conceptual entity, occupies a distinct sphere of activity that is separate from the rest of American society. This leads to a second consequence, namely that "most Americans still see this conceptual zone as being occupied, potentially at least, by alien, even hostile forces."[17] Those forces, for the most part, are politicians.

Thus, whereas Europeans accept government as inevitable, "Americans are still apt to wish, in a vague sort of way, that the whole business of government could be dispensed with."[18] This point echoes a now classic argument made by the political scientist James Morone, in which he suggested that "the democratic wish" in the United States consists of "a dread and a yearning." The dread is a fear of government power; the yearning is for the people to govern themselves, directly, with as little interference from government officials as possible.[19] The vision of governance without government relies on what the American public takes to be a simple truth: "The people are wiser than their governors."[20]

But the disdain for politicians must be based on more than the public's faith in the "wisdom of the crowd."[21] In fact, as noted in Chapter 1, Americans have a rather dim view of the capabilities of their fellow citizens. Is it possible, then, that attitudes toward politicians in the United States are simply the result of a unique commitment by Americans to status leveling?

Lipset has argued that there is a deeper commitment to egalitarianism in the United States than in virtually any other country (with the possible exception of Australia). And such a commitment shapes the relationships we have with those in authority. In egalitarian societies, according to Lipset, "the differences between low-status and high-status people are thought to reflect accidental and perhaps temporary variations in position, differences which should not be stressed in social relations, and which do not convey to the high-status person a general claim to social deference."[22] Thus, we should not expect politicians to be held in high esteem in the United States.

Equality as an ideal has certainly been part of the lifeblood of the United States since the founding of the American republic.[23] "Equality was in fact the most radical and most powerful ideological force let loose in the Revolution," writes the historian Gordon Wood. "Once invoked, the idea of equality could not be stopped, and it tore through American society and culture with awesome power."[24] Another eminent historian, Joyce Appleby, has noted that for "America's undistinguished citizens" in the early years of the nation, the values of American exceptionalism were to be found in the country's "institutional innovations, the leveling spirit—above all—the expanded scope of action for ordinary people."[25]

Indeed, early observers of American society claimed to find no distinctions in the United States based on birth or class. This is obviously more than a bit of mythmaking as tremendous inequalities, based on race, class, and gender, existed in the early United States.[26] Nevertheless, as far back as the 1780s, when the French-American writer J. Hector St. John de Crèvecoeur penned his *Letters from an American Farmer*, it has been believed, "The rich and the poor are not so far removed from each other as they are in Europe . . . [A visitor to America] must take some time ere he can reconcile himself to our dictionary, which is but short in words of dignity, and names of honour."[27] Tocqueville, too, thought he recognized a unique level of equality in the United States. "America therefore presents the strangest phenomenon in its social state," wrote Tocqueville. "Men show themselves to be more equal in their fortunes and in their intelligence or, in other terms, more equally strong than they are in any country in the world and than they have been in any century of which history keeps a memory."[28] That relative equality of station, he argued, would inevitably influence politics. The result would be a firm commitment in the United States to the sovereignty of the people. Indeed, as Tocqueville put it,

> If there is a single country in the world where one can hope to appreciate the dogma of the sovereignty of the people at its just value, to study it in its application to the affairs of society, and to judge its advantages and its dangers, that country is surely America.[29]

The observations of these particular men, well educated and wealthy elites that they were, may reflect a willful blindness to the myriad ways that the vast majority of Americans were unable to exercise such sovereignty. Indeed, for most Americans, for much of the nation's history, political equality has been elusive. But whether equal status for all citizens has been an empirical fact of democracy in the United States or not, the belief that no person is politically superior to another has been deeply held for as long as there has been a United States.[30]

Though the democratic temperament may not always and everywhere foster a belief in political equality, the American version of the democratic temperament does seem to do so. This is not, of course, the only explanation for our attitudes toward politicians. The next section will make the case that people are turned off by the way politics—and, by extension, democracy—operates. As a result, they blame those who appear to be responsible for the repellant state of affairs.

The Operation of Democracy

A familiar adage suggests that it is better not to see laws and sausages being made.[31] For most of the nation's history, citizens were indeed blind to the law-making process. With the advent of television, the curtain was pulled on that process. Cable television, of course, tore down the curtain, kicked in the window and put us seemingly right in the middle of the room with the legislators. But it isn't really the process of governing that 24-hour cable television, non-stop blogging, and instantaneous tweeting reveal to the public; it's politics. Today's citizen is bombarded with politics in a way that citizens of the past could not have imagined. Unfortunately, most people don't have much appetite for politics. This has been true for nearly all of American history. Though we think of the nineteenth century as a time of widespread political engagement—torchlight parades, well-attended (and lengthy) candidate debates—historians Glenn Altschuler and Stuart Blumin argue convincingly that fewer people were active in politics in the 1800s than is conventionally believed. One of the primary reasons people chose not to engage in politics, Altschuler and Blumin maintain, is that politics was perceived to be a "rude" activity.

> Blatant office-seeking and behind-the-scenes maneuvering, the cultivation of political loyalty among newly enfranchised workers and recently arrived immigrants, the inclusion in political organizations of saloonkeepers, street toughs, and other unsavory characters, the employment of manipulative techniques of mass appeal, and the equation of these techniques with other forms of crude humbuggery, imparted an unseemliness to politics that considerably complicated the simultaneous pursuit of respectability and an active political life.[32]

If politics was thought to be a rude affair, upstanding citizens could only conclude that its practitioners were riff-raff. Indeed, the late nineteenth-century politician was commonly thought to be uneducated and unsophisticated. First published in 1905, William Riordon's *Plunkitt of Tammany Hall* provides a portrait of what many took to be the typical turn-of-the-century big-city, machine politician. The book is a collection of informal commentary by New York State Senator George Washington Plunkitt. In one talk, Plunkitt defends Tammany leaders against charges that they are uncivilized. "You hear a lot of talk about the Tammany district leaders bein' illiterate men," says Plunkitt.

> If illiterate means havin' common sense, we plead guilty. But if they mean that the Tammany leaders ain't got no education and ain't

gents they don't know what they're talkin' about. Of course, we ain't all bookworms and college professors. If we were, Tammany might win an election once in four thousand years. Most of the leaders are plain American citizens, of the people and near to the people, and they have all the education they need to whip the dudes who part their name in the middle and to run the City Government. We've got bookworms, too, in the organization. But we don't make them district leaders. We keep them for ornaments on parade days.[33]

Complicating matters was the fact that, as political scientist Elmer Cornwell noted, "the classic urban machine and the century of immigration which ended in the 1920's were intimately intertwined phenomena."[34] Big-city politics was attractive to many immigrants because, in exchange for votes, party bosses could provide economic security and social integration. But in an age of pervasive ethnic prejudice, the party machine's reliance on immigrants as a base of support and the newcomers' prominence in the ranks of party operatives, led many to look down their noses at the entire business of politics.

The image of politicians was not helped, of course, by the bald corruption of the Gilded Age. There was a seemingly endless series of scandals in the years following the Civil War, including Crédit Mobilier, the Great Gold Conspiracy, the Whiskey Ring, and the Salary Grab, among others. Not surprisingly, the fiction and satire of that period, as Altschuler and Blumin document, began to reflect the unfortunate reality of political sleaze. Writers in the post-Civil War era included politics in their storylines to a far greater extent than antebellum authors had done and they "base[d] their political characters, episodes, and references on the judgment that public life in America was unseemly and corrupt."[35] But no fictional politician could have exemplified knavery as well as Plunkitt himself. Among his most famous insights are an explanation of the difference between dishonest and honest graft and a rationale for his own involvement in the latter—"I seen my opportunities and I took 'em."[36]

The Progressive movement emerged, in part, as a response to widespread political corruption and sought to limit the ability of "special interests" (by which they meant, primarily, monopolistic corporations) to manipulate the system for their own ends. Progressives looked to the state to eradicate the social ills they believed were caused by unfettered industrialization. But before the state could be expected to stand up to corporate interests, it had to be reformed.[37]

Perhaps the most significant barrier to a properly functioning, healthy democracy, according to Progressive reformers, was the power of party machines and the bosses that controlled them. In order to emasculate party bosses, Progressives assumed that parties themselves had to be weakened. According to Michael McGerr, one of the pre-eminent historians of the period:

> The evils of party ran through the whole reform litany. Recalcitrant parties thwarted reform goals, ignored issues or took the wrong side, controlled nominations, exploited public office for patronage, excluded good men, and fostered corruption. Party had grown out of proportion, the reformers believed, until it overshadowed the government itself.[38]

Though some Progressives worked to purify the parties from the inside[39]—and even formed their own party, which nominated presidential candidates in 1912 and 1924—most of them held deeply anti-party attitudes. As one Progressive leader wrote, "War begets war. Strife begets strife. Parties beget partizans."[40] And partisanship, of course, ran counter to the value Progressives held most dear—social harmony. Thus, Progressive reforms sought either to eliminate parties altogether—as in the case of non-partisan local elections—or to shift decision-making power within parties away from party leaders and toward the rank-and-file—as in the case of direct primaries.

Through other reforms, Progressives circumvented representative democracy in favor of direct democracy. Representatives, after all, are party politicians. So Progressives vigorously advocated initiatives and referenda, which give legislative power to "the people." They also sought to place considerable responsibility for administering government in the hands of unelected bureaucrats and experts in public administration. The council-manager model of municipal government, for example, originated during the Progressive era. Without partisan allegiances, professional civil servants could be trusted to protect the public interest.

Other Progressive reforms were aimed at preventing corruption at the polling place. For example, the secret, or Australian, ballot was introduced at the end of the nineteenth century and voter registration requirements were implemented or strengthened between the Civil War and World War I.[41] The Australian ballot had the dual benefit, in the minds of Progressives, of reducing corruption and weakening parties, as it was the parties that had previously printed and distributed ballots. But these anti-corruption reforms also reduced voter turnout dramatically.[42]

For Progressives, this was not an entirely unwelcome consequence. They believed that the uneducated and uninformed should not be encouraged to vote and, indeed, many believed they should not even be allowed to do so. This is an uncomfortable fact for those who look back at the Progressive era with fondness. For all their apparent reverence for "the people," the Progressives had a very narrow conception of citizenship.[43] As Michael Schudson describes it in his masterful book *The Good Citizen*, "The model citizen, in the reform vision, would be disciplined enough to register, educated enough to read, thinking enough to choose candidates with little or no party guidance, and docile enough to leave many matters to the experts."[44]

This is all in keeping with the Progressive vision of a well-ordered polity. More than anything, the Progressives disliked conflict—between classes or any other opposing interests—and sought to achieve social harmony with reforms that would take the politics out of politics. That lofty goal may appear to be desirable. But it is naively idealistic, if not utopian; indeed, it may well be dangerous. Can a nation of over 300 million people be expected to agree on the common good? It seems not only unlikely, but impossible. As the late British political scientist, and defender of politics, Bernard Crick, maintained, in a society without political conflict, "it is more likely that politics has been forbidden *in order* to try to reach such a unanimity rather than that it has withered away because there is unanimity already."[45]

If achieving some sort of national consensus is impossible, a free system of government (or what we typically call a democracy) must be designed to accommodate that fact and to manage the conflict of interests (or what we typically refer to as politics) that naturally arises in society. This, of course, is the very justification for the American system of government provided by James Madison in Federalist No. 10; namely, that the system must control factions. But it should not, indeed it cannot, eliminate them. To attempt to do so would be a "remedy . . . worse than the disease" because it would threaten liberty.[46] Thus, democracy requires politics.[47] As a result, the Progressives did extensive damage to democracy by disparaging politics and those engaged in it.

The anti-politics of the Progressive era continues to influence the thinking and the behavior of Americans today. Contemporary Americans are so turned off by politics that even when they are engaged in what most scholars would say is political activity, the typical person denies being political. Nina Eliasoph conducted a fascinating and illuminating exploration of this phenomenon by associating with members of voluntary, recreational, and activist organizations and listening to how they talked (or didn't talk) about civic affairs. Eliasoph found that people would go to great lengths to avoid what she calls "public-spirited political conversation."[48] They might, and often did, express political opinions in private. Indeed, they would often couch the issues upon which they were active as matters of considerable collective importance. But in a public setting, such as a meeting or a press conference, they would steadfastly avoid political disagreement.[49] Instead, they inevitably focused on the ways in which the issues affected them personally.

We might chalk this up to a general discomfort many people have with fighting and arguing. In their study of people's attitudes about how government should work, Hibbing and Theiss-Morse found that a quarter of the respondents in their national survey agreed "that political arguments in general made them feel uneasy."[50] In an attempt to better understand such discomfort, political scientist Carolyn Funk conducted an experiment in which she provided subjects with a written description of a congressional debate over Medicare. In one condition, the debate was described as acrimonious; in the other condition, disagreement was civil. Funk found that subjects reported higher levels of their own anger and disgust with the description of the acrimonious debate than with the civil one. Interestingly, the level of disapproval of the hostile debate was identical for those subjects who reported their own tendency to avoid arguing and for those who don't avoid arguing.[51] Thus, whether they themselves are likely to engage in arguments or not, people tend to dislike displays of animosity by others. To the extent that American politics has become more adversarial, and thus more acrimonious, in recent years, it is likely to turn off large segments of the citizenry. As Funk puts it, "The prevalence of animosity in elite policy debate is likely to amplify public distaste and contribute to dissatisfaction with politicians and politics."[52]

Of course, people do encounter disagreements in their everyday lives. And conflict, as Hibbing and Theiss-Morse point out, tends to draw the attention of Americans in many realms of life. Sports and reality television are inconceivable without it. In fact, Eliasoph observed arguments about the day-to-day operation of the organizations in which her subjects were involved. "Disagreement itself was not taboo," she maintains; "what was out of place was public-spirited conversation about discouraging issues and topics that volunteers assumed to be beyond their scope."[53]

Ultimately, Eliasoph argues that a kind of "political etiquette" influences the behavior of the typical American.[54] The function of the civic practices based upon this etiquette is, in part, to maintain optimism in the face of seemingly insoluble political problems. For the community activists that Eliasoph observed, talking politics meant "to stop trying so hard to keep up that can-do spirit and let some frightening uncertainty in. Actively ignoring [political] tensions was considered a positive good, a moral act."[55] Avoiding politics, then, helps to preserve the common good. The result is a "happy public discourse" according to which "the world is good, moral, and makes sense."[56] Politics, in short, is a downer.

Hibbing and Theiss-Morse offer a different explanation. They note that Americans believe there is a consensus among the public with respect to the most important problems facing the nation as well as to the solutions to those problems.[57] This belief, it should be said, finds support among some well-respected and well-informed observers. The columnist E. J. Dionne's explanation for why Americans hate politics is that our politics are stuck in a "phony polarization" between left and right as liberals and conservatives continue to fight the battles of the 1960s.[58] "America's cultural values," on the other hand, "are a rich and not necessarily contradictory mix of liberal instincts and conservative values."[59]

One might be tempted to argue that Dionne's work, now 20 years old, is outdated; though polarization may have started as an elite phenomenon, surely it has now seeped into the wider populace. But the renowned political scientist Morris Fiorina has more recently drawn essentially the same conclusion as Dionne. Fiorina maintains that the divide between "Red America" and "Blue America," or those on the right and those on the left, has been greatly exaggerated. "Elections are close," he acknowledges, "but voters are not deeply or bitterly divided. In both red and blue states a solid majority of voters see themselves as positioned between two relatively extreme parties."[60]

Perhaps not surprisingly, politicians also contribute to the view that there's a political consensus among Americans. None has done so more eloquently than Barack Obama. His keynote address to the Democratic National Convention in 2004, delivered when he was still just a candidate for the U.S. Senate from Illinois, reached a crescendo when he proclaimed, "there's not a liberal America and a conservative America; there's the United States of America." He went on to insist,

> The pundits, the pundits like to slice and dice our country into red states and blue states: red states for Republicans, blue states for Democrats. But I've got news for them, too. We worship an awesome God in the blue states, and we don't like federal agents poking

around our libraries in the red states. We coach little league in the blue states and, yes, we've got some gay friends in the red states.[61]

However, in a series of articles and a recent book, Emory University political scientist Alan Abramowitz has challenged the view that political polarization is a uniquely elite phenomenon. He finds "that the American public has become more consistent and polarized in its policy preferences over the past several decades."[62] This is primarily true of those he calls "politically engaged citizens," a group that has more than doubled in size over the past 50 years and that includes nearly half of all voters.[63] Ultimately, Abramowitz concludes that members of Congress, who everyone agrees have become highly polarized, "appear to be accurately reflecting the views of their supporters in the electorate."[64]

The extent to which the public is polarized is a complicated empirical question that depends, in large part, on how one defines and measures polarization. However, even if the public policy preferences of citizens are not wildly divergent, no political scientist would deny the recent "partisan sort" that has occurred in American politics. That is, a nearly perfect alignment between those on the left with the Democratic Party and those on the right with the Republican Party has emerged over the last 40 years.[65] To be sure, this process of sorting does not necessarily mean that voters have become more extreme (or more divided) in their ideologies or policy preferences, which is what we normally mean when we talk about polarization.[66] Nevertheless, partisan sorting certainly does lead to more partisan voting behavior and it produces divergent political evaluations, particularly of the president's performance.[67] Indeed, the gap between Democrats' and Republicans' approval of the president grew dramatically during the presidency of George W. Bush and it certainly did not abate when Barack Obama took office.[68]

Marc Hetherington and Jonathan Weiler have identified another dividing line within the American public. They argue that "preferences about an increasing number of salient issues are structured by a deeply felt worldview, specifically authoritarianism."[69] Authoritarianism, in turn, has begun to influence party identification and voting behavior.[70] Republicans, on average, now score higher on measures of authoritarianism than do Democrats.[71] This was not true, at least to a statistically significant degree, even a decade ago.[72]

At a minimum, then, the public is polarized along partisan lines. If one believes the evidence provided by Abramowitz as well as by Hetherington and Weiler, the public is also divided ideologically or by other measures of worldview. But, though the particular form polarization takes in the twenty-first century may be unique, deep-seated political animosity between Americans has a long lineage. We need not even mention the Civil War to make the point. (It is, however, indicative of the tenacity of Americans' political disagreements that even in the North itself, serious party conflict existed *during* the Civil War.[73])

Great divisions between Americans developed before they were even, technically, Americans. Indeed, the very idea of independence split colonists into Tory (or loyalist) and Patriot (or rebel) camps. Though loyalists were outnumbered (the best estimate is that roughly 20 percent of the white population at the time was loyalist[74]), there were enough of them—and in disproportionately high places—to cause a significant tear in the fabric of colonial America. The disagreement between the two camps was not simply intellectual; it was emotional and it was violent. Patriots often attempted to force fealty to the "glorious cause" by treating loyalists to tremendous indignities (e.g., tarring and feathering). As the historian Arthur Schlesinger put it, "Mass violence played a dominant role at every significant turning point of the events leading up to the War for Independence."[75]

Perhaps such disagreement, not to mention violence, is to be expected in the midst of revolution. Surely the nation would unite in the creation of the new government. As it happened, significant differences of political opinion emerged between Americans almost as soon as the ink was dry on the Treaty of Paris (which ended the Revolutionary War in 1783). Within only a few years, it became abundantly clear that the document in place as the nation's constitution, the Articles of Confederation, was severely deficient. Though there was broad agreement that something had to be done to fix the problems in the Articles, there was little agreement on what to do. Some believed that the only way to build a sustainable political system was to scrap the ineffective Articles of Confederation and grant substantially more power to the federal government through an entirely new constitution. Others viewed such a plan as a usurpation of state sovereignty, which they feared would ultimately threaten liberty. This group sought a mere revision of the Articles. Though this disagreement wasn't violent, it was heated and failed to result in any sort of consensus.

The dispute at the center of the debate over the Constitution was the locus of governmental power. The Articles placed ultimate power in the states. But they provided for an extremely weak (indeed, almost non-existent) federal government. That made it nearly impossible for the states to work together to achieve common ends, including a functioning national economy. In devising—or revising—a system of government, the Framers paid considerable attention to the preservation of liberty (if only for one segment of the population). Federalists believed, as Madison had argued so forcefully in Federalist No. 10, that liberty was best protected in an "extended republic."[76] With representation covering a large area, the ability of one faction to marshal a perpetual majority in its favor would be greatly reduced. Thus, tyranny would be least likely to take root at the federal level.

Anti-Federalists, on the other hand, believed that liberty was safer when states were the repository of power. They believed this, in part, because they (like Progressives a century later) thought that political conflict was ruinous and had to be not just controlled but eliminated. As "Brutus," perhaps the most famous Anti-Federalist, wrote in his first essay to the citizens of New York during the ratification debates, "In a republic, the manners, sentiments, and interests of the people should be similar. If this be not the case, there will be a constant clashing of opinions; and the representatives of one part will be continually striving against those of the other."[77]

Madison takes a more realistic view of political conflict. He notes, again in Federalist No. 10, that differences of opinion are natural and unavoidable. It is worth quoting him at length on the point.

> As long as the reason of man continues fallible, and he is at liberty to exercise it, different opinions will be formed ... The latent causes of faction are thus sown in the nature of man; and we see them everywhere brought into different degrees of activity, according to the different circumstances of civil society. A zeal for different opinions concerning religion, concerning government, and many other points, as well as speculation as of practice; an attachment to different leaders ambitiously contending for pre-eminence and power; or to persons of other descriptions whose fortunes have been interesting to the human passions, have, in turn, divided mankind into parties, inflamed them with mutual animosity, and rendered them much more disposed to vex and oppress each other than to co-operate for their common good. So strong is this propensity of mankind to fall into mutual animosities, that where no substantial occasion presents itself, the most frivolous and fanciful distinctions have been sufficient to kindle their unfriendly passions and excite their most violent conflicts.[78]

Differences of opinion, and the resulting conflict they engender, are natural. Pretending they don't exist is naive; but trying to eliminate them, as the Anti-Federalists hoped to do, is dangerous.

The Federalist vision of the extended republic won the day. Thus, written into the design of American government is the assumption that political conflict is unavoidable. Indeed, political conflict is even beneficial, if harnessed properly, in preserving and protecting liberty.

All of this is to say that the belief in a popular consensus about how to govern the United States is a fantasy. There have always been deep divisions in American politics and there is every reason to believe there always will be. But given that the public embraces the consensus fantasy, people naturally conclude, according to Hibbing and Theiss-Morse, that "conflict is unnecessary and counterproductive."[79] Thus, anyone engaged in such conflict—as politicians inevitably will be—is going to be viewed with suspicion.

Democratic Skepticism and Political Naivety

The two sources of anti-politician sentiment discussed in this chapter have very different impulses. One is, at root, well intentioned; the other is formed of naivety or ignorance (or both). As a result, the implications of these causes differ considerably.

The leveling spirit is premised on a deep commitment to equality.[80] This is precisely why it was so despised by the aristocracy. Indeed, the commitment to equality, as noted earlier, is a bedrock tenet of democracy: no person is to have more *political* worth than another. This is the basis, for example, of the principle of "one person, one vote." As much as is practically possible people are to be given equal respect or honor, regardless of their position in society. Thus, any tendency toward aggrandizement, especially of those who would wield power, ought to be checked in a democracy.

Wariness of those in power, therefore, is a positive disposition in a democracy. But when constructive wariness becomes cynical suspicion of everyone interested in serving the public in elected office, democracy will suffer. We've now reached the point where democracy is suffering as a result of public suspicion of politicians. Nevertheless, I recognize the value in not just holding politicians accountable for what they say and do, but also in preventing politicians from getting too puffed up. The leveling spirit at its core, then, is beneficial to democracy.

The other source of negative attitudes toward politicians, however, is based on a very simplistic view of how democracy ought to operate. It assumes, incorrectly, that we would all get along if it weren't for the politicians. Think of the Nextel ad I described in the preface to this book. Without politicians, problems would virtually solve themselves because the rest of us, not blinded by partisanship or ideology or special interest influence, would agree on the best course of action.

The next two chapters will examine the operation of democracy, otherwise known as "politics," in greater detail and will explain why politicians do what they do. For now, I simply want to maintain that Americans' tendency to recoil from politics is based largely on ignorance and naivety. It is based on ignorance because it reflects a misunderstanding of the way the American political system is designed, the incentives written into that system, and the myriad factors that influence politicians' behavior. It is based on naivety because it believes that we can have a society devoid of politics. However, as Crick reminds us, the truth is that "all known advanced societies are inherently pluralistic and diverse, which is the seed and the root of politics."[81]

If politics is inescapable, politicians are unavoidable. To indiscriminately despise them is to make the effective operation of representative democracy nearly impossible. Thus, unlike the leveling spirit, the disdain for politicians because they engage in politics is fundamentally dangerous to democracy.

Chapter 3

The Public Lives of Politicians
Do Politicians Pander?

In the last chapter, I discussed the public's distaste for politics and, in particular, for the conflict that politics inevitably entails. I suggested that this allergy to all things political makes the public hostile to those who engage in politics as a profession. In this chapter and those that follow, I will address the most common criticisms made of politicians. Here, and in the following chapter, I will discuss those that pertain to the public lives of politicians. That is, I'll examine charges leveled against politicians for what they do in their public roles as elected officials (or would-be elected officials). Chapters 6 and 7 explore accusations about the kinds of people politicians are; that is, they look at the private, or (perhaps more accurately) the inner, lives of politicians and ask, "Are politicians a different breed than the rest of us?"

Roughly speaking, there are three allegations made about the public behavior of politicians. One is that politicians pander. That claim will be the focus of this chapter. In Chapter 4, I examine the related charge that politicians only care (or, at least, mostly care) about getting elected as well as the claim that politicians are too ideological, too partisan, or both.

Before examining the charges leveled at politicians, I offer a brief description of the pressures the contemporary American political system places on those who hold (or would hold) public office. Constitutional design is responsible for some of these pressures, while others are the result of political reforms enacted over time, and still others have been produced by broader changes in society, culture, and technology.

The Thicket of American Politics

We're all aware of the constitutional design of American government.[1] Unfortunately, we sometimes forget to consider that design when we analyze the behavior of politicians. To refresh any memories that might need a quick primer, the national government of the United States has three co-equal branches of government including a legislative branch (Congress), an executive branch (the Presidency), and a judicial branch (federal district and appellate courts and the Supreme Court). The legislative branch is further divided into two chambers (the House of Representatives and the Senate). The concept behind dividing the government into three branches is the separation of powers. One faction (or even one party) cannot easily capture all the powers of government as long as those powers are distributed in separate parts of the government. When checks and balances, or the ability of one branch of government to constrain the exercise of power in another, are added to the equation, it becomes extremely difficult for any one group (again, including an entire political party) to work its will.

With respect to elected offices in the national government, the American system is premised on geographical (rather than, say, ideological) representation. To be precise, members of the House of Representatives come from relatively small districts, senators represent states, and the president is elected nationally (based on votes cast state by state). The terms of the elected officials differ such that members of the House serve for two years, senators (one-third of whom are elected every two years) serve for six years, and the president holds office for four years. The result of this design is that many different constituencies are represented in government, as are their different interests. Furthermore, the varied length of terms means that elected officials in different branches of government (or different chambers within the same branch) operate on different time horizons.

While most Americans master these basic facts in high school, I review them here simply to highlight a critical point about how that system is supposed to work: American government is sliced and diced in numerous ways in order to make the system operate deliberately. Indeed, nothing in American government is supposed to get accomplished without having been examined by multiple perspectives and run through a gauntlet of competing interests. Gridlock is purposely imposed by the structure of the system and conflict is, therefore, inevitable since multiple competing interests are inevitable. If anything is to get done, compromise is necessary. But because the system pits various interests against one another—in order, the reader will recall from the discussion of Federalist No. 10 in Chapter 2, to preserve liberty—conflict makes compromise extremely difficult.

There are other elements of the American system of government and politics that are outside the Constitution but are nonetheless vital for understanding how politics work in the United States. Political parties, for instance, are not mentioned in the Constitution but have been at the center of American politics since right after the Founding. George Washington, in his "Farewell Address" of 1796, had warned "in the most solemn manner against the baneful effects of the spirit of party."[2] Though there is some debate about when, precisely, we might say political parties formed in the United States, it is fairly clear that Washington's warning was too late; parties had already begun to form in the new republic.[3] And why had parties formed so quickly? The answer is that their existence is inevitable in a complex political system. As the late political scientist E. E. Schattschneider famously put it, "modern democracy is unthinkable save in terms of the parties."[4]

This is not the place to examine the factors that make political parties inevitable.[5] The point is simply that parties are an essential part of our political system. More importantly, for our purposes, is that once formed, parties exert pressure on politicians to behave in partisan ways.[6] This pressure, it must be said, is not entirely uninvited. After all, politicians create parties to help achieve certain goals, including not only re-election but efficient law-making. Nor is this pressure necessarily bad (as the pejorative use of the term "partisanship" would suggest). The function of parties is, at least in part, to encourage cooperation and enforce discipline among individual politicians who may not share all of the goals of their parties.

The direct primary, an election used to nominate a political party's candidates for office, is another extra-constitutional aspect of our political system that has significant influence in American politics. Though primaries had been used as early as the 1840s in the United States, it wasn't until the end of the nineteenth century that states began to consider using primaries for all (or nearly all) of their offices. By 1915, only Connecticut, Rhode Island, and New Mexico had not passed legislation making primaries mandatory for at least some offices.[7]

The main effect of the adoption of primaries has been to put candidates, rather than parties, at the center of the electoral process.[8] And those candidates face additional burdens that candidates in the pre-primary era didn't have to endure. For example, candidates have to build their own campaign staffs rather than rely on the party organization to run a campaign on their behalf. This is expensive, so candidates have to raise money just to get their party's nomination. If the primary is contested, a candidate has to raise even more money because he or she will need polling and advertising in order to mount a competitive campaign. Candidates' campaign strategies are also made more complicated by primary elections. If primary voters differ in their policy preferences from general election voters, candidates will feel pressure to align themselves with the primary electorate.[9] Of course, they'll face a different electorate in the general election and, consequently, will feel pressure to accommodate the wishes of those voters. Under these circumstances, it's not surprising that politicians sometimes flip-flop; the wonder is that it doesn't happen more often.

The conflicting demands placed on candidates by primary and general electorates is a particular instance of the general influence of public opinion on American politics. Prior to the middle of the twentieth century, it was much more difficult for public opinion to have an impact on politics because its systematic measurement was not yet possible.[10] With the rise of scientific polling, public opinion began to carry more weight in politics. Increasingly, all sides of a policy debate were able to wield poll results to claim that "the American people" backed their position. Today, poll results on every conceivable matter of public concern are released on an ongoing basis.

For their part, politicians faced a new dilemma as polling became ubiquitous—exactly how to respond to the "will of the people." Stick too closely to that will and be accused of pandering; ignore it and be denounced as out of touch. Assuming the path of least resistance is to follow the people's will, what is a politician to do when he or she believes the public is misinformed or is just plain wrong? And with which group of people is he or she supposed to comply in the first place? His electoral base? Her entire constituency? The broader public at the state, or national, level?

Interest groups, too, have a profound role in the American political system. Interest groups used to be referred to as "pressure groups" for a reason; they put pressure on politicians to advance the particular interests these groups are organized to promote. There have long been organized interests in the United States, but their numbers grew dramatically beginning in the 1960s.[11] Since then, these groups have become significant players in the halls of government as well as on the campaign trail. If lobbying doesn't achieve what an interest group wants to achieve, they can always turn to electoral remedies. In fact, there are now groups whose entire reason for being is to influence the outcomes of elections. It would be absurd, not to mention impossible, to kowtow to every interest group in existence. But every politician has a handful of groups that he or she must placate or face intense opposition at the next election.

This doesn't always require siding with the interest group over the wishes of the politician's constituency. In fact, it rarely does. That's because one of the most effective tactics an interest group can employ is "signaling" that its goals are consonant with the goals of a politician's constituency (or, at least, his or her key constituencies, such as an electoral base).[12] As political scientist Ken Kollman explains, "Interest group leaders mobilize people outside the policy making community to show policymakers the salience of policy issues among their constituents, who will decide their fate in the next election."[13] If an interest group can't credibly send the message that it has significant support within a politician's constituency, he or she won't feel much pressure to comply with its requests.

Still, there are times when politicians face pressure from powerful interest groups whose interests do not align with those of the politicians' constituency. The threat of vicious negative attacks unleashed during a campaign is enough to make any elected official consider a group's request, even if the threat is unspoken (as it virtually always is). Of course, if they decide to honor that request, they run the risk of angering their constituents. But if they don't, they will incur the wrath of the interest group. Regardless of what they decide to do in such situations, politicians will jeopardize their re-election chances *and* be accused of doing only what is best for their re-election chances.

The final piece of this brief, and overly simplified, review of the contemporary American political system is the media. As most readers will no doubt know, the media landscape has changed dramatically over the last 50 years. To access national news in 1960, people could choose between a newspaper, the radio, or one of three 15-minute network newscasts on television. Though news coverage on television would expand in the 1960s and 1970s, viewer choice was limited to three networks. Nevertheless, the news departments of those networks took journalistic standards very seriously, producing (almost exclusively) what we now refer to as "hard news."

With the rise of cable news, initiated by the launch of CNN in 1980, the nature of the news changed dramatically. In order to fill a 24 hour a day, seven day a week "newshole," cable news channels created programming that analyzed, rather than merely reported, the news. These programs "softened" the news in order to make it more entertaining and, thus, more appealing to audiences. But they also adopted a noticeably critical tone.[14]

While cable television gave the consumer of news added choice, the Internet has completely fragmented the media environment. There are now countless sites that are capable of breaking news at any moment of any day and just as many that promote a particular viewpoint. The result is that news consumers can tailor the information they receive to correspond to, and reinforce, their political prejudices.

Soft news may be entertaining, but it does nothing to help inform the audience.[15] And the Internet may put a world of information at one's fingertips, but it too easily enables citizens to avoid information that may conflict with what they prefer to believe.[16] For our purposes, the bigger problem caused by the rise of both soft news and the Internet is that politicians are too often forced to address "issues" that are not related to policy but are, instead, salacious and titillating. These include, of course, sex scandals (of which I'll have more to say in the Chapter 7). But some of the "controversies" that have attracted considerable attention in recent years are trivial and don't even have the virtue of being interesting. These include the cost of a candidate's haircut; the authenticity of a congressional leader's tan; the price tag on a bottle of wine ordered by a member of Congress; the schools to which various elected officials send their children; and the amount of credit a candidate has at an exclusive jewelry store. Stories such as these can be rationalized in all sorts of ways. They tell us something about a politician's lifestyle, which, in turn, is indicative of his or her ability to empathize with average Americans. Or they give us insight into their judgment. Or, similarly, they are windows into the character of politicians. Of course, by that logic *everything* a politician does is newsworthy.

In fact, that is the new standard of newsworthiness. Whereas in previous eras, politicians could expect a considerable amount of privacy, today they have none. Even fairly scandalous personal behavior was off-limits to journalists in the past. Nowadays, every move a politician makes is under surveillance. They cannot expect a moment of privacy. And every word they say is captured on tape, analyzed within minutes of its utterance, and archived by opponents for potential use at a later date. Every malapropism is subject to endless ridicule; every misstatement is taken to be a purposeful deception; and every claim that appears to contradict an earlier one will be used to suggest a flip-flop, or worse. Anyone who would like to imagine the intensity of such scrutiny should try the following: For the next month, assume that anything you say— on the phone, via e-mail, or face-to-face—can wind up on the front page of tomorrow morning's paper and broadcast on the nightly news. If you should take this challenge, you'll notice that, first of all, you say numerous things every day that you wouldn't want publicized in the news. And, second, it is extremely difficult to be on guard at all times. Even if you manage to avoid saying something that might embarrass you, the stress of having to watch everything you say is tremendous.

I can anticipate the response from many readers at this point. No one forces politicians into the arena, some will say. In other words, politicians know what they're getting into when they decide to run for office. Furthermore, they court media attention relentlessly; they can't object when that attention isn't always on their terms. The same is true for politicians' relationships with parties, interest groups, and voters. When politicians ask for support—in the form, for example, of campaign contributions or votes—they have to expect their supporters to ask for something in return. The pressure politicians feel from interest groups or their constituencies is simply the other end of the bargain. And politicians are as likely to try to manipulate public opinion as they are to be constrained by it.

There is some validity to these claims. I certainly don't mean to imply that politicians are innocent victims. But neither are they complete villains. Instead, they respond to incentives in the structure of the political system the way all rational human beings would respond. If their collective activity seems dysfunctional, it is not because there is a flaw in the individual politicians themselves. Instead, it's because the system pressures politicians to behave in ways that may be less than ideal. The fact that the public wants politicians to disregard such pressure leads to the first category of criticism I want to explore.

Politicians Pander

One of the most common allegations made against politicians is that they pander to the voters or to public opinion generally. Another way of putting it is to say that they are too responsive to the will of the people. They should do what is best for the country, say the critics, and not worry about how popular it is. However, in a republican form of government, where the people elect representatives to do their collective business, aren't politicians supposed be responsive to the public?

The debate over how responsive representatives should be dates to at least the eighteenth century. Hanna Pitkin summarized nicely what is often called the "mandate-independence controversy" in her classic work on representation *The Concept of Representation*. As Pitkin puts it, "Should (must) a representative do what his [sic] constituents want, and be bound by mandates or instructions from them; or should (must) he be free to act as seems best to him in pursuit of their welfare?"[17] Representatives who are bound to constituency mandates are often referred to as "delegates"; those who are independent are called "trustees."

Now at first blush, it might seem that democracy requires representatives to act as delegates. After all, we elect representatives to do what we would do were we to legislate directly. But, as Pitkin points out, the delegate's obligations quickly become problematic as one thinks about them further.[18] How is one person supposed to stand for hundreds of thousands (in the case of a member of the U.S. House of Representatives)? How could a representative ever know the true preferences of his or her constituency? What should the representative do if the people he or she represents are ill-informed? What if the constituents prefer a policy option that the representative firmly believes (based, perhaps, on information the constituents do not have) would be harmful to their interests? And what is the representative to do if his or her constituents' interests run counter to the interests of the nation? Is there any room for the delegate to compromise?

Satisfactory answers to such questions are hard to come by. As a result, many political thinkers have come to the conclusion that the trustee model of representation is best. One such thinker is Edmund Burke, the eighteenth-century political philosopher and member of the British House of Commons. In his famous speech to the voters of Bristol in 1774, Burke maintained,

> Government and Legislation are matters of reason and judgment, and not of inclination; and what sort of reason is that, in which the determination precedes the discussion; in which one set of men deliberate, and another decide; and where those who form the conclusion are perhaps three hundred miles distant from those who hear the arguments?[19]

In other words, the legislature is, or ought to be, a deliberative body. How can elected officials know the correct course of action *before* they've heard arguments on all sides? Indeed, representatives are chosen for this very purpose—to hear arguments, engage in deliberation, and settle on the best policy options available. What is the point of sending representatives to a legislature if they are to act only as rubber-stamps for their constituencies' opinions? "Your Representative owes you," said Burke, "not his industry only, but his judgement; and he betrays, instead of serving you, if he sacrifices it to your opinion."[20]

The American public largely disagrees with Burke and those who argue that representatives should not be constrained by constituency opinion. Though there has been very little research on the public's preference for representational style—and what has been done is now quite dated—the results of that research make clear that Americans want their representatives to act as delegates. The earliest evidence for this conclusion comes from public opinion polls conducted before the United States entered World War II. Between November 1938 and April 1940, four polls asked Americans their preference in the delegate vs. trustee debate. In three of those four, between 61 and 66 percent of the respondents chose the delegate model of representation.[21]

The questions in those pre-war polls were of the either/or variety. That is, respondents were required to indicate a preference for either the delegate model or the trustee model. In 1965, Carl McMurray and Malcolm Parsons published the results of research they did based on a survey that asked respondents to agree or disagree with separate statements describing the delegate and trustee models of representation.[22] This allowed for the possibility, as illogical as it is, that some respondents would favor both the delegate and the trustee models.

McMurray and Parsons found that 69.1 percent favored the delegate form of representation for members of Congress (and slightly higher percentages favored it for state legislators and city councilors). But when asked about the trustee model, 45.9 percent favored it as well.[23] In the end, less than half (47 percent) the respondents favored the delegate model and opposed the trustee model; but only 18 percent favored the trustee model while opposing the delegate model.[24] Interestingly, over a quarter (26 percent) of the respondents favored representatives *always* being both a delegate and a trustee. Another 9 percent took the view that a representative should not be either a delegate or a trustee exclusively, a view referred to in the literature as the "politico" model of representation.[25]

It should be said that the sample used by McMurray and Parsons has some limitations. For example, their results are based on the responses of 207 individuals in the Cape Kennedy area of Florida in 1962.[26] Nevertheless, their findings suggest two important conclusions for our purposes. First, Americans tend to favor the delegate model of representation over the trustee model.[27] This is a conclusion supported by most of the research done subsequent to the McMurray and Parsons study.[28] The 1978 American National Election Study (ANES), for example, asked respondents the following question:

> Sometimes voters want their U.S. representative to do something the representative disagrees with. When this happens, do you think the representative should do what the voters think best, or should the representative do what he or she thinks best?

A majority of voters (55.4 percent) wanted the representative to do what the voters think best (i.e., the delegate model). Not quite 30 percent (29.8) trusted the representative to do what he or she thinks best while 11 percent held the politico view, saying, "it depends."[29]

In addition, Roger Davidson asked respondents on a national survey to "describe the job of being a Congressman" or, in other words, "what are the most important things you think he [sic] should do in Washington."[30] Davidson found that, first and foremost, people wanted members of Congress to act as "Tribunes." In such a role, the representative acts "as discoverer, reflector, or advocate of popular needs and demands."[31] Implicit in this view, according to Davidson, is a preference for the delegate model of representation.

Second, and perhaps more importantly, the McMurray and Parsons results indicate that a significant portion of the public want representatives to play contradictory roles simultaneously. Recall that over a quarter of the public agreed that legislators ought to *always* vote according to the voters' wishes and they should *always* vote according to their own best judgments. As a result, elected officials will inevitably disappoint, if not anger, these people.

To a large extent, then, the question of whether representatives should be delegates or trustees is linked to the leader-and-follower trap described in Chapter 1. A sizeable percentage of the American public apparently wants politicians to lead, or act as trustees, but also to follow, or act as delegates. Having said that, nearly two-thirds (65 percent) of the respondents in the McMurray and Parsons survey landed consistently on the side of either the delegate view or the trustee view. In at least one sense (i.e., consistency), this is encouraging.

But, in truth, it is unrealistic to expect representatives to *always* (as the survey questions stipulated) act as a delegate or a trustee. A more reasonable view to take on this debate is that representatives should be politicos, acting as delegates in some situations and as trustees in others. Perhaps, for instance, the representative should do as his or her constituents wish when those constituents are well informed on a given issue and have reached something of a consensus on it; otherwise, he or she should act as a trustee. Regardless of whether the politico model is a more realistic or reasonable view of representation than the delegate or trustee models, it is not popular with the American public. Only 9 percent of the respondents in the McMurray and Parsons study, and only 11 percent in the 1978 ANES survey, expressed the view that elected officials shouldn't be confined to only one representational style.

To be fair, there is some evidence that the public holds somewhat nuanced views of the role elected officials ought to play. According to Lee Sigelman, Carol Sigelman, and Barbara Walkosz, "people do not appear to have a generalized preference for one kind of leadership or another."[32] Sigelman and colleagues conducted an experiment in which subjects were given vignettes about the decision-making process of a hypothetical elected official named Wayne Fowler. Several pairs of variables were combined in various ways to create 64 different situations. The key variable pairings were whether Fowler was an executive (i.e., governor) or a state legislator; whether the issue under consideration was complicated or largely symbolic and easy to understand; whether Fowler's ultimate decision complied with his constituents' preferences or was opposed to them; and whether the rationale given for Fowler's decision was principled or self-serving.[33]

Among the main results of the experiment is the finding that "Fowler was evaluated more favorably when he did the people's bidding than when he followed his own instincts."[34] That is, people generally preferred Fowler to act as a delegate than as a trustee. That preference, however, was stronger when the hypothetical politician was depicted as a legislator than when he was governor. So the public may have some sense that the behavior of elected officials should differ depending on the office they hold. But, for the most part, the subjects in this experiment preferred their elected officials to be delegates.

At the same time, the subjects responded more positively to a decision that was described as principled than to one that was, as the authors put it, "politically expedient."[35] Since subjects appear to want a delegate who acts on principle, the only logical conclusion a politician could draw from these findings is that his or her principles had better comply with the preferences of his or her constituents. How voters could be certain that those principles are sincere, but just happen to be compliant rather than being the product of political expediency, is not entirely clear. Given the public's dim view of politicians, they are likely just to assume that any decision that complies with voters' wishes is purely self-serving and not based on principle.

Sigelman and his co-investigators provided some insight into people's assumptions about politicians by asking subjects how typical they found Fowler's behavior to be. When Fowler's decision was explained in self-serving terms, and when he acted as a delegate, subjects were significantly more likely to describe him as typical of elected officials. "These findings suggest," the authors write, "that respondents tended to view most politicians as delegates, but as unprincipled ones, concerned primarily with hanging on to their offices."[36] In other words, politicians pander.

But is there any evidence that politicians pander? Anecdotally, the evidence seems overwhelming. Republicans pander to the wealthy, Democrats to unions. Conservatives pander to pro-life and pro-business organizations; liberals pander to pro-choice and pro-environment organizations. Regardless of party, members of Congress from agricultural districts or states favor subsidies to farmers. Politicians of all ideological stripes promise to protect Social Security and Medicare. No elected official seems willing to even consider, let alone vote for, a tax increase on the "middle class," defined so broadly as to include nearly all Americans.

Examples such as these have led political scientist Paul Quirk to offer "a high-pandering, limited-autonomy account of the contemporary politics of law-making in the US."[37] According to Quirk, new technologies have made it easier for ordinary citizens to obtain information about public policy and to act on that information to influence elected officials. In addition, the increased competitiveness of elections since the 1990s has encouraged parties and politicians to do whatever is necessary to garner votes.[38] The combination of these factors has led to "*all pandering, all of the time.*"[39]

But to whom are politicians pandering? Those making the allegation rarely answer this question specifically. Typically, the implication is that politicians are courting public opinion. Whether it's national public opinion or opinion within a particular district or state is not often clear.

Quirk, however, provides an answer. Politicians, he argues, are responding to the policy demands of "mass constituencies," by which he means "the relatively extreme ideological constituencies of various kinds that are manifestly crucial in contemporary congressional politics."[40] Elsewhere, Quirk narrows the category a bit. In a 2011 article, he refers to "less encompassing mass constituencies" that "include the core constituencies of each party."[41] These core constituencies, otherwise known as the parties' "bases," include organized interests, citizens' groups and political movements, party activists and contributors, and various groups of voters such as the elderly, religious conservatives, and racial minorities. The key point, for Quirk, is that these constituencies do not consist of elites, which he describes as being employed in politics or government and who "do politics or government all day."[42] Thus, unless one makes a living in politics or government, one is part of the masses.

We could, of course, quibble with Quirk's equating party bases with "mass constituencies." This seems a sleight of hand intended to capture the vague sense that pandering is a response to public opinion, broadly construed (i.e., to *mass* constituencies), while also acknowledging the reality that the parties' bases have outsized influence in an era of partisan polarization. But whether or not Quirk is justified in referring to the parties' core supporters as mass constituencies is not critical. More important is his argument that politicians are pandering to those constituencies.

The real problem with Quirk's view, and with all claims that politicians pander, is that any sign of responsiveness is taken as evidence of pandering. Indeed, anytime a politician's position is in alignment with that of some constituency group or other, that politician will appear to be pandering. But unless a politician takes a position that has yet to be articulated, there will always be a group that has advocated for the position the politician ultimately adopts. As a result, the politician in question will appear to be pandering to someone.

Of course, the chances that a politician's position is aligned with not only a key constituency group, but with most constituency groups and voters within his/her party, are now much higher given the partisan sorting that has occurred in recent decades. That is, Democrats are much more uniformly liberal than they used to be, just as Republicans have become, to one degree or another, conservative.[43] Because both elites and rank-and-file partisans have sorted themselves in this way, it should not surprise us that the preferences of politicians are in line with those of their supporters.

In addition to the logical critique of the pandering allegation, there is also empirical evidence against it. In a particularly compelling book entitled *Politicians Don't Pander*, Lawrence Jacobs and Robert Shapiro conducted case studies of the attempt by Bill Clinton to enact health care reform and of the Republican "Revolution" of the mid 1990s.[44] Jacobs and Shapiro argue that politicians are motivated by both policy objectives (few of which reflect centrist opinion) and re-election. Though the two goals are quite often in conflict with one another—because the pursuit of policies on the right or left jeopardizes swing votes—politicians attempt to accomplish them by engaging in what Jacobs and Shapiro call "crafted talk." That is, "politicians craft how they present their policy stances in order to attract favorable press coverage and 'win' public support for what they desire."[45]

Far from being overly responsive, according to Jacobs and Shapiro, politicians pursue policies they find desirable and attempt to steer public preferences in the direction of those policies. When they are successful, the process will "simulate responsiveness" because policies will correspond to public opinion.[46] But it does so only because politicians first had to move opinion in the desired direction. In other words, rather than pander to public opinion, politicians manipulate it.

Politics, in this scenario, becomes a game of tug-of-war with public opinion as the flag in the middle of the rope.[47] The more one side (i.e., party) can pull opinion in its direction, the better its chances of winning policy debates and elections. If the people and their preferences dominate American politics in Quirk's view, they are victims in Jacobs and Shapiro's.

Neither portrait of contemporary American politics is desirable. Fortunately, neither is entirely accurate. Given the deep divide between the parties on just about every significant issue (and many quite insignificant ones), at least half of all politicians can't be pandering to the public at any given time. Quirk gets around this fact by arguing that politicians pander not to the public but to their bases; as a result, they are all in a constant state of pandering. But, as noted above, this argument leads one to the ridiculous conclusion that any responsiveness on the part of politicians, or indeed any policy agreement they may have with any group whatsoever, is pandering. We may consider this pandering if we wish, but it could just as easily be considered an essential element of democracy.

Jacobs and Shapiro, on the other hand, leave an impression that overstates their case. Though they occasionally describe politicians as pursuing policies "they and their supporters favor,"[48] they more often than not neglect to mention the supporters. The emphasis in *Politicians Don't Pander* is clearly on what politicians do and say (notwithstanding three chapters' worth of analysis of the media's role in the process). The influence of interest groups, think tanks, party activists, campaign donors, and primary voters on politicians' policy preferences gets very little attention from Jacobs and Shapiro. But that influence is substantial.

Indeed, it can be traced to changes that began to take place in American politics as far back as the 1940s. Following World War II, activists with unambiguous ideological perspectives began organizing to voice their concerns and to advocate for their legislative agendas. For example, a group of liberal activists formed Americans for Democratic Action (ADA) in 1947 to pressure the Democratic Party to move left at a time when conservative southerners held considerable sway in the party.[49] Activists like those who formed ADA would become a highly visible force in American politics by the 1960s.

Before nearly anyone had noticed them, such activists caught the attention of the Harvard political scientist James Q. Wilson, who in

1960 and 1961 interviewed dozens of these political "amateurs" (as well as their professional counterparts) in three American cities. For Wilson, the amateur politician is not, as the adjective "amateur" would suggest, someone who engages in politics solely as a hobby. Instead, it's a person for whom a cause is more important than personal or partisan gain. Wilson described "the amateur spirit" in the 1966 preface to *The Amateur Democrat* as animated by

> the belief that the proper motive for political action is a concern for the ends of politics, that participation in the management of the affairs of the party ought to be widespread and in accord with strictly democratic procedures, and that party leaders and elective officials ought to be directly responsive to the substantive goals of the party activists.[50]

Later in the book, Wilson notes that amateurs favor programmatic parties, or those that offer "a real policy alternative to the opposition party."[51] Amateurs, in other words, are ideologically motivated political purists who are uninterested in compromising with the other side. Indeed, as Wilson suggests, this new brand of party activist "sees each battle as a 'crisis,' and each victory as a triumph and each loss as a defeat for a cause."[52]

Since the 1960s, amateurs have come to play a central role in both political parties. According to political scientists Marty Cohen, David Karol, Hans Noel, and John Zaller, groups of what they refer to as "intense policy demanders" form coalitions that back one party or the other.[53] In fact, these coalitions are now thought to constitute the political parties or, at least, to act as extensions of the parties.[54] As a result, intense policy demanders have significant influence over the political parties. In recent decades, for example, they have been able to exert considerable influence over whom each party nominates for president.[55] Furthermore, party activists have been identified as a leading contributor to—if not the primary cause of—the partisan polarization that has increased so dramatically in recent decades.[56]

If party activists have significant control over the parties, then they drive much of what happens in American politics today. In one sense, then, Quirk is correct; politicians are not entirely autonomous actors. They must be responsive to their base if they wish to stay in office and carry out a legislative agenda. But the relationship is a symbiotic one. Politicians rely on party activists to support their election bids, but intense policy demanders need politicians to not only put themselves forward as candidates for office (something even most political activists are loath to do), but to enact favorable legislation once in office. Furthermore, politicians are the primary spokespersons for the agenda.

It is fruitless to wonder who is calling the shots in this relationship. Nowadays activists and politicians tend to be on the same page ideologically. That is, while there may be differences of opinion over the strategy and tactics needed to accomplish their goals, intense policy demanders and politicians agree on matters of public policy. Increasingly, large segments of the electorate also fall in line with the issue positions of activists and politicians in their own parties.[57]

Recall from the previous chapter the discussion of the "partisan sort." The sorting process has created parties that are more ideologically cohesive than they've been in decades. Engaged voters who identify with a political party, the activists within the party network, and the politicians who stand for the party are increasingly cut from the same ideological cloth. Thus, the question of why politicians take the positions they take is something of a political chicken-and-egg. The politicians who are most successful are those who start their careers with policy positions that are consonant with those of the party's base. Politicians don't have to pander; they're already in agreement with the people they need in order to win elections.

There is nothing nefarious in this arrangement, but it doesn't sit well with the American public. Undoubtedly, it is the case that politicians appear compelled to be responsive—whether to their base or their constituents, or to public opinion generally—because they want to stay in office. It's not the responsiveness but the desire to stay in office that people seem to dislike. One might wonder how responsive an elected official would be if he or she did not care to remain in office. Nevertheless, there is something about the politician's wish to be elected that bothers people. Much of that desire is rooted in ambition, a character trait I'll address in Chapter 6. But some part of it is simply a requirement of the profession. If you want to be an elected official, you must win elections. And given the frequency with which we hold elections in the United States, an elected official must constantly be in campaign mode. I take up this aspect of politicians' public lives—as well as the allegation that they are blinded by ideology, partisanship, or both—in the following chapter.

Chapter 4

The Public Lives of Politicians
Election (or Ideology, or Party) Above All Else?

In the last chapter I argued that, generally speaking, politicians are guilty of neither pandering to public opinion nor manipulating it. They are simply responsive to groups of activists and voters that make up their party's base. In fact, policy responsiveness on the part of politicians is largely a by-product of the fact that the parties are increasingly ideologically cohesive. It is not, as the pandering allegation would suggest, the result of politicians determining which positions are popular and then adopting them.

Nevertheless, politicians may still be guilty of placing their election above all else. In other words, politicians may focus too much of their efforts on winning elections and not enough on doing the "people's business." Furthermore, given the ideological compatibility between politicians and party bases, one could argue that politicians have become too ideological, too partisan, or both. This chapter takes up these allegations.

Is it All About Getting Elected?

That politicians care about winning elections is undeniable. But exactly why they seem so desperate to win is unclear and, in fact, is probably unknowable. That's because asking them is not a reliable way to uncover their actual motivations. I have never heard a politician say, "I first ran for office because I wanted fame and power." They'll tell you, I believe sincerely, that they entered politics to make a difference. Often, they first ran for office to try to fix a very specific problem that no one else was addressing. Perhaps, once in office, their motivations change. But they aren't likely to admit publicly that, though they entered politics to do good, they want to stay in office for selfish reasons. I doubt that, were the latter really true, many politicians would acknowledge that fact even to themselves. People rarely ascribe disreputable motives to themselves.

Motivations are quite complex and people, including politicians, are unlikely to be fully aware of what is motivating them. In fact, politicians are likely to be motivated by multiple goals simultaneously. As Joseph Schlesinger noted in his classic study, *Ambition and Politics*, "Politicians are no more driven by the single motive of office than businessmen are guided solely by the desire for profit or doctors by the urge to heal. Each has a life beyond his [sic] occupation which impinges on the way he performs."[1]

Politicians are, no doubt, driven by self-interest, just as we all are. But it takes more than self-interest to motivate a person to run for office. Keeping in mind that the vast majority of politicians in the United States operate at the state or local level, one realizes that any benefits that could possibly accrue to individuals by entering politics are actually quite limited. Salaries are low (or, in the case of citizen legislators, non-existent), the level of prestige is minimal, and very few individual politicians wield much power. Furthermore, the work is largely thankless. Even most members of Congress could acquire more for themselves outside of politics. As congressional scholar Patricia Hurley has observed, "There are plenty of other jobs that pay more money, are less demanding, and even feed one's ego more generously than those of U.S. representative or senator."[2]

Viewed from this perspective, it is a wonder anyone willingly endures the significant hardships of running for office. That they do is an indication that there is more than self-interest shaping the behavior of politicians. What might an additional motivator be? John Kingdon has suggested "ideas" as a catch-all to "refer either to goals or motivations other than self-interested pursuits or to theories about how the world works."[3] Ideas include, I would add, solutions to public problems (i.e., policy proposals).

Kingdon argues that we can't separate ideas from self-interest. Politicians use ideas to help them get elected and getting elected helps them advance ideas. Keep in mind that elected officials became elected officials in the first place by agreeing with their constituents, or at least a plurality of those who vote, on the broad direction in which public policy should be headed and, more than likely, on specific positions on major issues. Thus, even a politician who cared about nothing other than getting elected would have to champion ideas that are held by the people in his or her party's base and by most of the voters in his or her area.[4]

Just taking the correct positions, however, would not be enough to guarantee success, as there are dozens of other potential candidates with the same positions in each district or state. Thus, candidates who can best communicate ideas are likely to have an advantage at election time.

Those candidates, in turn, are likely to be the ones who embrace ideas most sincerely. The alternative is to argue that the candidates most likely to be successful are simply those who can *act* as if they embrace ideas sincerely. I'll take up this argument in Chapter 6. For now, suffice it to say that this assumes a level of mendacity that simply could not be sustained across all levels of our political system.

The flipside of the candidate who takes all the right positions but for the wrong reasons (i.e., for his or her election) is the candidate who wants nothing more than to make good public policy. But even that candidate would have to have election as a proximate goal. That is, before a politician can pursue a policy agenda, he or she has to win an election. And to win an election, one has to run a campaign. That, in turn, requires a great deal of effort, all of which necessarily revolves around the candidate. So the politician who only wants to do well by the public must first act for him or herself in the short run.

This is why Kingdon concludes, "Most of the time, legislators take *both* the expedient course *and* the principled course at once."[5] In other words, we can never determine exactly what the balance of influence between ideas and self-interest is for any given action by a politician. Rather than assume it is always one or the other, we should accept that it is both. Perhaps one or the other holds a bit more (or even quite a bit more) sway at any given time. But politicians want to win elections and they want to achieve public policy goals. Trying to figure out which one they want *more* is not only impossible, it is pointless.

Admittedly, it often appears that politicians care more about winning elections than anything else. But that's simply a result of the frequency with which we hold elections. In the American system, politicians are constantly running for office because we are constantly holding elections for office. Frequent elections make politicians act like politicians—rather than, say, statesmen and stateswomen—all of the time.

The United States holds more elections than just about any other country in the world. "Among advanced democracies," writes Mark Franklin in a comprehensive study of comparative voter turnout rates, "only Switzerland and the United States call their voters to the polls more than once a year on average."[6] Why do we hold so many elections? In short, it is because we distrust politicians so much.

At the time of the constitutional debates (1787), the British Parliament had a maximum tenure of seven years, which had been increased from three by the Septennial Act of 1716. For the Framers, seven years between elections was far too long at least for the House of Representatives. Some, including James Madison, argued for three-year terms. Others wanted annual elections, which was the common practice for the state legislatures. Annual elections, according to Elbridge Gerry of Massachusetts, were "the only defence [sic] of the people ag[ainst] tyranny."[7] "By remaining at the seat of Gov[ernment]" for too long, argued Roger Sherman of Connecticut, representatives "would acquire the habits of the place which might differ from those of their Constituents."[8] Essentially, the Framers believed that frequent elections kept elected officials well behaved.

On the other hand, some of them realized that holding elections too frequently also posed risks. As Daniel of St. Thomas Jenifer (of Maryland) maintained, "the too great frequency of elections rendered the people indifferent to them, and made the best men unwilling to engage in so precarious a service."[9] Similarly, Alexander Hamilton sought to strike a balance in the frequency of elections. He argued, "There ought to be neither too much nor too little dependence, on the popular sentiments" and that holding elections too often "tended to make the people listless to them; and to facilitate the success of little cabals."[10] This, Hamilton claimed, was a complaint heard in all of the states.

Though all of the Framers argued for frequent elections, then, the question was just how frequently they should be held. At first, those who wanted a bit more breathing room for elected officials (including senators and the president, though those offices were not to be directly elected by the people) seemed to have won. The Constitutional Convention initially voted for terms of office of three years for the House, seven years for the Senate, and seven years for the president. Of course, these terms would eventually be shortened to two, six, and four, respectively. For the House and Senate, these terms were compromises between the very frequent and the not so frequent camps. For the president, four years was the shortest term proposed.

Nearly all office-holders in the United States, including those at the state and local levels, are elected frequently. And because some state elections are held in odd years (so as not to compete with federal elections for the voters' attention) and many local elections are held in the spring, it appears that some group of politicians or another is constantly running for office. None of this, of course, is to mention the use of direct primaries.

Primaries are not widely used outside the United States, but they are used to nominate candidates for many types of offices at all levels of American government. As noted in Chapter 2, direct primaries are a creation of the Progressive era. As such, primaries are typically thought to have been an anti-party reform and, indeed, for Progressive reformers they were. But Alan Ware has made a convincing case that politicians weren't always opposed to the adoption of the direct primary.[11] Indeed, without the support of elected officials, the legislation required to make primaries the legally required method of nominating candidates couldn't have passed. Of course, anti-party reformers were central to the movement to adopt direct primaries. As Ware notes, they helped "transform a debate about a highly complex issue—nomination reform—into one in which a 'solution' (the direct primary) came to the forefront."[12] But politicians—unaware though they may have been of the long-term consequences of primaries—were also critical to the implementation of the primary as a standard feature of the American electoral system.

At the time, primaries were thought by many party leaders to solve several problems that had begun to plague the old caucus-convention system of nominating candidates.[13] Primaries were also a response to public opinion, which, as discussed in Chapter 2, had begun to sour on parties by the end of the nineteenth century. Ware downplays public opinion as a factor in the adoption of primaries, though he does admit that it served as a "constraint" on the alternatives politicians could realistically consider.[14] He also denies the influence of a general anti-partyism.[15] Surely, however, the long history of anti-party sentiment in the United States helped to bolster arguments for what many believed to be a reform whose goal was to weaken political parties.[16]

One of the most significant consequences of the use of primaries was to make candidates reliant on themselves, rather than the party organization, to build their campaigns. As mentioned in the previous chapter, with the advent of primaries, candidates had to build their own campaign staffs, develop their own strategies (and concomitant "messages"), and raise the money necessary to mount a serious campaign. Perhaps most importantly, they had to do all of these things not once, but twice in each election cycle. Given the short terms of most American elected officials, the process has become a perpetual one.

Despite the fact that politicians had a hand in piling election upon election in the American system of politics, the justification for all of these elections is, at root, the distrust of politicians. From one perspective, what the Framers and the Progressive reformers wanted to achieve was accountability. This principle is essential to a properly functioning democracy. That is, in a democracy, we expect representatives of the people to be responsive to those people. Just how responsive representatives must be is up to the people themselves. Thus, elections ensure that elected officials are held to account by the ultimate authority in a democracy—the people. Frequent elections, in turn, ensure that the ultimate authority renders judgment regularly. Otherwise, so the theory goes, the sovereignty of the people is jeopardized.

The irony, though, is that our preferred method for holding elected officials accountable—which is not elections, per se, but rather frequent elections—forces them to behave in precisely the ways people find unacceptable in public servants. We do not want politicians to constantly think about their elections, but we make them endure elections constantly. We make politicians feel intensely vulnerable, and then blame them for acting in ways that might alleviate their vulnerability. We do this, I suppose, because we want politicians to *be* vulnerable, but not *feel* vulnerable. The absurdity, not to mention the unreasonableness, of this desire should be patently obvious.

Of all the behaviors that frequent elections produce, the most distasteful (to the public and most politicians alike) is the so-called "money chase." In order to run an effective campaign, candidates must raise an incredible (some would say insane) amount of money. The median amount raised by winning candidates for a seat in the U.S. House of Representatives in 2010 was just over $1 million.[17] To put that in perspective, serious House candidates had to raise roughly $10,000 per week, beginning the morning after Election Day 2008. For Senate candidates, the situation is even worse. They have to raise over $19,000 per week for six years.[18] This explains why it is not uncommon for elected officials to spend over half of their time fundraising.

To raise the kind of money they need to be competitive, politicians must turn to wealthy donors and political action committees (PACs). This creates the concern that they "owe" their wealthy contributors something in return for the campaign donations. There may be anecdotal evidence to suggest that money influences policy outcomes. But the political science research on the question is mixed, at best. In fact, one review of the literature concludes, "PAC contributions show relatively few effects on [legislators'] voting behavior. In three out of four instances, campaign contributions had no statistically significant effects on legislation or had the 'wrong' sign—suggesting that more contributions lead to less support."[19] This is not to say that money *never* influences the policymaking process and, indeed, systematic evidence does exist to support the view that wealthy contributors get favorable treatment at least some of the time.[20] However, the idea that there is a quid pro quo between elected officials and their well-heeled backers is not supported by the scholarship.

One of the reasons it will always be difficult to isolate the impact of contributions on votes is that money may follow, rather than precede, votes. Contributors, being strategic, are more likely to give money to elected officials and candidates who have already established a record of support for the contributors' interests than to give to a politician whose support is less certain. That is, the real effect of campaign contributions may be to help sympathetic politicians stay in office (or win in the first place) rather than to persuade legislators with unclear intentions to vote a particular way. In the end, it is much easier to help friends than to create them.

If this is an accurate portrayal of the way money is typically used in politics, then we are left with a very different image of politicians than we usually have in mind. Rather than opportunists who have fingers in the wind, waiting to be captured by the highest bidder, politicians may well be principled actors with a clear set of issue positions who raise money from allies in order to compete in increasingly expensive elections. Of course, some will still find fault with this image. The principled politician is, according to these critics, a mere ideologue and his or her relationship with allies is nothing but blind partisanship.

Ideologues and Partisans

There is no doubt that most politicians hold distinct ideologies and many hold them dearly. Increasingly, politicians in the same party also happen to share a commitment to the same ideology. Indeed, as Figure 4.1 illustrates, the two parties are now highly polarized along ideological lines. Despite the fact that this phenomenon is often discussed in apocalyptic terms, the level of polarization today isn't particularly unique in American history. At the turn of the twenty-first century, polarization was no greater than it had been in the 1910s and early 1920s or in the 1890s.[21] There was, however, far less polarization between the 1930s and the 1980s and it is that "golden age" of bipartisan moderation that many observers pine for today.

What is the normal state of political affairs in a two-party democracy like ours? I argued in Chapter 2 that deep divisions between Americans have existed since the Founding of the Republic. In truth, then, the supposedly golden age of moderation in the middle of the twentieth century was an historical anomaly. The polarization we're witnessing today is really a return to form after an unusual period of ideological pluralism in the two parties. That period was caused by an extraordinary event, the Great Depression. The Depression allowed Franklin Roosevelt to unite southern conservatives, who had been "yellow-dog Democrats" since the Civil War, with more liberal members of the party from outside

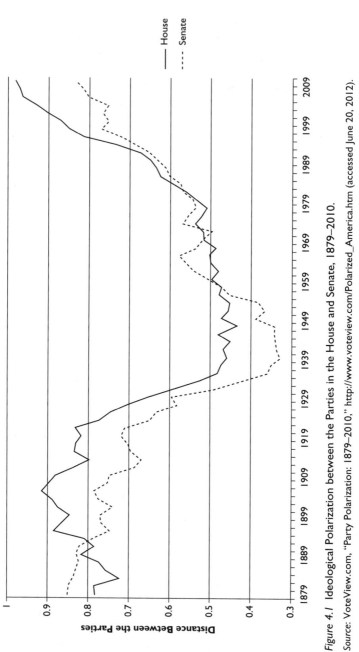

Figure 4.1 Ideological Polarization between the Parties in the House and Senate, 1879–2010.

Source: VoteView.com, "Party Polarization: 1879–2010," http://www.voteview.com/Polarized_America.htm (accessed June 20, 2012).

Note: The numbers on the Y-axis represent the distance between "the Republican and Democratic Party means on the first DW-NOMINATE dimension" (ibid.). The range of DW-NOMINATE scores is −1.0 (most liberal) to 1.0 (most conservative).

the South. This "New Deal Coalition" was fragile from its inception and it wasn't likely to hold together for long.

As early as Roosevelt's second term, fault lines in the Democratic Party were beginning to appear. By 1937, a "conservative coalition" between Republicans and southern Democrats had formed in the House of Representatives.[22] Initially, southern Democrats defected on labor issues and those involving civil liberties, but disagreements arose over social welfare in the 1940s and foreign policy in the 1950s.[23] Of course, the most contentious issue was civil rights. In 1948, half of the Alabama delegation and the entire Mississippi delegation walked out of the Democratic National Convention after states' rights resolutions were defeated and a strongly worded civil rights plank was inserted into the platform.[24] Over the next 20 years, the New Deal Coalition would continue to fracture until, by 1968, it was completely destroyed (at least at the presidential level).

The fact that politicians are normally divided by ideology doesn't mean this is a positive aspect of American politics. People long for the golden age of moderation not because it is the norm, but because they believe it to be a model for how American democracy should work. But that golden age may not have been as golden as we like to remember.

Liberal northeastern Republicans and conservative southern Democrats certainly did provide opportunities for bipartisan cooperation in the middle of the twentieth century. But they also confused matters for many voters. Which party, for example, was the party of civil rights in the 1950s and 1960s? (After all, a larger percentage of Republicans in the House voted for civil rights acts in 1957, 1960, and 1964 than did Democrats.) Which party believed in an active federal government? Which favored a robust internationalism in foreign policy? Put simply, Democrats and Republicans in the 1950s and 1960s were not fulfilling one of the most important functions of political parties in a representative democracy; namely, they weren't clarifying choices for the voters. This is why George Wallace's famous claim that "there's not a dime's worth of difference" between the two parties resonated with so many voters in 1968. When Ralph Nader made similar claims in 2000, far fewer took it seriously.

This lack of distinct agendas between the parties, and the resulting lack of a clear choice between them for voters, is precisely why the Committee on Political Parties of the American Political Science Association called for more "responsible" parties in a 1950 report. A healthy democracy, argued the Committee, requires parties that present real policy alternatives to the public. "When there are two parties identifiable by the kinds of action they propose," the Committee wrote, the voters have an actual choice. On the other hand, the sort of opposition presented by a coalition that cuts across party lines, as a regular thing, tends to deprive the public a meaningful alternative. When such coalitions are formed after the elections are over, the public usually finds it difficult to understand the new situation and to reconcile it with the purpose of the ballot. Moreover, on that basis it is next to impossible to hold either party responsible for its political record. This is a serious source of public discontent.[25]

Curiously, the Committee on Political Parties believed that parties could become more responsible—that is, they could establish party cohesion around distinct policy alternatives—and, yet, not "erect between themselves an ideological wall."[26] It is hard to imagine what programmatic and cohesive but non-ideological parties would look like. In fact, many politicians were driven by ideologies even in the golden age of moderation. The parties just looked non-ideological (or moderate) because the lack of party unity disguised the ideology, in the aggregate, of individual elected officials. But this was precisely the problem the Committee on Political Parties sought to address. When the parties included both liberals and conservatives among the ranks of their elected officials, it was very difficult to know what any individual Democratic or Republican candidate believed. Finding out what candidates up and down the ballot stood for, of course, required an enormous amount of effort on the part of voters, effort many of them simply couldn't exert. As a result, the ability of the electorate to hold parties and politicians accountable for their actions was severely compromised.

Today, we have something very close to the responsible parties that the Committee on Political Parties envisioned. As Nicol Rae notes, "The party scholars behind the 1950 report would certainly be pleased to see the development of more coherent and effective parties in the United States and the end of the organizationally ramshackle and ideologically incoherent parties of the post-New Deal era."[27] But with this development came polarization between the parties. That was inevitable. Despite the optimism of the Committee on Political Parties, once political elites began to sort themselves along programmatic lines, the ideological wall the Committee dismissed was, in fact, erected.

So the polarization we see in American politics today is merely a sign of the fact that Democrats and Republicans are now ideologically distinct. But this ideological distinctiveness, and the polarization it has produced, is far better than the alternatives. One alternative, the one

I've just been discussing, is for parties to be an ideological mish-mash. Ideology, in this scenario, might be an important element of politics but the two parties would contain politicians representing all (or at least most) points along the ideological spectrum. This alternative, as has been noted, confuses voters and hampers democratic accountability.

Another alternative to ideologically distinct, if polarized, parties would be parties that lack any ideology whatsoever. Though most Americans are likely to find this appealing, we cannot evaluate such an alternative until we know what would take the place of ideology. I suppose most people would expect that, free of ideology, politicians and their parties would pursue the best course of action for the nation. But, as I've already suggested, this is a pipedream. Indeed, if it were possible, we would only need one political party. Everyone would simply see the virtue in pursuing a particular course of action. Perhaps we could even dispense with elections!

Of course, one-party states are not democratic states. Differences of opinion, as we've established, exist among Americans and they will always exist. Consequently, the dream of political parties and politicians driven by nothing other than "what is best for the country" is not realistic. Once we begin to define "what is best," different perspectives will emerge. Those perspectives are rooted in ideologies; people who share an ideology are likely to join together in an organization that will further the ideology (i.e., a political party); and, therefore, parties will almost always be ideological.

In reality, political parties devoid of ideology—that is to say, parties made up of politicians who are not committed to principle—are very likely to be parties that are driven by spoils and patronage. We might say such parties are "pragmatic," but a better descriptor may be "opportunistic." Without policy goals to motivate them, parties would be concerned with little more than securing goodies for their constituents, their preferred interest groups, or themselves.

Ideology, then, provides a sound foundation for politicians' actions. It also helps to mobilize the electorate. According to Alan Abramowitz, "The strongest predictors of political engagement in 2004 were ideology and partisanship, followed closely by age and education."[28] Indeed, a long line of scholarship has established the fact that the more committed a person is to a cause, the more he or she is willing to incur the costs of participating in civic life. If widespread political participation is important in a democracy, we should embrace ideology, not lament its influence. Ideology provides clarity and passion in political debates and that, in turn, stimulates engagement by the public.

The immediate response to a suggestion that we welcome the role of ideology in our politics is to express the concern that compromise will be impossible if politicians cling to their ideologies. Of course, "clinging" to anything would make it hard to compromise. But there is no reason to believe that holding an ideology, and using it to guide one's thinking about matters of public policy, necessarily means that the ideology will be held dogmatically. Politicians, like all of us, are capable of holding ideologies and still compromising.

Admittedly, that may be easier said than done. There is a danger that one's ideology will blind him or her to certain facts about the world. We know, for example, that people tend to readily accept information if it confirms their prior beliefs, but to be skeptical of it if it contradicts those beliefs.[29] We also know that when people *only* surround themselves with like-minded individuals, and when they *only* use sources of information that share their ideological perspective, they not only become more confident in their point of view, but that point of view becomes more extreme.[30] Compromise under these circumstances would be difficult.

However, the problem is not ideology per se, but the manner in which information is processed and deliberation takes place (or doesn't). There are also personality attributes that influence one's willingness to compromise. Of the "Big Five" personality traits, for instance, agreeableness has been shown to correlate with a tendency to cooperate.[31] Furthermore, the process of negotiation is also vital to achieving resolution of disputes. Compromise is never easy, particularly when principles and values are at stake. But when values can be decoupled from interests, or when an understanding of the opponent's values is facilitated in some way, compromise is more likely than when values and interests are closely linked in the minds of those negotiating.[32]

The challenge we face is to find politicians who are committed to a set of principles and, yes, an ideology, but who are able to cooperate with those with whom they disagree. If, in recent years, we seem not to have met this challenge—and I am not convinced we haven't (see the case study in Chapter 5)—it is not because politicians hold ideologies. Instead, it is because the constitutional design of American government, and the incentive structure of American politics, makes compromise extremely difficult.

Others will argue that it is not ideology that concerns them but partisanship. Indeed, politicians motivated by principle would be welcome. But too often, so the argument goes, politicians act not on principle but simply to gain advantage for their party.

This argument finds some scholarly support in the work of Frances Lee. In her book *Beyond Ideology*, Lee examines the influence of ideology on roll-call votes in the U.S. Senate from 1981 to 2004. She finds that 44 percent of the votes that divided a majority of Democrats from a majority of Republicans (i.e., "party votes") contained no discernible ideological content.[33] Why would so much of the party conflict in the Senate be unrelated to the fundamental principles of the parties? Lee suggests that it is the result of "legislative partisans' collective electoral and power goals."[34]

Though it is a careful and impressive study, we could quibble (as one always can) with certain aspects of Lee's work. Most importantly, some of the issues she codes as non-ideological may, in fact, have ideological underpinnings. "Measures to promote electoral integrity," for example, seem uncontroversial and Lee codes them as "good-government causes" that "cannot be classified on the left-right continuum."[35] That may be true for some issues related to election administration. But there are others, such as voter registration and voter identification laws, for which ideology surely contributes to the disagreement. Indeed, the parties' positions on voter registration and identification reflect competing views about the desirability of eliminating barriers to the polling place. Philosophical disputes about that issue extend at least as far back as the eighteenth century.[36]

Of course, it is also the case that the positions the parties take on voter registration and voter identification align with their political interests. Presumably, the higher the bar to voting, the better Republican candidates are likely to do because the kinds of people most likely to be frustrated by voting regulations—the poor and the less well-educated—would disproportionately vote Democratic. Thus, policy disputes may be ideological and partisan at the same time. The mere fact that a party will benefit politically by its positions on issues does not preclude an ideological justification for those positions.

The critic who believes politicians are too partisan may be tempted to dismiss ideological justifications as rationalizations. The language of principles, he or she might argue, is window dressing meant to distract us from the real goal of the politician, namely, partisan advantage. I have no doubt that many people believe this, but I can think of no good reason to draw such a conclusion. As long as there is a recognizable ideological rationale for a policy position, an observer cannot possibly know whether the position is *mostly* the result of partisan considerations or of principled ones. (Conversely, if parties cannot muster a recognizable ideological rationale during a partisan dispute, or if the rationale is a stretch to any fair-minded observer, that would indicate that little more than jockeying for partisan advantage is behind the quarrel.)

It is important to recognize, too, that an increasing number of seemingly non-ideological issues in Congress are rooted in debates over the budget. Those debates, in turn, reflect the parties' most basic principles, namely those about the size and role of government. Thus, when Republicans in the House of Representatives voted to eliminate the Election Assistance Commission in 2011, surely a vote Lee would have coded as non-ideological, they did so primarily to "eliminate unnecessary government spending and help reduce the deficit."[37] There doesn't appear to be any partisan advantage to be gained by Republicans in eliminating a commission whose responsibility is to provide guidance to the states on matters of election administration. Instead, a general anti-government ideology appears to be the motivation.

Even partisan battles that are rooted in nothing other than an attempt by one party to gain an advantage over the other may, in fact, be a means to an end. In order to enact their policy agenda, a party has to secure a majority in Congress. "Partisan bickering," as Lee calls it at one point,[38] is not aimed at winning elections as the final goal. Winning elections, which requires some amount of partisan sniping, is required for controlling government, which, in turn, is required to advance a policy agenda.

Of course, the end, as worthy as it may be, doesn't justify the use of all means to accomplish it. But partisan bickering is a relatively harmless way—particularly in the context of the long, and quite bloody, history of power struggles between human beings—to help realize a party's goal of enacting legislation it views as beneficial to society. Furthermore, purely partisan votes in Congress don't occur as often as it might seem. In 2008, for example, 53 percent of all votes in the House of Representatives pitted a majority of Democrats against a majority of Republicans.[39] If less than half of those party votes lacked ideological content (based on Lee's estimates), than no more than a quarter of all House votes were purely partisan.

Part of the reason partisan strife seems to be ubiquitous is that the media puts a spotlight on conflict. Bipartisanship simply isn't newsworthy. Of course, party conflict could be covered in a way that makes policy alternatives clear and explains the ideological reasoning behind those alternatives. Instead, the media treat politics as a game and they place a heavy emphasis on the strategies that each player employs.

This approach to media coverage is most obvious in reporting about campaigns and elections.[40] Increasingly, however, it is being applied to coverage of the policymaking process.[41] Rather than examine the details and potential consequences of a policy proposal, journalists find it more intriguing, or perhaps just easier, to reveal the strategic machinations of the parties and to identify the political motivations of the politicians who support or oppose the proposal. To political junkies, the media's "game schema" is, indeed, interesting. But it comes at a cost. In the context of campaigns, strategic frames have been shown to hinder people's ability to retain substantive information.[42] And there is ample evidence that, regardless of the context, coverage of politics as a game increases cynicism about politics and government.[43] Because the only experience most of us have with politicians is through the media, and because the media tend to portray politicians "as calculated and deceitful users or, worse, manipulators of the media to their advantage,"[44] it's no wonder we conclude that they are driven by partisan concerns and not principle.

Some may still claim that politicians are only portrayed in the media as they "really" are. That is, they are deceitful and manipulative, and that's why they appear that way in the media. I'll deal with the character of politicians in Chapters 6 and 7. For now, I want to consider one of the most despised aspects of politicians' public behavior. Because it seems so willfully deceptive, "spin" is taken to be the prototypical political activity.

There is no widely accepted definition of spin, though William Safire's is probably as good as any. Spin, according to Safire, is "Deliberate shading of news perception; attempted control of political reaction."[45] It's not entirely clear what Safire means by "shading." It may suggest something like "conveying less than the truth." But spinning is not lying. If a politician tells a lie, we call it a lie; we wouldn't say he or she was merely spinning. So shading may mean that a politician in spin mode is only telling part of the truth. When a monthly jobs report indicates that hundreds of thousands of jobs were created but, at the same time, the unemployment rate rose as more people entered the job market looking (unsuccessfully) for work, the president's party can be expected to trumpet the number of jobs created and the opposition party will point to the increase in the unemployment rate. Neither is lying. They are simply interpreting the data in a way that puts their best foot forward. We can't seriously expect individuals (or groups of individuals) in a competitive setting to make the opposition's case for them, can we? I think we would all recognize that this is not a tactic unique to politicians. And there is nothing inherently dishonest about it.

Notice, too, that what is being shaded in Safire's definition is not the truth, but "news perception." Spinning is used to influence public attitudes about oneself, one's party, or one's position on an issue. This fact is captured in the second part of Safire's definition, "attempted control of political reaction." This is precisely what Jacobs and Shapiro mean by "crafted talk." Recall from Chapter 3 that politicians use such talk to garner positive media coverage and to guide public opinion toward support of their positions.[46] For Jacobs and Shapiro, crafted talk is manipulative behavior. This is not the place for an extended discussion of what constitutes manipulation.[47] But if by that term we mean something like attempting to influence others to act in ways we want them to act, then manipulation may well be an inherent part of communication.[48]

If manipulation is an attempt to get others to do what one wants them to do, how does it differ from persuasion? Theoretically, there are several differences.[49] First, persuasion helps the listener realize his or her own interests; manipulation is an attempt to further only the speaker's interests. Second, an attempt to persuade someone of something is an interactive process in which the speaker and the listener engage in dialogue. A manipulative speaker isn't interested in the views of the listener. Indeed, victims of manipulation are treated as things, as tools to be used or machines to be operated. Finally, persuasion is rational. Manipulation relies heavily on non-rational, especially emotional, appeals.

It is not at all clear to me that political spin is manipulative given these distinctions. Surely politicians believe that their plans for improving the country are in the interests of all, or at least most of, the voters. While spin may be used to gain a partisan (or personal) advantage in a political debate, the ultimate goal, as noted earlier, is to enact public policy that politicians and their parties believe is best for the nation. Spin, like partisan bickering generally, is a means to that end.

In addition, politics is little more than an ongoing, collective dialogue. A politician who ignored the views of his or her audience would not long command their attention and certainly wouldn't enjoy their support. Interestingly, one of the supposed signs of manipulative spin is a heavy reliance on polling. But polling is a kind of dialogue. The feedback from the public may not be as nuanced as we would like. But in a nation of over 300 million people, or even in congressional districts of over 700,000 people, a rich dialogue between politicians and the people is simply not possible. Polling does have the advantage of capturing a representative expression of the public's opinion. This is something town hall meetings, for instance, do not offer.

Jacobs and Shapiro argue that the use of polling allows politicians to simulate responsiveness without actually being responsive. According to this argument, politicians shape public opinion, based on information gleaned from polling, so that the public embraces the course of action politicians wanted to take in the first place. The feedback loop that includes politicians, the media, and public opinion creates an appearance of responsiveness when, in fact, politicians have stacked the deck.

Of course, it's very difficult to tell where the feedback loop begins. We might assume that politicians start the process and that may be true, at least in cases where much of the public has no opinion, or not a well-developed opinion, on a particular issue. But on most issues, the public knows where it stands. So it is also the case that politicians' actions are constrained by existing public opinion. In fact, Jacobs and Shapiro have argued elsewhere that politicians try to intentionally "prime" voters, or alter the criteria by which they make political judgments.[50] The priming process, however, takes as a given both the voters' priorities in terms of the most salient issues facing the nation and their positions on those issues.[51] Politicians have their own policy agendas, but they cannot successfully pursue those agendas outside the context of what public opinion will allow. Thus, there is a dialogic element to the use of polling and the priming process.

The final distinction between persuasion and manipulation is that the former is rational while the latter is not. Defining "rationality" is extraordinarily difficult and there is a huge literature on the subject, encompassing both theoretical and practical considerations.[52] Suffice it to say that it is far from clear what would be required for a political appeal to be considered rational. However, one might suggest that at a minimum it would have to avoid excessive emotion. Notice that it would not have to avoid emotion altogether. Though reason and emotion were once thought to work at cross-purposes, we now recognize that the two interact in complex ways and that "affective states may diminish or stimulate the capacity for deliberation."[53] Merely appealing to emotion, therefore, is not enough to declare spin manipulative.

But what constitutes *excessive* emotion? That, of course, is a subjective judgment. Does a majority of the appeal have to be emotional or would some lower proportion allow us to conclude that there was too much emotion being used? Regardless of where we set the threshold, I would argue that spin as it is currently employed relies on emotion only minimally.[54] This is an empirical claim and, admittedly, I have no systematic evidence to support it. To this point, no one has attempted to measure the ratio of emotional to rational appeals in spin.[55] But I would maintain that simple observation of politicians defending opposing positions on cable news shows, or of debates between candidates, will reveal far more arguments based on reason and logic—flawed though it may often be—than on emotion.

Spin, then, is more an act of persuasion than of manipulation. Rather than crafted talk, it is more accurate to say that politicians use rhetoric, or persuasive speech, in making the case for their candidacies and their parties. There is, of course, a very long history of the use of rhetoric in politics. We may think, romantically, of the Athenian Assembly in the fifth and fourth centuries BCE as a model of direct democracy, but rhetoric flourished in this period.[56] Indeed, citizens who wished to assume a leadership role in the Assembly could hire teachers, the Sophists, to improve their rhetorical skills.[57]

Like today, there were critics of the use of rhetoric in Athenian democracy. The arguments, by and large, were the same as those made by contemporary critics. Particularly skillful speakers could manipulate the people, it was alleged, getting them to make bad decisions or to act against their collective interests.[58] But many of the arguments against rhetoric were little more than attacks on democracy itself.[59]

What would it mean for politicians to try to gain the assent of the public without using rhetoric or spin? It's unimaginable. That's in part because, as the experience of ancient Athens suggests, rhetoric is a natural element of politics. It is also a normal part of everyday human interaction.[60] Indeed, a provocative recent argument by Hugo Mercier and Dan Sperber suggests that the purpose of human reasoning is not to help us deliberate better but to argue more effectively. That is, the function of reasoning is "to devise and evaluate arguments intended to persuade."[61] If this view is correct, persuasive speech—whether we call it rhetoric or spin—is not the antithesis of reason; it is reason's progeny.

The only realistic alternative to spin, therefore, is for politicians to refrain from appealing to the public for their support. There was a time when politicians in the United States did just that. Candidates, for example, "stood" for office and didn't "run."[62] Asking voters for their support was undignified and threatened the early American notion of republican virtue. Nor did politicians argue in front of the public as they do on our television screens on a daily basis today. Political deliberation was an elite activity and it was done within the confines of capitol buildings, often behind closed doors.

As a more democratic sensibility began to emerge in the nineteenth century, politicians began to engage the public. Not surprisingly, they relied on rhetoric almost as soon as they began doing so. For instance, though the Lincoln–Douglas debates of 1858 are often held up as the standard for a rational and substantive exchange of ideas, the communication scholar David Zarefsky has shown that they contained many of the elements that people believe are the hallmark of contemporary political debates. According to Zarefsky, "Candidates traded unsupported charges and personal attacks, digressed from the issues, and pandered to the audience."[63] In fact, Lincoln and Douglas are likely to have gotten away with much of that behavior because there wasn't a ubiquitous media to fact-check every utterance as there is today.

In a pluralist democracy, different visions of the good society must compete for the approval of the people. For this process to work effectively, the people are expected to pay attention, evaluate rival visions, and decide which one is best. (We'll leave aside a consideration of whether the people are any more likely than politicians to do so without relying on ideology and/or partisanship.) At the same time, those presenting the visions must be allowed—in fact, they should be encouraged—to put forward the best case for their perspective. That will include, it should be said, pointing out the flaws in the competing visions. But it is only after politicians have done their best to convince the people, using all the powers of persuasion they can muster, that we can be confident that the public's judgment is a reasoned one. The alternative would be coming to judgment based on *nothing* but party identification, on an irrelevant factor like a politician's looks or personality, or, indeed, on no deliberation at all. In this sense, rhetoric and, yes, spin, are essential to democracy.

Of course, this is not to say that every instance of spin is valuable for democracy. Politicians do sometimes stretch the truth to the point of all but lying. They may also obfuscate, blurring distinctions between themselves and their opponents in order to confuse citizens. Sometimes they exaggerate for effect. At other times, they avoid being accused of some wrongdoing by defining terms so narrowly that they are technically innocent of the charges. Fortunately, when politicians employ these tactics, they are routinely called to account by not only the media, but by their political opponents who, as part of their own efforts at spin, will be quick to point out acts of deception on the part of their rivals. And empty rhetoric is easily recognized for what it is. As a result, it is rarely effective. American political discourse is not perfect. But it is far from the demagoguery it is often portrayed to be.

Ideology and partisanship are central features of politics for a reason. They reflect divergent sets of principles and different coalitions of interests that exist organically in our society. Though the value of ideology ought to be clear (at least upon reflection), people often have a difficult time acknowledging the usefulness of partisanship. But "party spirit" is a positive force in democracy. Among its virtues, partisanship develops in people a commitment to a set of beliefs and to policies that seek to improve the lives of fellow citizens. Partisanship also encourages individuals to participate in a collective political effort. That effort, admittedly, is to build a majority for one's own party. But the process of building majorities forces partisans to think, and to argue, in terms that extend beyond their own narrow self-interests. Though it may sound counter-intuitive, partisan goals promote concern for a common good and, thus, inclusiveness in those who hold those goals. As Russell Muirhead puts it, partisanship "displays a democratic sympathy, a willingness to compromise, to give and to take, and (perhaps most of all) to bear the burdens of standing with one's fellow citizens."[64] It is not, then, an exaggeration to say that partisanship fosters a "democratic ethos."[65]

If ideology is, at times, held dogmatically and if partisanship often makes compromise difficult, the solution is not to excise ideology and partisanship. Instead, it is to encourage politicians, not to mention party activists (and, indeed, voters themselves), to strike a balance between their principles and loyalty to their allies, on the one hand, and a willingness to work with those with whom they disagree. As human beings, they (and we) will never get that balance exactly right. But asking them to discard ideology and partisanship is as harmful to democracy as it is unrealistic. If we want to find a culprit for what appears to be dysfunction in our political system, it is (as I suggested in the previous chapter) the design of our system of government that we should interrogate.

Chapter 5

The 2011 Debt Ceiling Debate
A Case Study

By many accounts, the debt ceiling debate of 2011 marked a low point in recent American political history. Indeed, it may be elevating the behavior of elected officials to call it a "debate" when it seemed that very little rational discourse was taking place. Perhaps, instead, we should call it a "crisis," one brought on by political obstinacy and, if the commentary of the chattering classes is correct, petty disagreements.

It is worth taking a detailed look at this episode because it seems to encapsulate everything that is wrong with the public behavior of politicians. Upon closer inspection, however, this incident actually illustrates the tensions produced by the design of the American political system. American government is structured to hinder activity while the party system encourages decisive action on the part of parties in the majority. These two tendencies work at cross-purposes and make it extraordinarily difficult to govern effectively. In short, elected officials have to operate within a system designed to frustrate their intentions. The result is exasperating for the public and elected officials alike. But central features of the system, not the politicians, bear most of the blame.

The Context

Unlike virtually all other developed nations, the United States establishes a "debt ceiling" by law.[1] The debt ceiling is the total amount of money the federal government is permitted to borrow to meet its obligations. In February of 2010, the Democratically controlled Congress raised the ceiling from $12.4 trillion to $14.3 trillion in anticipation of the federal debt reaching the lower cap. The $14.3 trillion limit, in turn, was to be surpassed sometime in the spring of 2011, though the Department of the Treasury announced in May of that year that they could take "extraordinary measures" to meet federal obligations until August 2.[2] That set the stage for a major summer battle over how to control the nation's growing debt.

Not raising the debt ceiling would have negative, some have said disastrous, consequences for U.S. citizens and the economy. Simply put, the federal government would find itself without enough money to pay all of its bills. Payments to individuals and day-to-day operations would have to be prioritized. As the *New York Times* explains:

> if the government were to choose to pay the interest on its debt, Social Security benefits, Medicaid and Medicare payments, defense contractors and unemployment benefits, it could not have enough left to pay for the salaries of federal workers and members of the military, Pell grants for college, highway construction or tax refunds, among other things.[3]

Even if a default on government debt could be avoided—and it wasn't at all clear in the summer of 2011 that it could—the government would have to shut down. The process would spook potential creditors, harming the government's creditworthiness and raising interest rates, which would increase the cost of borrowing money and, with it, the chances that the government would default on its loans at some point in the future. There's no telling how calamitous that would be for the United States and, indeed, the global economy.

Following the midterm elections of 2010, attention began to turn to the looming debt limit because many Republicans in the new House majority had vowed during the campaign to vote against raising the ceiling. They did so because the voters who helped nominate them, and who would ultimately be responsible for putting them in office, demanded that they do so. But they also believed that raising the limit was bad public policy. As Rep. Steve Stivers (R-OH) said on the campaign trail, raising the debt ceiling "shows a reckless desire to spend money we don't have, and borrow money we can't afford to pay back."[4] In the view of many Republicans, especially those first elected in 2010, Washington was addicted to spending, and raising the debt limit was simply enabling the addict to continue its destructive ways.[5] Some Republicans believed that the consequences of a default had been exaggerated.[6] Others felt that, even if the results were terrible, it was the kind of shock to the system Washington needed in order to get its fiscal house in order.[7] Real cuts in spending would only occur if Congress was forced to take this awful medicine.

Much of the hard-line stance against raising the debt limit reflected the Tea Party's influence in the Republican Party. But it wasn't just Tea Partiers who opposed raising the cap. Polls in early May, when most Americans were just beginning to pay attention to the issue, showed that only one in five people, and only 8 percent of Republicans, wanted to increase the debt limit.[8]

If public opinion was so clearly against raising the debt ceiling, why were President Obama and congressional Democrats committed to doing so? One could argue that they were simply willing to do the right thing, even though it was unpopular. Despite what the "default deniers" were claiming, not raising the debt limit would likely have had serious, even catastrophic, consequences. It wasn't just the Obama Administration making that claim. Leading bankers and fund managers warned Congress and the president repeatedly throughout the ordeal of the dangers of not raising the debt ceiling.[9] In April of 2011, the credit rating agency Standard & Poor's threatened to downgrade U.S. debt.[10] And in late June, the International Monetary Fund predicted "a severe shock to the economy and world financial markets" if the debt limit wasn't raised.[11]

There is one problem with the argument that Democrats were simply "doing the right thing." In 2006, while George W. Bush was president, every Senate Democrat, including Barack Obama, voted against raising the debt ceiling (then just under $8.2 trillion). However, this was little more than gamesmanship and posturing, as there was never any doubt that the cap would be raised. In fact, votes on the debt ceiling are usually—though in important ways, not always—partisan votes. Between 2002 and 2010, the debt ceiling had been raised 10 times. In seven of those instances, the Senate held stand-alone votes (that is, not tied to another measure like an economic stimulus bill) on the debt limit.[12] When Democrats controlled the White House and the Senate, in 2009 and 2010, the debt ceiling was raised with Democratic votes almost exclusively; only one Republican voted to raise the cap in 2009. When Republicans controlled the White House and the Senate, in 2002, 2003, and 2006, almost all Democrats voted against the increase (with the exception of three votes in 2002 and two in 2003) and Republicans shouldered the burden of raising the ceiling. However, when the presidency and the Senate were controlled by opposite parties, as they were during debt ceiling votes in 2002 and 2007, there were bipartisan votes in the Senate to raise the cap.[13] This suggests a willingness by both parties to "do the right thing" when they have responsibility for governing.

The Two Sides Square Off

Having noted this recent history, there is an important difference between the debt ceiling debate of 2011 and prior debt ceiling votes. In 2011 there was a real effort to defeat the attempted increase. Conservative Republicans appeared willing to let the federal government crash into its borrowing limit. Refusing to go along with the debt ceiling increase wasn't a partisan ploy to gain electoral advantage. It was an attempt to extract significant budget cuts from President Obama and the Democrats. Republican obstinacy was a negotiation tactic to get concessions that they truly believed were necessary for the fiscal health of the nation.

They also faced considerable pressure from their base. Tea Party activists threatened Republicans in the House, including the party's leadership, with primary challenges if they gave in on the debt ceiling.[14] And whereas two-thirds of all Republicans in a *Washington Post*–Pew Research Center poll in July said they were more concerned with raising the debt ceiling than with what would happen if it wasn't raised, three-quarters of those who identify with the Tea Party felt the same.[15] More telling was a separate Pew poll in July showing that while a majority of Republicans wanted "lawmakers who share your views on this issue" to "compromise, even if it means they strike a deal you disagree with," 53 percent of Tea Party supporters wanted the opposite; they wanted their lawmakers to "stand by their principles, even it means the government goes into default."[16]

Some powerful groups within the Republican Party's coalition lobbied Republican Members of Congress to oppose an increase in the debt ceiling. In the summer of 2011, for example, the Club for Growth ran ads in Utah and Indiana urging Senators Orrin Hatch and Richard Lugar, respectively, to vote against raising the limit.[17] Both senators, it should be noted, faced re-election (and, thus, re-nomination) in 2012. And both undoubtedly had in mind the fate of former Utah Senator Robert Bennett who, despite an 18-year record of conservatism in the Senate, was refused re-nomination by Tea Party activists in 2010. His vote in favor of the 2008 "bank bailout" is said to have motivated the activists to oust him. It also would not have been lost on Senators Hatch and Lugar that the Club for Growth "spent more than $200,000 on a combination of television ads, direct mail pieces and phone calls designed to influence the 3,500 (or so) delegates who attended . . . [the] state convention" that rejected Senator Bennett.[18]

Another important player in this drama was Grover Norquist, the president of Americans for Tax Reform (ATR). Though he is a bogeyman of the left, and though the media portrays him as a singularly powerful operative, it is impossible to determine exactly how influential Norquist is. Nevertheless, he undoubtedly wields considerable power. His organization is well funded, though its finances and donors are not publicly disclosed, and he functions at the center of a network of conservative organizations whose goal is to limit the size and scope of government. The threat of public criticism by Norquist is enough to force most (though not all) Republicans into line.[19] Throughout the debt crisis, Norquist insisted that the more than 250 Republicans who had signed ATR's pledge never to raise taxes remain faithful to that pledge. And at one point in the battle over the debt, he suggested raising the ceiling slightly every two months "because each time you could get something reasonable [from President Obama and the Democrats]."[20] Norquist's clout was enough to give this proposal serious consideration among many Republicans.

The Democrats, for their part, wanted to fend off deep cuts to domestic programs they have long defended. Though they were willing to accept some cuts in spending, they sought a balance between cuts and increased revenue, which would be generated by raising taxes on the wealthiest Americans.[21] This general approach had significant support within the public.[22] In a July Gallup poll, just 20 percent of the public favored reducing the deficit "only with spending cuts."[23] Based on some reasonable assumptions, the New York Times blogger and statistical analyst Nate Silver used the results of this Gallup poll to estimate the mixture of spending cuts and tax increases favored by the public. His conclusion was that Americans preferred a debt deal consisting of 65 percent spending cuts and 35 percent tax increases.[24]

In actuality, and perhaps not surprisingly, public opinion sent mixed messages to lawmakers. In a Gallup poll from January of 2011, 50 percent of the respondents wanted the debt ceiling raised "only if Congress can agree ahead of time on measures to reduce the deficit in the future" and just 16 percent wanted to raise the limit "to avoid a government shutdown even if Congress cannot agree on measures to reduce the deficit in the future."[25] This was pretty clear evidence that the public wanted deficit reduction. Yet, in the same poll, respondents were asked if they favored or opposed spending cuts in nine budgetary areas including funding for the arts and sciences, defense, anti-poverty programs, education, Medicare, and Social Security. In all areas but one—foreign aid—a majority opposed spending cuts.[26] So a majority of the public wanted deficit reduction without cuts in spending. We might forgive elected officials for being confused.

Democrats were undoubtedly emboldened by the support in the polls for their general approach. But they also had pressure from groups in their electoral coalition. Allied Democratic organizations fought cuts to popular programs on a number of fronts. One of the largest and most influential unions in the country, the American Federation of State, County and Municipal Employees (AFSCME), held rallies in several states in opposition to cuts in Medicaid.[27] They also mobilized thousands of their members to contact Democratic lawmakers. "Our goal," said AFSCME's chief lobbyist, "is to keep Democratic defections to a minimum."[28]

At one point fairly late in the process, the media reported on a potential agreement between President Obama and Speaker Boehner. The deal allegedly included cuts to entitlement programs but no new tax revenues, at least in the short run.[29] Liberal organizations, including MoveOn.org, Democracy for America, the Progressive Change Campaign Committee, the AFL-CIO, and the Service Employees International Union (SEIU) reacted to the news immediately by asking hundreds of thousands of activists to call Democratic members of Congress and urge them to oppose the deal.[30] Buoyed by such efforts, liberal leaders in Congress vocally opposed any deal that did not include an increase in taxes for the wealthy.[31]

On July 31, just a day and half before government borrowing hit the debt ceiling, the President, Senate Democrats and the House Republican leadership were able to reach an agreement. The deal raised the debt ceiling by $2.1 to $2.5 trillion in two stages; paid for part of that increase with $1 trillion in cuts to defense and domestic spending over 10 years; created a Bipartisan Joint Committee of Congress to identify another $1.5 trillion in spending cuts; authorized automatic cuts in spending, 40 percent (or $600 billion) of which would come from defense, if the so-called "Super Committee" couldn't compromise on cuts by November of 2011; required a vote in Congress on the Balanced Budget Amendment by the end of the year; and included no new tax revenues.[32]

Given that it contained no tax increase on the wealthy, and no guarantee that Medicare would be protected, liberals were quite displeased with the final deal. At the same time, conservatives were dissatisfied with the lack of entitlement reform and the fact that Social Security and Medicaid were shielded even from the automatic cuts that would take effect if the Super Committee failed to act. Conservatives were also concerned about the possibility that the Super Committee would propose tax increases and they found unacceptable the large defense cuts that would be triggered in the event that the Super Committee deadlocked. As a result, both liberals and conservatives were unhappy with the deal.[33]

With a compromise reached, one might have thought that the American public would have been satisfied with the settlement. Instead, the public was ambivalent at best. Only 39 percent approved of the agreement while 46 percent, including 64 percent of Republicans, disapproved.[34] Surely at least some of this reaction is the result of opposition to the details of the deal. But much of the dissatisfaction was based on process itself. In a Pew Research Center poll taken in late July 2011, nearly three-quarters of the respondents used negative terms to describe the debt negotiations, frequently calling it ridiculous, disgusting, and stupid.[35]

Critics Pounce—and Get it Wrong

There was, of course, a great deal of commentary, both during and after the stalemate, about the behavior of the participants. Much of this commentary was by seasoned observers of politics, but all of it expressed the same sense of exasperation found in the public at large.[36] In an essay entitled "What Were They Thinking?" the journalist Elizabeth Drew, a keen observer of American politics for over 40 years, wrote, "Were they all insane? That's not a far-fetched question."[37] Later in the piece she suggests, "It was all about theater and politics." In a *New York Times* column, Thomas Friedman imagined a press conference in which President Obama and Speaker Boehner promise to work together for the sake of future generations and in which they announce a "Grand Bargain" that puts everything on the negotiating table. The column ends with a lament. "What's sad," writes Friedman, "is how much this is a fantasy and how easily—with just a little political will—it could be a reality."[38] At the height of the battle over the budget, National Football League (NFL) owners and players reached an agreement that ended the 132-day lockout. In a statement about the NFL agreement, New England Patriots owner Robert Kraft proclaimed, "I hope we gave a little lesson to the people in Washington because the debt ceiling is a lot easier to fix than this was."[39] And during a discussion of the debt ceiling debate on a morning cable news talk show, publisher and editor Mort Zuckerman declared, "I think we probably could figure it out sitting around this table. I don't think it would be that difficult."[40]

Really? Is it reasonable to ask whether the elected officials involved in this debate were *insane*? It was *all* theater and politics? It would only take a *little* political will to reach a compromise? A negotiation that must find agreement between 435 members of the House and 100 members of the Senate plus the president, all of whom must answer to constituencies and are under intense pressure from political allies, is analogous to five talking heads sitting around a table, answerable to no one? And the NFL lockout was *more difficult* to settle than an agreement on the U.S. budget?

Such criticism, with all due respect to those quoted above, is just ridiculously simplistic. Even within her own piece, Elizabeth Drew pointed to acts of principle and acknowledged the complexity of the issue. At one point, she quotes an exasperated President Obama as saying, "I'm the President of the United States; my words carry weight" in response to Democratic members of Congress who wanted him to let them know if he was intending to capitulate to Republican demands.[41] In the account of this exchange, both the Democratic members of Congress and President Obama are operating above mere theater and even above partisan game playing. The congressional Democrats wanted an assurance that the president would fight for their policy preferences. The president, for his part, recognized that every word he utters has significant policy ramifications. This anecdote is not about how Democrats can come out of the fight looking good or how their positions will help at the next election. It portrays them as concerned with policy and with governing.

Drew's piece also recognized how difficult Speaker Boehner's task was. In order to increase the debt ceiling, Boehner was going to have to limit defections in his own party and pick up enough Democratic votes to cobble together a majority. That was going to be difficult because Tea Party Members of Congress were "on principle" (the quotation marks are Drew's) opposed to raising the debt ceiling and raising taxes.[42] By using scare quotes around "on principle," Drew is suggesting either that there wasn't much principle behind the Tea Party position or that the principle itself was absurd. In fact, she appears to believe the latter. She writes at one point in the essay, "The Republicans embraced a philosophy of no new taxes or revenue that had little relation to reality—except for the fact that their long-standing goal has been to shrink the size of the federal government."[43] So Republicans were out of touch with reality because they were pursuing a "long-standing" philosophical goal? Drew may find the principle outrageous, but it is a principle nonetheless.

Interestingly, there was very little criticism of the public and their contradictory priorities in the debt ceiling debate. If a politician simply wanted to do what the majority of the public thought should be done, he or she would have had absolutely no guidance from public opinion.

The public wanted compromise, but of what sort? Perhaps there was general agreement that taxes would have to be raised, but there's rarely a consensus on who should bear the burden of tax increases. A reduction in spending was recognized to be necessary, but very few categories of spending garner anything near majority support for cuts and those that do are minuscule parts of the budget.

If the critics found the public's role problematic, it was not because the people somehow thought we could balance the budget with minimal taxes and virtually no spending cuts. It was because politicians were too concerned with potential public reactions to their decisions. This presumably manifested itself in the alleged obsession with re-election that I discussed in Chapters 3 and 4. Politicians, according to the critics, seemed to care more about staying in office than about finding the best solution to the debt crisis. Drew makes this point repeatedly in her essay. In the House, she says, "Boehner didn't want his flock to have to cast a controversial vote anytime close to the election." But in the Senate, where 23 Democrats were going to be up for re-election in 2012, Minority Leader Mitch McConnell "was looking for a way to force a controversial vote closer to the election." In the White House, according to an insider Drew quotes, "Everything is about the reelect." And the fact that Republican leaders ultimately agreed to a deal was "because they feared the political consequences of not *appearing to be responsible*."[44]

When we boil it down to its essence, the critics' primary objection to the behavior of both sides in the debt ceiling debate is that neither appeared to be willing to "do the right thing" for the country. Perhaps elected officials were doing what their constituents wanted or what groups that are allied with their party demanded. But they should have been less concerned with the next election and more concerned with the next generation.

Leave aside for the moment the odd suggestion that representatives in a democracy should disregard the potential response of the electorate to their actions. Doing so undermines accountability, a principle that is absolutely essential to democracy. I'll have more to say about democratic accountability when I discuss ambition in Chapter 6. But it should be obvious that elected officials have to be held accountable for their actions. The mechanism we have for holding them accountable is an election. Asking elected officials not to think about the next election is giving them license to ignore the will of the people.

Leave aside also the curious assumption that doing the right thing requires risking re-election. Why should that be the case? If the best course of action were obvious, wouldn't everyone recognize it? If decisions were obviously right or wrong, there'd be no controversy. Liberals and conservatives, Democrats and Republicans, would agree and representatives wouldn't have to be implored to throw electoral caution to the wind. Doing the right thing would also be doing the popular thing and re-election would be assured.

In fact, the choice is rarely between the best option and the popular one. That's because what politicians think is the best option also happens, by happy coincidence, to be the option most of their voters would choose as the best course of action. As it turns out, that's not a coincidence at all. Democracy enables voters to choose representatives who, to a large degree, agree with them on major issues or, at least, on the direction in which the country should be headed.

Critics of politicians are likely to respond that doing what one's constituency wants is not *necessarily* doing the right thing. That is undoubtedly true, but how are we to know when the right thing and the popular thing are not the same? We'd have to be able to step outside our own ideologies and partisanship to objectively determine what the best course of action is in any given situation. Of course, we can't do this, though many people (perhaps especially the critics of politicians) believe *they* can do it and that it is others who are blinded by ideology or partisanship. Needless to say, this is a biased belief in itself.

The core problem with the suggestion that politicians "do what is right and forget the next election" is that it presumes that whatever the matter at hand may be, it is the most important matter that an elected official is ever going to confront. But how is an elected official to know which issue, or which vote, is critical enough to sacrifice his or her career over? In just the first session of the 112th Congress (2011), critical votes were taken to keep the federal government operating in the absence of a final budget for Fiscal Year 2011; to raise the nation's debt ceiling; and to extend a payroll tax cut (which many economists thought was vital to the economic recovery but that would add considerably to the deficit). In each of these cases, and several others, Members of Congress were asked to "do the right thing." But critical votes would surely be taken in the second session, and then in the 113th Congress, and in all future Congresses.

The plea for politicians to do the right thing is a plea for current elected officials to fall on their swords to avert a crisis; once they've done so, the implication seems to be that everything will be fine from that point forward. But, of course, the next crisis is only just down the road. When it arises, a new set of elected officials will be asked to sacrifice re-election for the good of the country. And because crises are ever present in a democracy, this cycle will be perpetual. Elected officials will be asked to do the right thing, which (for some reason that remains unclear) is also an unpopular thing to do, so they'll likely lose re-election and a new set of elected officials, faced with a new crisis (or an old one re-emerged), will also do the right thing and then lose, and so on.

It should be fairly apparent that a process such as this would be far from ideal. It is not clear how it would even be democratic. Elected officials might be doing, in some abstract sense, the "right thing," but the people wouldn't like it and so the voters would continue kicking them out of office, only to be replaced by another set of unresponsive, but supposedly brave and clear-sighted, politicians. At that point, why hold elections at all? A benevolent dictator could accomplish the same ends.

Expecting politicians to do the right thing even if it is unpopular presents us with a complicated paradox. We want the kind of people in politics who are willing to sacrifice public office to do the right thing. But if such elected officials were actually to sacrifice public office over a single critical vote, they would likely be replaced by politicians who wouldn't be willing to do so. So we have a choice to make as voters. Either we give elected officials some breathing room, or we guarantee that those in power won't take risks to pursue the greater good.

Systemic Dysfunction

The criticism of politicians we hear today is really dissatisfaction with our constitutional system masquerading as frustration with the actions of individuals. The American system, quite frankly, may be working too well. Elected officials are highly responsive and the separation of powers is producing conflict and gridlock as well as it ever has.

Technically, the problem we're facing today, and that we've faced throughout our history to one degree or another, is that American politics is designed to produce majorities but our government was created to thwart them. In his comparative examination of 36 democratic countries, the eminent political scientist Arend Lijphart described two models for the operation of democracy. One is the majoritarian model (sometimes referred to as the Westminster model after the British parliamentary system), which "concentrates political power in the hands of a bare majority." This model allows the majority party to work its will. The second approach is the consensus model, which "tries to share, disperse, and limit power in a variety of ways."[45] Here, parties must work together if they are to accomplish anything.

Lijphart identifies 10 institutional characteristics of democracies whose forms are shaped by either the majoritarian or consensus principle. These characteristics include executive power concentrated in a single-party cabinet as opposed to a multiparty coalition; a two-party as opposed to a multiparty system; a unicameral legislature versus two powerful legislative chambers; and flexible versus rigid constitutions.[46] The 10 characteristics can be grouped in two dimensions, the first of which Lijphart calls the "executives-parties dimension." This dimension concerns "the arrangement of executive power, the party and electoral systems, and interest groups."[47] The second is the "federal-unitary dimension," which includes not only "the contrast between federalism and unitary government" but matters of constitutional change and interpretation.[48]

Democracy in the United States is an almost perfect balance between the majoritarian and consensus models, with a slight tilt toward the latter. That may sound ideal; a balance between extremes is typically a good thing. But our particular combination, which is quite rare among the 36 countries in Lijphart's study,[49] is a recipe for dysfunction.

On four of the five characteristics in the executives-parties dimension, the United States is majoritarian. The electoral system, for example, produces a two-party system. Consequently, one of the two parties will have a majority in the House of Representatives and the Senate. The same party may have a majority in both, or (as was the case during the debt ceiling debate) one party may control the House and the other the Senate. In addition, the executive power resides in a president, who will inevitably come from one of the two parties, and a cabinet made up (by and large) of the president's fellow partisans. Finally, the interest group system in the United States is pluralist. That means that, unlike corporatist systems in which the relationship between interest groups and the government is cooperative, interest groups in the United States compete mightily for influence. For most interest groups, the optimal strategy for gaining influence is to align with one of the political parties. Thus, the interest group system contributes to the pursuit of majorities.

The one executives-parties characteristic on which the United States is not majoritarian is the balance of power between the executive and the legislative branches. In addition, all five characteristics on the federal-unitary dimension operate according to the consensus principle. Governmental power is federal and decentralized; there are two powerful chambers in the legislature; the constitution is rigid, which means that the majority party cannot easily change it; legislation is subject to judicial review; and the central bank is not dependent on the executive. Each of these elements of the American system of government makes it impossible for majorities to govern unilaterally.

Keep in mind that the consensus model limits power and encourages cooperation between parties if government is to be effective. Because more than half of the central features of American government adhere to this model, our system is designed primarily to hinder the exercise of power. And, yet, our political system (i.e., certain elements of the executives-parties dimension) is designed to produce majorities. Majorities, in turn, expect to wield power.

The frustration so many Americans felt during the debt ceiling debate was caused by this schizophrenic arrangement. Majority parties in the House and Senate and a single party in the executive were given the power to govern by the voters. But the separation of powers and other features of the consensus model in our system won't allow those parties to fulfill their mandates.

Elected officials may have appeared to be acting recklessly during the debt ceiling crisis. House Republicans, in particular, were pilloried for their inflexibility. But we could just as easily describe them as having acted responsively. Key Republican constituencies wanted massive spending cuts and opposed tax increases, Republican elected officials agreed with those priorities, and they held out for as long as they could in pursuing them. In the end, however, House Republicans were neither reckless nor particularly responsive. Nearly three-quarters of them voted in favor of the final debt deal, even though almost two-thirds of Republican voters disapproved of it. Even a majority of the House Tea Party Caucus (32 of 62) voted in favor of the deal and were quickly branded "traitors" to the Tea Party movement for doing so.[50] Isn't this, in its own small way, an act of political courage?

Individual behavior can be perfectly rational in a system that produces irrational collective behavior. House Republicans, Senate Democrats, and President Obama all had some responsibility for governing. They also had different priorities, based on different values, as well as different interests to represent. Add to the mix Senate Republicans who, though in the minority, had the filibuster to use as a cudgel to protect their interests (which, incidentally, were not exactly those of their fellow partisans in the House). Each of these actors doing what they were elected to do—namely, represent the voters who sent them to Washington—created a situation that brought the government and the economy of the United States to the edge of a cliff. None would have done so if they had sole responsibility for governing. But splitting up that responsibility, and yet giving different actors majority control of one part of the system, encourages one big game of budgetary chicken.

This is not the place to make recommendations for reform. I will note, however, that we ought to decide whether we want a majoritarian system or one that works toward consensus. Changing to a purely majoritarian system would require moving to a Westminster style arrangement. One easy way to start would be to get rid of the filibuster. But to adopt a truly majoritarian system, we would have to consider a unicameral legislature and we would also have to contemplate eliminating the presidency in favor of a prime minister. That, quite frankly, will never happen.

The alternative is to reform those aspects of our system that are majoritarian in favor of a purely consensus model. Essentially, this would require changing our electoral system. If we adopt one that would produce more than two parties, it could draw the ideological center of gravity toward the middle of the spectrum as the two major parties compromise with third parties to build governing coalitions in Congress.[51] An advantage of the consensus model is that it comports with the distrust of government that is deep-seated in American political culture.

No system of government is perfect. But as long as we continue to have a hodge-podge system that puts majority parties in control of parts of the government but forces them to operate in institutions designed to thwart majorities, we will have the sort of gridlock and bickering that we saw in the 2011 debt ceiling debate. Crises like that one will occur with regularity. But that is primarily a systematic problem, not one caused by the bad behavior of politicians.

Chapter 6

The Private Lives of Politicians
Ambition and Hypocrisy

Much of the discussion in this book has examined the public actions of politicians. I have argued that those actions are reasonable given the design of the American system of government and politics. But underlying much of the criticism of politicians is an assumption, sometimes implicit though at times quite explicitly stated, that anyone who would enter politics must be flawed in some fundamental way.

What kind of people are politicians? Do they differ, in important ways, from the rest of us? And if they do differ, is this necessarily a bad thing? Or might the differences between us and them be beneficial for democracy? To answer these questions, we must consider what I would call the private lives of politicians. By "private lives," I do not mean what politicians do in the privacy of their own homes or even what they do away from the Klieg lights of politics, though that is part of a private life. I mean, instead, something like the inner lives of politicians. Some elements of this interiority are on display publicly, so the line between the "private" and "public" lives of politicians is not especially bright. The distinction, however, is useful in examining what is believed to be the character of politicians.

This chapter begins by establishing a context for understanding the ways in which people think about, and judge, other people. We will see that our impressions are not always entirely accurate. I then turn to the basic personality traits of politicians, with special attention paid to ambition given the public's wariness of that particular trait. That discussion is followed by a consideration of hypocrisy. The following chapter will address the question of whether or not politicians are more dishonest than the rest of us. As we will see, it is not at all clear that politicians are any more flawed than the public at large (though, admittedly, it is impossible to quantify such things). Furthermore, in those instances in which they do differ from the rest of the public, that fact often redounds to the benefit of democracy.

How We Think About Others

Before examining the ways in which politicians are thought to be personally flawed, it is important to take a moment to understand how human beings make judgments about other people. None of us know with certainty why people do what they do. As psychologists Daniel Gilbert and Patrick Malone note, "Character, motive, belief, desire, and intention play leading roles in people's construal of others, and yet none of these constructs can actually be observed."[1] Given that fact, we would probably be better off following the Biblical injunction to "judge not . . ." And, yet, we all make judgments. With no direct evidence of the innermost forces driving a person's behavior, however, we can really only speculate. When we do so we are, in effect, trying to read the minds of others.

Of course, our speculation about others is often incorrect. We know this from decades of research in social psychology. "When people observe behavior," write Gilbert and Malone, "they often conclude that the person who performed the behavior was predisposed to do so—that the person's behavior corresponds to the person's unique dispositions— and they draw such conclusions even when a logical analysis suggests they should not."[2] This mistake in judgment is called the "correspondence bias" or the "fundamental attribution error."

The problem with the correspondence bias is that it ignores situational factors that influence behavior. Though we would all acknowledge that behavior is at least sometimes, and perhaps always, influenced by the circumstances in which we find ourselves, people will nevertheless attribute another person's actions entirely to dispositional factors.

In one of the classic experiments in this area of research, conducted in the late 1960s, students were asked to read essays that either supported or opposed the Castro regime in Cuba. When students were told that the authors of the essays got to choose the side they would defend, the students naturally concluded that the essays revealed the authors' true beliefs. However, when students were told that the authors were randomly assigned to defend one side or the other, they continued to assume that the authors believed what they wrote (though not, admittedly, to the same extent as those in the "free choice" condition).[3] Ignoring the situational factors that might have led an author to write in support of Castro, namely that he or she was randomly assigned that task, the subjects in this experiment could not help but assume the author actually believed what he or she wrote.

This leap of judgment has been shown to occur in numerous studies in recent decades. Exactly why we do this is not entirely clear, though there is likely an evolutionary explanation. For instance, the bias of attributing actions to dispositions may help reduce the risk that we will mistakenly overlook another person's bad intentions.[4] Perhaps our tendency to engage in the correspondence bias with politicians is a way of protecting democracy against those who would deceive us or who desire too much power. But Americans appear to assume the worst in *everyone* who runs for office, regardless of the evidence of their deceptive or power-hungry nature. At some point, this primal defense mechanism becomes an impediment to a healthy democracy.

Think of the way candidate behavior on the campaign trail is treated. If a candidate confuses facts or makes an inarticulate statement, we conclude that he or she lacks intelligence, not that he or she might be exhausted in the midst of a stressful and grueling campaign. If a candidate exaggerates in reporting an anecdote, he or she is a liar, not someone who may have simply forgotten details and filled them in as memory served.

Highlighting the fact that humans are susceptible to the correspondence bias is not meant to suggest that we should not pass judgment on what politicians *do*. The point is just that we should be hesitant to draw conclusions about who they *are*. When a politician tells a lie, we have no idea what his or her intention is. Perhaps he or she had incorrect information; or maybe the lie was intentional. We simply cannot know for sure. That does not stop us from calling the statement a lie, but it should keep us from making a blanket determination that the politician lies as a matter of course (i.e., that he or she is a "liar").

In addition to the correspondence bias, there are other cognitive biases that influence how we think about politicians. For instance, the information people process about politicians is subject to the availability heuristic and the confirmation bias. The former is defined as "the process of judging frequency by 'the ease with which instances come to mind.' "[5] Thus, people are likely to believe the incidence of personal scandals involving politicians is much higher than it really is because they can easily recall several such scandals.

People are also likely to rely on a confirmation bias when they test beliefs or hypotheses about the world around them, including those concerning other people. The confirmation bias is the propensity of people to "seek data that are likely to be compatible with the beliefs they currently hold."[6] That is, we tend to search for evidence that confirms what we already believe.

A better approach, one suggested by the philosopher Karl Popper, would be to search for evidence to falsify our beliefs. Those for which we cannot find contrary evidence can justifiably be held until falsified; those for which we find disconfirming evidence ought to be discarded.[7] Of course, most people do not employ the scientific method in everyday life. Nevertheless, we ought to be careful in jumping to conclusions about politicians based on evidence that confirms what we believe about them. There is plenty of contradictory evidence if we are only open to considering it.

The biases in the way we think are obviously relevant to our judgments about politicians. They should remind us that we are likely to be wrong—or, at the very least, we cannot be certain—about the private lives of politicians. In the absence of reliable knowledge about who politicians are as people, we can assume the worst or we can give them the benefit of the doubt. I will argue in the final chapter that it is better for democracy if we do the latter. For now, I suggest that unless we have systematic evidence to the contrary, we assume that politicians are just like the rest of us and that, were we in their shoes, we non-politicians would behave in ways very similar to politicians. Furthermore, the ways in which any randomly selected group of citizens would differ from politicians are likely to be ways that put the politicians in a relatively decent light.

What follows is a discussion of whether the character of politicians differs from that of non-politicians in significant ways. I will begin by examining basic personality traits, paying particular attention to ambition, then hypocrisy, an aspect of character that is thought to be especially prevalent in politicians.

Ambition and Other Personality Traits

This is largely speculation, but I am convinced that the primary reason people dislike politicians so much is that they think anyone who would be attracted to a career in politics must be very different from the rest of us. What kind of person would go into politics and why would anyone want to? Obviously, such a person must be ambitious. Indeed, the level of ambition necessary to enter politics must seem astronomical to most Americans. Because he or she cannot relate to that level of ambition, the average person naturally questions the politician's motives. Excessive ambition surely indicates an unacceptable level of self-interest and this, in turn, must be incompatible with a commitment to the common good. Alternatively, it might suggest a dangerous personality flaw.

Suspicion of those who seek power is not only a popular prejudice. It has a scholarly lineage dating to the post-World War II era. Most notably, Harold Lasswell hypothesized that what he called the "political type" (i.e., "power seekers") was attracted to politics as a way of compensating for personal deficiencies.[8] As Lasswell explained, "Power is expected to overcome low estimates of the self."[9] People seek positions of leadership, according to this view, in order to make themselves feel wanted or valuable.

This "compensation hypothesis" does not enjoy much empirical support. As Paul Sniderman has shown, those who get highly involved in politics (not as politicians, per se, but as party activists) actually have higher levels of self-esteem than those not active in politics.[10] Though the differences in general self-esteem levels between "leaders" and "followers" are reduced when socio-demographic factors (e.g., income, education, etc.) are controlled, political activists still show considerably higher levels of interpersonal competence.[11] This trait is "an individual's self-confidence about his [sic] capacity to deal with other objects in his environment."[12] Similarly, a recent study of potential candidates for public office found that those who have considered running for office are significantly more likely to see themselves as qualified to hold office than those who have not considered running.[13]

Politicians, we may therefore conclude, are likely to feel more confident than the typical citizen in their ability to influence those around them. This enhanced sense of efficacy also extends to the ability to shape processes. Such confidence is undoubtedly necessary for leadership and, thus, we should not only expect politicians to have it, but we should welcome it.

Studies of actual politicians' personalities, as opposed to those of political activists generally, are quite rare. As one might imagine, it is extremely difficult to get elected officials to fill out the standard personality tests used to determine a person's dispositional makeup.[14] Nevertheless, there are "at-a-distance" studies that attempt to assess the personalities of leaders. These studies examine biographical facts in a politician's life, or the words he or she uses in speeches and interviews, to infer personality traits.[15] While these studies contain important insights about particular politicians, they tend to focus on the highest offices (e.g., the presidency) and their aim is not to compare politicians to non-politicians. Instead, the goal is usually to identify traits that are likely to indicate success in office.

Despite the difficulty in directly assessing the personalities of politicians with standard measures, there has been at least one recent attempt to do so outside the United States.[16] Though we have to be careful about applying the results to U.S. politicians, and while the study has some methodological limitations, the findings are worth considering. They suggest that those attracted to politics, generally speaking, have traits that make them well suited for public life and that give us little cause for alarm.

In 2001, a team of researchers asked Italian elected officials to complete a questionnaire that would allow the politicians' personalities to be assessed.[17] Psychologists who study personality generally agree that there are five traits that constitute human personality. Individuals score higher or lower on measures of each of the "Big Five" factors, which include conscientiousness, agreeableness, neuroticism, openness to experience, and extraversion.[18] In the 2001 Italian study, elected officials had significantly higher scores than the general public on extraversion (which these scholars refer to as "energy") and agreeableness. This should not be much of a surprise. Because they need to be comfortable in groups of people, and because running for office requires a great deal of energy, we would expect politicians to score highly on extraversion. Furthermore, a disagreeable politician is not likely to make it very far. As a result, we might expect elected officials to be more agreeable than the average citizen.[19]

Beyond the Big Five personality dimensions, Italian politicians were also found to have significantly higher levels of social desirability than the average person. That is, they have a greater need to project a positive image of themselves than does the typical Italian. This, too, is unsurprising. Given the fact that anyone entering politics is subjecting his or her entire life history to public scrutiny, a person who voluntarily does so is likely to want to make a good impression (and to believe that he or she can make such an impression).

Does this desire imply that the compensation hypothesis might be correct? Do some people enter politics seeking affirmation, validation and praise? Undoubtedly, some do. But that does not mean that politicians pursue power to compensate for low self-esteem, as Lasswell argued. In fact, a recent review of the literature on social desirability concluded that this trait indicates "an agreeable, emotionally stable and interpersonally adjusted personality profile."[20] Furthermore, a high score on social desirability measures seems to indicate that an individual understands social norms of appropriate behavior and has a need to follow them. In this way, the desire to be viewed by others in a positive light serves as a check on improper behavior. As the review just cited notes, the "core characteristic" of social desirability appears to be a "self-regulatory capacity."[21]

Though we must be careful about generalizing the findings of one study in Italy to politicians in the United States, it is quite plausible that our politicians, too, are more extraverted (or energetic) as well as more agreeable than the average person. They may also score higher on social desirability measures. But as each of these traits is positive, the basic personality differences between politicians and non-politicians appear to be no threat to democracy and may even be advantageous.

Surely that is not true of the outsized ambition that many, perhaps most, politicians seem to possess. Though we have no reliable way of determining this, politicians must certainly have more ambition than the average person. Does such ambition suggest that politicians are interested in fame and glory? And does that reflect a level of self-interest that is incompatible with serving the public?

Before addressing these questions, it should be noted that politicians are likely to be no more ambitious than other professionals. Of course, people who seek positions of prestige, whether in business, law, medicine, academia, or other professions, can reasonably be expected to have more ambition than the average person. But there is no good reason to believe that politicians would be more ambitious than the typical professional. In fact, there is some empirical evidence that among individuals in professions that routinely produce politicians (e.g., law, business, education), those who have considered running for office do not express higher levels of ambition, in career or material terms, than those who have not considered entering politics.[22]

One might argue that, unlike business, law, and medicine, politics offers notoriety and it is the potential for accolades that draws certain people to this field. This argument ignores the fact that most politicians have very little notoriety and hardly any get accolades. Few elected officials, including most members of Congress, would be recognized by more than a handful of people at the local mall on any given weekend. And, as I documented earlier in this book, those who enter politics can expect disparagement rather than praise.

To be sure, elected officials are introduced as dignitaries at all sorts of public events. Some, at the highest levels of government, are afforded formal respect. But the appeal of such treatment can hardly outweigh the costs of running for office. Whether intentionally or not, we have created a grueling obstacle course politicians must navigate on their way to public office. In Chapter 1, I alluded to some of the indignities candidates have had to face on the campaign trail in recent years. Candidates are routinely asked to throw back shots at local bars, milk cows and feed baby animals at farms, participate in various athletic activities, and eat unique regional foods that, if the truth be told, even many locals do not enjoy. There is nothing inherently wrong with any of these things. But often candidates are uncomfortable with one or another of them—as, for example, Barack Obama was with bowling in 2008 or Mitt Romney was talking about grits while campaigning in the South in 2012—and, yet, they are expected to engage in them willingly and with aplomb. They get no credit for trying and are mocked for making mistakes.

Being demeaned on the campaign trail is not the only cost of running for office. Campaigning is physically and mentally exhausting. Candidates face constant travel, very long days, and "trackers" from the opposing campaign who follow them around recording every move and every utterance they make. They must familiarize themselves with not only the most important issues facing the country (or their city or state), but with a panoply of issues, many of which will be important to only a handful of constituents. In addition, they have to raise mind-boggling amounts of money in order to mount a serious campaign.

Of course, no one is forced to enter politics. Those who decide to throw their hat in the ring know what they are getting into. That is true enough. But why would we want to make public service such a miserable experience? After all, representative democracy requires representatives. We cannot expect individuals to volunteer for such an important role and then treat those who do like pariahs. On second thought, we can do that and, in fact, we do. But then we have to realize that, eventually, the only people who will be willing to run for office are the kinds of people who live down to our expectations.

We should keep in mind that the campaign process is stress-inducing not only for the candidate but for his or her family as well. Campaigns inevitably intrude on the lives of all candidates' family members. Connie Schultz, a Pulitzer Prize-winning newspaper columnist and the wife of Ohio Senator Sherrod Brown, starts her memoir about life on the campaign trail as a candidate's spouse with a telling anecdote. One morning very early in Brown's 2006 campaign for the Senate, Schultz noticed two men in suits jump out of a van and start rummaging through the couple's garbage. Startled, she and the family's dog (Gracie) ran outside yelling,

"Hey! Hey! Drop that trash! Drop that trash!"

On cue, Gracie started barking so hard only one of her paws was touching the ground. That got their attention. The men in suits took one look at me and the beast, dropped the bags, ran to the white van, and tore off.

"You're kidding," Sherrod said when I finally reached him after calling his cell phone, his Blackberry, his desk phone and his scheduler.

"Do I sound like I'm kidding?"

"Oh, my God."

"Yeah."

"Did you get their license?"

"What?"

"Their license plate number? Did you get it?"

I wanted to say, "Oh, sure, I whipped out the binoculars we don't own, focused the infrared ray we also don't have, and nailed the suckers."

Instead, I started to cry.

"Who would do this to us?" I blubbered. "Who would care about our trash?"

Sherrod hesitated, then sighed.

"I'm sorry, honey," he said. "Welcome to the campaign."[23]

Opposition research goes beyond digging through garbage. Spouses' lives often receive intense scrutiny. A spouse's financial dealings and employment history, not to mention past improprieties like drug use, are all fair game. So are any marital problems the political couple may have had. Occasionally, even the children of politicians become the focus of public attention. Typically this only happens to *adult* children of politicians and only when the son or daughter has done something wrong.[24] Politicians' children rarely choose to live in the public spotlight; nevertheless, that is where they often find themselves.

To be sure, politicians often use their families to court votes. They cannot very well enjoy the political benefits of having a family but expect to keep hidden those aspects of their families that are less than perfect. However, we should keep in mind that part of the reason politicians feel compelled to parade their families in front of voters—and the reason they engage in so many demeaning activities—is because voters appear to want them to. Voters want evidence that a candidate has a loving family. They also want to know that a politician understands average folks, where they "come from," and what they face on a daily basis. To reassure voters, therefore, a candidate must demonstrate a commitment to family. To connect with them, a politician must prove that he or she is ordinary (but not too ordinary).

That some of our fellow citizens voluntarily enter this minefield is fairly astonishing. For most Americans it is also proof that those who do must be at least a little untrustworthy. More generously, we might simply conclude that, to those who seek it, elected office must really be worth the hardship of attaining it.

Indeed, it is. But in what way is elected office worth the stress and strain of winning it? Perhaps its value lies in the fame and glory it promises. However, I have already noted that few elected officials gain much notoriety. Alternatively, those who enter politics may believe they can benefit financially by doing so. But the plausibility of that proposition is diminished by the fact that so many politicians are wealthy *before* they enter politics. A recent study by the Center for Responsive Politics found that nearly half of the Members of Congress are millionaires.[25]

Members of Congress, admittedly, are more financially atypical than politicians at the state and local levels. Nevertheless, politicians at all levels tend to be wealthier than their average constituent because only those with financial security can typically afford to run for office. To begin with, candidates need a great deal of time away from work in order to run for office. In addition, legislative pay is not particularly lucrative. Some states only pay legislators on a daily basis. Alabama, for example, pays legislators $10 for every day the legislature is in session (though there is a per diem worth $3,958 a month to cover expenses while the legislature is in session, which is typically about three and a half months). Most states pay an annual salary to legislators, but the amounts vary considerably. California pays $95,290.56 a year while New Hampshire pays $200 per two-year term (with no per diem).[26] A 2010 study found that the average legislative pay for states that provide an annual salary was $33,983.[27]

Low pay for elected officials creates a dilemma. Unless we want only the rich to serve in public office, we have to make it easier for people of average means to enter politics. One way to do that would be to pay elected officials more. (This would not, of course, address the problem that running for office requires time away from work and an income while on the campaign trail.) However, if we pay politicians more, then we are likely to attract a greater number of people who enter politics solely (or largely) for the money. In truth, there is not much danger of that because the pay will never be so great that it overwhelms, in and of itself, the disincentives to run for office. Therefore, I would argue that we should pay elected officials more.

Exactly how much to pay elected officials at different levels and in different branches of government is not entirely clear. But, in general, it is worth supporting higher pay for politicians primarily because it might diversify the pool of people who enter politics. It would also send a message that we appreciate those who are willing to serve in offices that conduct the public's business.

The point of this extended discussion of politicians' pay is that very few people enter politics to get rich. The opportunities to do so simply do not exist in the way, or to the extent, that the public thinks they do. (I will deal with "honest graft" in the next chapter.) Even the opportunity to parlay a political career into a lucrative job once one leaves office is a long shot. Few politicians gain the clout necessary to make themselves valuable to a firm once they have retired from politics. Some do, of course, but it is hard to believe that those individuals entered politics and spent years working their way into positions of real authority, while enduring frequent elections and nearly constant fundraising, just for the possibility that they *might* get a high paying job in the end.

If it is not notoriety or money that politicians are after, why do they put up with the hardships of politics? This question takes us back to the claim made at the outset of this section, namely, that those who enter politics are ambitious. What, then, do we mean by ambition if it is not the pursuit of personal glory or material enrichment? Surprisingly, studies of ambition rarely define the term directly. For example, Joseph Schlesinger, the author of a classic work on political ambition, writes, "In politics . . . immediate personal success is so obviously the goal that the social scientist does well to give it primary consideration."[28] For Schlesinger, then, ambition is something like a desire for "immediate personal success." But success, we might ask, at what?

Perhaps the answer is success at winning office. At another point in his book, Schlesinger notes, "The attainment of office remains the one observable goal that we have in politics."[29] So political ambition becomes the desire to hold public office. Indeed, Schlesinger often uses the phrase "office ambition" as a synonym for "political ambition."

Given the structure of the American political system—including federalism and the separation of powers—political ambition may take several forms or directions (as Schlesinger puts it). Ambition may be "discrete," wherein a person seeks a particular office, serves a term, and leaves the political sphere when that term is up.[30] Many, maybe even most, individuals who enter politics do so with discrete ambition. This makes it unlikely that they would be considered politicians by most people. For instance, if a neighbor decides to run for the school board and serves one term, is she a politician? She will surely not consider herself one, nor will her acquaintances (at least those who like her). But why? Is it the once-and-done nature of her foray into politics? Why should that matter? If she runs for a second term, does she then become a politician?

Certainly, those who want to make a career out of politics are considered politicians. Their ambition can take two directions. Some will have what Schlesinger calls "static ambition." That is, they would like "to make a long-term career out of a particular office."[31] Members of Congress, in both the House and Senate, are the most likely politicians to have static ambition, but some state legislators make a career out of serving in the State House.

Finally, Schlesinger notes that some politicians have "progressive ambition." By that, he means they have designs on an office higher than the one they currently seek or occupy. "A likely assumption," he writes, "is that progressive ambitions dominate and are suppressed only when they appear unreasonable in terms of the chances."[32]

Indeed, Americans are suspicious of those who would like to spend their lives in politics and they may be particularly leery of those who want to climb the political career ladder. But as Gordon Black noted in another early study of political ambition, a politician's evaluation of other offices changes as he or she holds any given office. That's because, "some part of [the politician's] investment in politics is transferable to the pursuit of other offices, and the ability to transfer investments increases his [sic] expected return from higher offices. Thus, each step in a political career sequence alters one's evaluation of the other step."[33] A person may not have sought a seat on the city council with an eye toward the state legislature, let alone Congress after that, but once he or she serves as a city councilperson, other offices may become more attractive. This is not because politicians are power hungry, but rather because new opportunities present themselves. Undoubtedly, some people also find that they enjoy public service or they are encouraged to seek higher office by those around them. At any rate, Black concludes,

> This description of the development of ambition differs markedly from the view that sees the politician as a driven man [sic] who decides his course early and plans his whole life accordingly. Perhaps there are such men, but we suspect they are a distinct minority. The

tides of politics are too great to permit men to chart an undeviating route through the uncertain and troubled waters of political life.[34]

Incidentally, ambition does not tell us anything about why people want to hold office. In Chapter 4, I argued that there are likely to be multiple reasons that a person would enter politics. Some of these, undoubtedly, are self-serving. But I made the case that public policy is at least as powerful a motivator as self-interest.[35]

Ultimately, though, politicians' motivations do not matter as much as we tend to think they do. The very fact that they want to hold elected office—the fact that they have political ambition—serves the public's interest. It does so by ensuring that we have a sufficient pool of potential public servants. If no one had political ambition, who would ever voluntarily put him or herself through the intense public scrutiny that politicians receive?

Believe it or not, political ambition also helps to constrain politicians' behavior. Because they want to remain in office, or move on to other offices, politicians must be mindful of the public's wishes. In fact, progressive ambition plays a particularly critical role in linking elected officials to the people. One study of state legislators in eight states found that progressively ambitious legislators spent significantly more time monitoring constituent opinion than did those who were either not ambitious or statically ambitious.[36] Without the desire to move up the political ladder those who run for office may pay less attention to the concerns of their constituents.

Furthermore, political ambition makes elections all the more powerful as instruments for accountability. To stay in a given office, or to move to a higher one, politicians must face elections on an ongoing basis. This allows the voters to regularly hold them responsible for their actions in office. An elected official who plans to leave office after only a few terms, or who is more than happy to leave the political scene at any moment, lacks a fear of electoral defeat. That fear is the mechanism that ensures democratic responsiveness and accountability. Without it, elected officials are free to ignore the public's wishes. Of course, they may choose to do what the public wants anyway. But there is no guarantee that they will do so.

Does the fear of electoral defeat lead to the opposite problem, namely, a willingness to pander to voters? I suppose it could if the fear is great enough. I argued in Chapter 3, however, that the allegation of pandering is largely baseless. As it turns out, one person's act of pandering is another person's fealty to the will of the people.

Admittedly, staying in office requires more than currying favor with the public. Given the astronomical cost of campaigning, politicians must also be attentive to potential campaign donors, including interest groups. The result is some, perhaps even considerable, tension between responding to the concerns of the public and those of organized interests.

Many people simply assume that elected officials respond to this tension by favoring contributors over the public. However, there is very little empirical evidence for this assumption. The policymaking process is extraordinarily complex, with pressures in every direction, and the tendency is for the status quo to be maintained. As a recent magisterial study of lobbying influence concludes, "public-policy disputes are almost always related to existing public policies and . . . efforts to change an existing policy orientation usually fail."[37]

Of course, the status quo may simply reflect previous efforts of the wealthy (i.e., well-financed interest groups) to secure their interests. But when less wealthy groups are well organized and mobilized to compete with more privileged groups on a given issue, "there can be no prediction as to whether the next adjustment [to the policy equilibrium] will be toward further advantage to the wealthy or away from that position."[38] Indeed, Mark Smith's study of the political power of the business community, which is often thought to be the most powerful sector in American society, found that business interests are not as successful in shaping policy as is often assumed.[39] According to Smith:

> Business normally does not go from winning to losing, or vice versa, because of the effectiveness of its own efforts to influence policy. Instead, public opinion and elections remain the most important forces determining fluctuations in policy even when the analysis considers possibilities for influence by a unified business community.[40]

Ambitious politicians, then, are not puppets controlled by wealthy and powerful interests. But they do pay close attention to the opinion of voters. If they hope to stay in office or move up the ranks, they have to respond positively (though not slavishly) to that opinion. And if they should become too cozy with powerful interests, or begin to ignore the wishes of the people, the voters have an effective means of punishment. They can deny the ambitious politician something of real value, namely, re-election. Ultimately, political ambition acts as a guarantor of democratic responsiveness and accountability. As Joseph Schlesinger put it:

To slight the role of ambition in politics, then, or to treat it as a human failing to be suppressed, is to miss the central function of ambition in political systems. A political system unable to kindle ambitions for office is as much in danger of breaking down as one unable to restrain ambitions. Representative government, above all, depends on a supply of men [*sic*] so driven; the desire for election and, more important, reelection becomes the electorate's restraint upon its public officials. No more irresponsible government is imaginable than one of high-minded men unconcerned for their political futures.[41]

Hypocrisy

If ambition has some redeeming qualities, hypocrisy surely does not. Here, I use the term "hypocrisy" broadly, following the Cambridge political theorist David Runciman's understanding of it as "the construction of a persona ... that generates some kind of false impression."[42] Typically, the term refers to behavior that contradicts one's stated principles. The hypocrite says one thing and does another. But insincerity is also a form of hypocrisy according to Runciman. Regardless of the specific form it takes, hypocrisy is troubling to people because it is a kind of deception.

One of the most popular criticisms of politicians is that they are "fake." Because they must constantly put on an act, or at least feel as though they must put on an act, the public never knows for sure who these people really are. That is disturbing in a democracy because voters have to make determinations about those running for office. If we cannot know with any degree of certainty what politicians are like, we could easily make mistakes in the voting booth.

There is a great deal of truth to this claim. However, its truth derives not from the unique nature of politicians but from the fact that all human beings put on acts. When we hire someone, for example, we can never know whether we have hired the right person. An individual will behave in a certain way during the interview but may turn out to be considerably different once he or she has the job. The same can be said about finding a romantic partner. People behave differently during courtship than they do once in a committed relationship. This fact surely contributes to the high divorce rate in the United States.

I often ask my students if they act the same way around their friends as they do around their grandparents. They always laugh at the question because it would be absurd to answer, "Yes." I assume that the difference is that they clean up their language and maybe mind their manners a little more around their grandparents. Behavior such as this was examined in Erving Goffman's classic work of sociology, *The Presentation of Self in Everyday Life*. According to Goffman, "when an individual appears in the presence of others, there will usually be some reason for him [sic] to mobilize his activity so that it will convey an impression to others which it is in his interests to convey."[43]

There are two aspects of this passage that are important to consider. First, notice that Goffman is describing something that happens dozens, maybe hundreds, of times every day. When we interact with another person, we will "usually" have reason to alter our behavior in an attempt to manage an impression. Second, we all attempt to manage impressions. We want employers, potential spouses, and grandparents to think highly of us. So we "mobilize our activity" to convey positive impressions. Of course, we cannot be too obvious in our efforts to control how others view us. They are, nonetheless, aware of what we are up to because they engage in the same behavior. That fact forces us to act with "calculated unintentionality."[44] That is, we must purposefully act as though we are not acting purposefully. This dynamic creates "a kind of information game—a potentially infinite cycle of concealment, discovery, false revelation, and rediscovery."[45] That sounds like an accurate description of the relationship between voters and candidates. But Goffman is describing ordinary human behavior.

We might say that we are all acting as politicians when we control the presentation of ourselves in everyday life. But it makes more sense to me to conclude that politicians are simply behaving as normal human beings when they manage impressions of themselves. We all want to hide our flaws and put ourselves in the best possible light. The difference is that politicians have to do this in full public view. This means that they find themselves especially susceptible to a disadvantage faced by all "actors" in the everyday drama of self-presentation. As Goffman explains:

> the arts of piercing an individual's effort at calculated unintentionality seem better developed than our capacity to manipulate our own behavior, so that regardless of how many steps have occurred in the information game, the witness is likely to have the advantage over the actor.[46]

In other words, people are better at identifying insincere behavior than hiding their insincerity. That is unfortunate for politicians, because it means they will inevitably be thought of as insincere. If their attempts to project a positive image are clumsy, they will appear obviously manipulative. If their self-presentation is smooth, they are just "slick." When the public is constantly on the lookout for insincerity in politicians, they will find evidence of it everywhere. Again, this is not because politicians are uniquely insincere. Rather, people—politicians and non-politicians alike—are always acting.

Of course, most people believe that one can avoid being accused of insincerity by simply being one's self. But Goffman's work, and a great deal of recent research in psychology and neuroscience, suggests that the "true self" is a fiction.[47] When are my students acting more like their true selves—when they are with their friends or with their grandparents? According to the psychologist Bruce Hood, the social environment we inhabit determines our sense of self. But because the context we find ourselves in varies so often, if not continually, our selves are often morphing to match our surroundings. "There is not one self or multiple selves in the first place," writes Hood. "Rather, it is the external world that switches us from one character to another."[48] After showing that people are quite "susceptible to group pressure, subtle priming cues, stereotyping, and cultural cuing," Hood concludes, "the notion of a true, unyielding ego self cannot be sustained."[49]

If it is difficult to know ourselves, how can we ever know what another person is "really" like? It is especially difficult—if not impossible—to know someone's essential self if we have never met him or her. Since we rarely meet politicians, or do so only superficially, can we really claim to know anything about them as individuals? We think that because we see them on television so often, we have special insight into their character. But all we really know is how they act when they are on television as elected officials.

All of this suggests to me that our attempts to test politicians' sincerity are likely to backfire. Rather than reveal their real nature, which they could not convincingly do even if they wanted to, politicians will simply respond to such a test as any person would: they will try to *appear* sincere. The result is that we are forcing politicians to behave in precisely the way we deplore. Worse, we have created a self-perpetuating cycle of politicians acting sincere, the public doubting their sincerity, and politicians redoubling their efforts at acting sincere. In these circumstances, even a politician who is actually being sincere will be viewed with suspicion.

Assuming that the pursuit of sincerity is futile, can we at least insist that politicians avoid the form of hypocrisy wherein people say one thing and do another? We certainly can expect consistency in our politicians, can we not? But, once again, we would be expecting them to behave in ways that most human beings do not (and perhaps cannot). As the psychologist Robert Kurzban argues in his fascinating book *Why Everyone (Else) is a Hypocrite*, "The very constitution of the human mind makes us massively inconsistent."[50]

Kurzban posits a "modularity" theory of the human mind. According to this theory, "the mind consists of many, many parts, and these parts have many different functions."[51] Different modules, or parts of the mind, rely on different pieces of information, some of which is contradictory. As a result, we often hold mutually exclusive beliefs simultaneously. Furthermore, our behavior does not always match our stated principles. "Modularity," says Kurzban, "explains why everyone is a hypocrite."[52] Of course, few (if any) of us recognize our own hypocrisy, but we are very good at detecting it in others. This is particularly true with respect to politicians, as Kurzban himself notes. It is worth quoting him at length on this point.

> My guess is that—and maybe I'm just naïve—politicians, despite appearances, aren't actually all that much more hypocritical than the rest of us. It's just that the rest of us skate by without anyone noticing ... Because politicians have to express moral condemnation publicly, when they commit immoral acts they can be found to have condemned them, on the record, in the *New York Times*. Having to say that many things are wrong, combined with public scrutiny, makes hypocrisy among politicians and other publicly visible moralists, such as religious leaders, easy to spot. For the rest of us, well, hypocrisy is part of the modular design. We condemn because our moralistic modules are designed to constrain others but there is nothing that keeps our behavior consistent with our condemnation. And we can get by with a great deal of inconsistency because it's not always easy for others to notice it. We can be as inconsistent as others allow us to be.[53]

Some experimental evidence does exist to suggest that those with power may act more hypocritically than those without power.[54] However, the generalizability of this evidence is limited. The one study directly examining this question was conducted with Dutch students who were assigned a high or low level of power and asked to simulate the roles of, for example, a prime minister or civil servant.[55] That students in these conditions played stereotypical roles should not surprise us and is not indicative of the way actual prime ministers, or others in positions of power, behave.

Nevertheless, political hypocrisy is inevitable—not because politicians are politicians, but because they are human. Should we, therefore, just accept hypocrisy in our politicians? It depends, argues David Runciman, on what kind of hypocrites we want in politics.[56]

Runciman is most concerned, rightly I would argue, with hypocrisy that makes it difficult to practice politics effectively. So, for example, demanding sincerity when we know (or should know) that insincerity is a normal part of politics, not to mention life generally, is a kind of hypocrisy that is problematic in a democracy. When we have these unrealistic expectations it is nearly impossible for elected officials to function legitimately. For Runciman, "it does not matter whether or not our politicians are all wearing masks, if that is what is needed to make our form of politics work. What does matter is if people are hypocritical about *that*."[57]

There are, essentially, two levels of hypocrisy at work in politics. Runciman refers to these as first-order and second-order hypocrisy.[58] "First-order hypocrisy," writes Runciman,

> is the ubiquitous practice of concealing vice as virtue, which makes up the parade of our social existence. Second-order hypocrisy is concealing the truth about this practice, and pretending that the parade itself is a form of genuinely virtuous, and therefore self-denying, behavior.[59]

First-order hypocrisy, as noted earlier, is part of human nature. As much as we might like to eradicate it from politics, we will never do so completely and attempts to do so are likely to be counterproductive. But second-order hypocrisy is problematic and we ought to try to eliminate it entirely.

Second-order hypocrisy is, in effect, hypocrisy about hypocrisy. Politicians engaged in this level of hypocrisy use the fact of first-order hypocrisy for political gain. They make a show of their anti-hypocrisy as they portray themselves as unsullied by the dirty work of politics. Such politicians may truly believe that they are not hypocrites, that they act authentically, and that they are offering a way out of "politics as usual." That, however, is self-deception. And it is a dangerous move in a democracy for it produces an environment in which a naive search for authenticity, and a desire to transcend politics, pervades civic life. As Runciman maintains, "Second-order hypocrisy, because it makes a mockery of the whole business of public enactment, is corrosive in ways that first-order hypocrisy is not."[60]

In a review of Runciman's *Political Hypocrisy*, Jeremy Waldron describes the political environment created by second-order hypocrisy. "It is a climate," he writes, "in which everyone is on the alert for hypocrisy and lying, and in which other forms of wickedness are put to one side in the all-consuming quest to uncover a mismatch between a politician's public professions and the genuine sentiments of his soul."[61] For Waldron, politicians themselves have created this environment. But it is not just politicians who engage in hypocrisy at this level; the people are second-order hypocrites as well. Time and again they vote for the politician who has affected the most anti-political posture and then are dismayed when that politician fails to change politics. Barack Obama and the Tea Party class of 2010 in Congress are just the latest examples.

When people come to believe, as the American public has done, that politics is an act of truth-seeking rather than of collective problem-solving, they are engaged in a serious form of hypocrisy. Politics requires a certain amount of winking and nodding, but the public refuses to play along. Some political motives must remain hidden, but the public piously demands full transparency. The people, assured in their belief that only politicians wear masks, want to unmask the impostors. Democracy can withstand only so much of this.

In the end, Runciman argues that politicians "should be sincere about maintaining the conditions under which democracy is possible, and should place a higher premium on that than on any other sort of sincerity."[62] They will not—they cannot—do that, however, if the public will not let them. It would be a mark of a mature democracy to accept a certain level of innocent and inevitable (i.e., first-order) hypocrisy for the sake of preserving the political system. Whether the American public can develop such an acceptance is unclear.

Chapter 7

The Private Lives of Politicians

Dishonesty

Perhaps ambition and hypocrisy can be tolerated in democracy. Dishonesty, on the other hand, surely cannot be. To the average person, dishonesty seems rampant in politics; it is, according to conventional wisdom, part of the very nature of the enterprise. That, in turn, means that politicians must be dishonest people *by nature*. How could one prosper in such an environment if he or she was not dishonest?

Of course, dishonesty comes in many forms. Lying, cheating, and stealing are all dishonest acts and politicians have been known to engage in all three. But so have non-politicians. An important question, therefore, is whether politicians do so to a greater degree than the rest of us. More fundamentally, can we conclude that politicians are—inherently—liars, cheats, and thieves?

This chapter will look at each of these forms of dishonesty in turn. I begin with lying because it appears to be ubiquitous in politics. I then turn to cheating and to a particular type of stealing, namely, financial impropriety. Far more than the previous chapter, this chapter explores the basic morality of politicians. It seeks to determine whether politicians are the moral cretins they are often made out to be and, regardless of their level of moral turpitude, how much they differ from the rest of us on this score.

Lying

Much of what passes for lying in politics is simply "spin." However, as I argued in Chapter 4, spin is more often an act of persuasion than manipulation. It is an attempt to frame a situation according to a particular interpretation. In any event, it is not lying, which is a statement that deliberately contradicts what the speaker believes to be true.

So how often do politicians lie? As one might imagine, an attempt to quantify the amount of lying that goes on in politics would be nearly impossible. One would have to gather every statement made by politicians in a given period of time and determine which of them is true and which false. But if a precise answer to the question is not possible, perhaps we can offer a relative one. Are politicians more or less likely to lie than the rest of the population?

We know from experience that people tell lies all of the time. In fact, we also have ample systematic evidence that they do so. According to one scholarly review of deception research, "the findings of all studies measuring the frequency of deception converge to the same conclusion: lying is a frequent event."[1] One study found that in a 10-minute "get-acquainted" meeting with strangers, people lied, on average, more than twice and 78 percent of the participants admitted to having lied during the session.[2] In another, college students reported telling two lies a day (on average) while older participants in the study told one.[3]

Of course, many of the lies people tell are "little white lies." They say a meal was tasty when it wasn't; they tell someone they like her shoes or his tie when they don't; they tell their children Santa Claus brings Christmas presents when he doesn't even exist. These lies do no real harm and many are virtually required as part of normal human interaction. Politicians certainly tell these sorts of lies. They may say that they really enjoy being in such-and-such a town in their district when they do not really like the town at all. But these lies are inconsequential.

What about more significant lies? Average people frequently tell these kinds of lies as well. They do so when they feel that lying is the only way to achieve a particular goal.[4] Typically, it is done to avoid the negative consequences of actions, but it may also be done to gain some kind of benefit or reward. The significant lies politicians may tell are related either to themselves and their records or to public policy.[5] The temptation to tell such lies could arise from a politician's desire to win an election or from an attempt to pass, or defeat, a particular piece of legislation. Nevertheless, there is reason to believe that politicians tell few significant lies, or at least fewer than most people would assume.

Nearly everything a politician says receives intense scrutiny. A politician's election adversary, for example, will search for any and all signs of dishonesty in his or her past. Opposition researchers get paid, in part, to find inaccuracies in the public statements of their clients' opponents. In addition, the media pay close attention to claims made by politicians. Journalists examine campaign ads using the "ad watch" format in which misleading or deceptive statements are labeled as such.[6] (Incidentally, the tendency of reporters to focus on ads containing false statements and to virtually ignore truthful ads skews our view of the veracity of campaign ads—and candidates—in a negative direction.[7]) There are also several projects devoted to ascertaining the truthfulness of politicians' statements. FactCheck.org and PolitiFact are the best known of these projects, but fact-checking is now a widespread phenomenon in the media and on the Internet.[8]

The likelihood that any lie a politician tells will be identified, labeled as such, and disseminated widely via well-trafficked websites (the headlines from which will then be used in campaign ads against the politician) is a powerful disincentive to lie. Of course, that does not mean lying never occurs in politics. But the microscopic inspection of everything politicians say forces them to be far more careful in their choice of words than the rest of us have to be. Perhaps this is why politicians often appear evasive. Too much concern that one's statements might be declared untrue encourages the use of ambiguous language.

Of course, there is a countervailing incentive at work in politics. Especially during campaigns, the pressure to obtain votes may lead politicians to promise voters the moon. Do they really intend to keep every campaign promise once in office? If not, is this a form of lying?

It would, indeed, be lying if politicians made promises they had no intention of keeping. But there is no evidence that they do not intend to keep their promises. In fact, there is good evidence that they are true to their word.[9] Most of the research on this question focuses on presidential candidates because the data is much more readily available for them than it is for other politicians. One of the earliest, and most widely cited, works is Jeff Fishel's *Presidents & Promises*. Fishel found that the presidents in his study "submitted legislation or signed executive orders that are broadly consistent with about two-thirds of their campaign pledges."[10]

More recent examinations of presidential accountability confirm Fishel's basic conclusion.[11] In her study of the first year of the George W. Bush, Bill Clinton, and Barack Obama Administrations, Michele Claibourn found that these presidents followed through on the issues they emphasized in their campaigns with only rare exceptions (i.e., Bush on Social Security reform and Medicare prescription drug coverage; Clinton on middle class tax cuts).[12] Why would there be any exceptions at all? Keep in mind that this study looked at only the *first* year of a president's term. President Bush, for example, neglected prescription drug coverage in 2001. But legislation creating Medicare Part D passed in 2003. The only other priority that President Bush neglected in his first year was Social Security reform. He did establish a presidential commission on the subject in May of 2001.[13] But the complex nature of the issue, and the events of September 11, 2001, meant that serious, sustained attention to Social Security reform would have to wait (until after his re-election in 2004, as it turns out, when he did make a concerted effort to sell his plan for "partial privatization").

When presidents fail to act on the agenda they proposed during the campaign, it is almost always because circumstances demand attention be placed elsewhere. President Clinton abandoned tax cuts for the middle class when he learned, before he had even been inaugurated, that the budget deficit was larger than had previously been realized. The choice, as he saw it, was between addressing a significant, and growing, problem (the government's structural deficit) and remaining true to a pledge made when that problem's seriousness was not entirely understood. Indeed, as President Clinton wrote in his memoir, "I hated to give up the middle-class tax cut, but with the deficit numbers worse, there was no choice."[14] So presidents do not lie when they make promises during a campaign, but events can conspire to thwart their best intentions.

The little research that has been done on whether members of Congress keep their promises indicates that they, too, are trustworthy. One study of positions taken on environmental policy during the 1996 campaign concludes that "representatives generally vote consistent with their campaign promises, and that these promises are powerful predictors of congressional behavior."[15] More broadly, Tracy Sulkin's impressive examination of the campaign agendas of successful House and Senate candidates in 1998, 2000, and 2002 confirmed the conclusion that members of Congress keep their promises.[16] "Contrary to the popular wisdom," writes Sulkin,

> that campaign appeals are meaningless and that candidates regularly lie in their campaigns, saying one thing but then doing another once elected, representatives' and senators' claims often serve as good signals about the issues they will pursue and what they will accomplish in their next terms.[17]

Does every member of Congress pursue only the agenda he or she proposed while running for office? Of course not. Has a representative or senator ever cast a vote that contradicts a position that he or she took on the campaign trail? Certainly. But members of Congress, like presidents, can be trusted to do in office what they say they will do when they are asking for votes. The same, one assumes, can be said for elected officials at the state and local levels as well.

Cheating

Of course, lying is not the only form of dishonesty. People also cheat and they appear to do so quite readily. Indeed, after a series of experiments on cheating, Duke University psychologist Dan Ariely and his colleagues concluded, "when people had the ability to cheat, they cheated." To be fair, "the per person magnitude of dishonesty was relatively low (relative to the possible maximum amount)."[18] The result, according to Ariely and his colleagues, is that people "behave dishonestly enough to profit, but honestly enough to delude themselves of their own integrity."[19]

Once again, the standard by which we should judge politicians is the typical person. If people cheat when given the opportunity, we should not be surprised that at least some politicians will also cheat when they have the chance. The truth, however, is that politicians have few opportunities to gain personal advantage by cheating. Indeed, it is not even clear what form cheating by a politician would take. At *what* would he or she cheat? Politicians are extremely unlikely to cheat on their taxes, for example, because their financial records are on full display for the media to examine. Of course, there have been high profile cases of public servants failing to pay the full amount of what they owed in taxes, but these cases typically involve appointees, not politicians in the sense that I have been using the term (that is, elected officials and those seeking to become elected officials). Furthermore, such cases are few and far between. The percentage of politicians, or even appointees, who cheat on their taxes simply cannot match the 15 percent of the American public who admit to doing so.[20] (This number, incidentally, probably underestimates the actual percentage of tax cheaters because many of those willing to cheat will not acknowledge their dishonesty on a survey.)

Given the scrutiny politicians face, they would likely get caught if they were to cheat in any way. As the odds of getting caught increase, the costs of cheating rise; and when the costs of cheating outweigh the benefits of doing so, very few people will cheat. Because the costs of cheating are higher for politicians than for the typical person, we can be fairly confident that politicians are not cheating to an extraordinary, or even an ordinary, degree.

There is, however, one situation in which politicians might find it beneficial to cheat. During an election, a dishonest candidate could benefit from campaign dirty tricks or even election fraud. Just how widespread such practices are is hard to say.[21] Few people cheat in broad daylight. There are certainly lots of anecdotes about campaign dirty tricks, though there are relatively few actual violations of campaign law. The same is true with respect to election fraud, despite the claims of widespread illegal voting or voter suppression.[22] Moreover, in the few cases in which there have been prosecutions for violations of campaign law or election fraud, the candidate him or herself is almost never charged.

Of course, cheating is unethical, if not always illegal. It is not illegal to send a "mole" into an opposing campaign to spy on it; it is, arguably, unethical. So how ethical are campaigns? The answer to that question depends on the ethical standard one employs.[23] Needless to say, there is considerable disagreement over such standards. Generally speaking, campaign operatives believe that they have a fiduciary duty to the candidates who hire them. Their first, and perhaps only, responsibility is to help the candidate win. That means they should do whatever it takes, short of breaking the law or violating universal moral norms (e.g., those against lying, cheating, and stealing) to accomplish the goal.

The rub, of course, is determining when universal moral norms have been violated. As it turns out, campaign operatives will not be as quick to find violations as will journalists, academics, and certainly the public. Is it cheating to send a spy into the opposing campaign? Many of us would say yes; most operatives are likely to say no.

Before we conclude that those who work for politicians are the real cheaters, it might be worth noting another study by Dan Ariely. He and his colleagues conducted one of their cheating experiments with congressional staffers in Washington, D.C. and with bankers in New York City. Bankers, it turns out, cheat twice as often as the "junior politicians" (to use Ariely's humorous phrase for the staffers).[24]

At any rate, when violations of campaign ethics occur, it is campaign operatives, not the candidates themselves, who usually commit them. Candidates do not run their own campaigns and they are unlikely to be aware of even half of what is done on their behalf. Perhaps this ignorance is willful. The "don't ask, don't tell" approach gives candidates plausible deniability and an innocent conscience. But it may be worse than that. Supposed ignorance, and the resulting silence from the candidate, about questionable campaign tactics may be a form of consent by the candidate. Allen Raymond, a campaign operative who was convicted of a felony for jamming the phone lines of political opponents, has written that one of the lessons he learned as an operative "was that the candidate who asks 'Is it fair to get me elected this way?' is the candidate who's never won."[25] So perhaps savvy candidates know not to ask, thereby giving their operatives a green light to play fast-and-loose with ethical boundaries.

Candidates, then, are ultimately responsible for what happens in their names. They should make it clear to the operatives they hire that they want to run a clean campaign. But, given the division of labor in campaigns, it is very often the case that they do not know what operatives are doing behind the scenes. Campaigns are frenzied and the pace of activity, especially as the election approaches, does not allow for the sort of oversight a principal would normally have in an organization. These are not excuses; they are simply facts of life in a campaign.

Another fact of campaign life is that the pressure to win is intense. The pressure a candidate feels to win an election comes not just from him or herself. It comes from all those who put their faith in the candidate, including party activists, campaign contributors, rank-and-file party members, and those who intend to vote for him or her. If the candidate occasionally turns a blind eye, willfully or not, to what operatives are doing, it is understandable if not any less inexcusable.

There is one other way in which politicians have been known to cheat. Indeed, there were at least five examples of this form of cheating that garnered significant media attention, and several others that were not as newsworthy, during the writing of this book.[26] The kind of cheating I have in mind here is not political in nature. Instead, it is a violation of one of the most important personal commitments an individual makes in his or her life.

Sadly, politicians are not immune from infidelity. Of course, we cannot know how many politicians cheat in this way. Thus, we can only speculate as to whether more of them engage in extramarital affairs than do non-politicians. The best estimates are that 28 percent of all men, and 15 percent of women, cheat on their spouses.[27] As of this writing, there are 357 men and 78 women in the U.S. House of Representatives.[28] If the estimates for the public at large were to hold in the House, 100 men and 12 women would be guilty of having had an affair at some point in their lives. Whether these numbers are at all accurate cannot be said with certainty. But it would be reasonable to conclude that they are far too high. Given the probability that affairs involving public figures are more likely to come to light than those of private individuals, and given the fact that there have been no more than about a dozen representatives even accused of extramarital affairs between 2000 and 2012, it is unlikely that there are currently 112 U.S. representatives who have had, or will at some point have, affairs.[29]

Nevertheless, observers have offered multiple reasons why politicians might be more likely to engage in affairs than non-politicians. Some suggest that politicians have more opportunities to cheat on spouses because they travel often and have many admirers among the numerous people with whom they interact. Other observers point to factors that are related to politicians' personality traits. Politicians are self-confident, for example, so they may believe that they are more likely than others to get away with indiscretions. Having power, or at least a desire for power, may also encourage infidelity. It might do so, as does self-confidence, by contributing to a politician's sense of invulnerability. Finally, politicians may have a heightened need for excitement in life and may, as a result, engage in more "thrill seeking" behavior.[30]

There is some empirical evidence, based on research from the Netherlands, that a person's power within an organization is positively correlated with self-reports of past infidelity as well as a willingness to behave adulterously.[31] Of course, this research applies to those in positions of power in all fields. There is no reason to single out politicians as particularly susceptible to power's nefarious influence. Furthermore, as those who conducted this research admit, a correlation between power and infidelity does not imply that power *causes* infidelity. That is, some individuals may have personality traits (e.g., self-confidence) that make them both predisposed to engage in extramarital affairs and to reach the upper echelons of their chosen professions.

While power may be related to infidelity, recall that one of the traits politicians seem to have in greater abundance than the typical person is a desire for social acceptance. Recall, too, that high levels of social desirability tend to indicate an enhanced capacity for self-regulation. Concern for how one is viewed by others encourages a person to behave appropriately. When that behavior is under a constant spotlight, this trait is even more likely to be effective at discouraging improper activity. The upshot is that politicians are no more likely than other people who hold positions of power to engage in extramarital affairs. There is even reason to believe that they are less likely to do so.

Stealing

The last type of dishonesty to consider is stealing, though with respect to politicians we are not concerned with shoplifting or petty theft. Instead, the concern is public corruption and financial impropriety. In recent years, there have been several high profile corruption cases in the United States. Perhaps the most infamous involved the former governor of Illinois, Rod Blagojevich, who was convicted in 2011 of "17 counts of wire fraud, attempted extortion, soliciting bribes, conspiracy to commit extortion and conspiracy to solicit and accept bribes."[32] Other recent cases include those of Representative Randy "Duke" Cunningham, who pleaded guilty to bribery in 2005 after prosecutors charged him with having "taken bribes from contractors, which enabled him to buy a mansion, a suburban Washington condominium, a yacht and a Rolls Royce";[33] and Representative William Jefferson, who was convicted of several corruption charges in 2009 after federal investigators videotaped him taking $100,000 in bribery money and then found $90,000 stashed in his freezer.[34]

The Public Integrity Section of the U.S. Department of Justice prosecutes roughly 900 "public officials" for corruption in a given year.[35] That number includes all public employees, in all branches and agencies of government, at the federal, state, and local level. Of that 900, just a fraction is made up of elected officials. But even if all 900 public officials who are brought up on corruption charges in a year were *elected* officials, that would be a minuscule percentage of the over 500,000 elected officials in the United States.[36]

Indeed, while cases of corruption like the ones identified above become front page news, and media coverage of such cases gives the impression that "they're all doing it," the fact is that government in the United States is quite clean compared to most other countries. According to Transparency International's Corruption Perceptions Index, out of 183 countries in the world, the United States was the 24th least corrupt.[37] That puts the United States slightly behind most of Western Europe, but our score on the corruption index is comparable to other developed democracies. Germany, for example, had a score of 8.0 (with 10 being perfectly clean) in 2011, while the United Kingdom's was 7.8 and France's was 7.0. The United States had a score of 7.1.[38]

Of course, it may not be actual corruption but "honest graft" that concerns Americans. A recent *60 Minutes* report, for example, suggested that members of Congress are exempt from insider trading laws and can use non-public information they obtain as representatives to buy and sell stocks.[39] In fact, members of Congress are *not* exempt from insider trading laws.[40] But they do have information "about government activities that could affect publicly traded companies."[41] Some certainly trade on this information, but it is not clear how widespread the practice is. The *60 Minutes* report was based, in part, on the work of Peter Schweizer, a fellow at the Hoover Institution.[42] When asked on a radio program how common it is for Members of Congress to use such information for private gain, Schweizer acknowledged, "It's hard to say."[43]

Nevertheless, Schweizer believes the practice is "fairly common."[44] But when making allegations of unethical behavior against an entire group of people—Schweizer's book, after all, is titled *Throw Them All Out*—one really should be more exact. Just how common is "fairly" common? Schweizer offers no estimates of the number of elected officials who engage in questionable financial dealings. Instead, he provides circumstantial evidence that members of Congress get rich while in office. Members of the House, for example, do better in the market than the average American investor.[45] Presumably, they are also better educated (with a better understanding of the economy and the market) than the average American investor and are more likely to get professional investing advice.[46] But the claim that politicians do better in the market than the average investor is intended to sound alarm bells.

In addition to circumstantial evidence, Schweizer offers anecdotal evidence to support his argument. His book provides several case studies of members of Congress benefiting from financial deals that appear to be shady. Of course, appearances can be deceptive and there is always another side to the story.[47] But even if we believe that many members of Congress are using their positions for private gain, there is no reason to think they are unique in this behavior. Many businesspeople, for example, use their influence in the same way. Part Two of Schweizer's book examines several cases of "businessmen and investors who get rich through their political connections, tilting the playing field of the free market by lobbying for handouts."[48]

Indeed, the financial crisis of 2008 was precipitated, at least in part, by the greedy behavior of some in the financial industry.[49] And there are countless examples of corruption on Wall Street and throughout the business world. Yet the term "businessperson" does not automatically conjure thoughts of swindlers who are only concerned about enriching themselves.

Though it is not likely to quell criticism of Congress, it should be noted that President Obama signed into law the Stop Trading on Congressional Knowledge (STOCK) Act in April of 2012. This law makes explicit the ban on insider trading by members of Congress and requires disclosure of financial transactions, including the terms of mortgages, within 45 days of any deal. In addition, the law forbids members of Congress from taking advantage of preferential access to initial public stock offerings and requires members of Congress to forfeit their federal pension if they are convicted of a public corruption felony.[50] There are additional steps that could also be taken to reduce the potential for honest graft. Members of Congress could, for instance, be required to place all of their investments in a blind trust upon taking office. Nevertheless, the point of this discussion is that very few elected officials engage in illegal financial activity. And while more of them may take advantage of their offices for personal gain, we have no systematic evidence to suggest that this practice is widespread. Furthermore, and more importantly, such behavior does not appear to be unique to politicians. How many average citizens, if placed in a position to use *legal* means to make extra money, would refuse to do so simply because the ethics of doing so could be questioned? Given evidence from the business world and research on the typical person's honesty, my guess is that the percentage taking advantage of privileged information would be similar to the percentage of elected officials who currently do so. This is not meant to imply that honest graft is acceptable. Instead, it is meant to suggest that politicians should not be considered any more (or less) likely to engage in questionable financial activity than any other human being. When an elected official behaves unscrupulously, we should roundly criticize him or her. But we have no basis for accusing them all, out of hand, of unethical behavior.

Even if one is willing to admit that politicians are not that different from the rest of us, one could conclude that once in office elected officials lose their ethical bearings. Power corrupts, as the old saying goes. So even if those who enter politics are good people, the trappings of office, not to mention the "way the game is played," encourages elected officials to engage in activity they would ordinarily deem inappropriate.

Notice, however, that this argument suggests it is the system, not the politicians, who are to blame. As is often said, *anyone* would be sullied by politics. This is the tack taken by Harvard Law professor Lawrence Lessig in his impressive critique of the current campaign finance system, *Republic, Lost*.[51] Money corrupts American government, argues Lessig, but it is "a corruption practiced by decent people, people we should respect, people working extremely hard to do what they believe is right, yet decent people working within a system that has evolved the most elaborate and costly bending of democratic government in our history."[52] Elsewhere, Lessig urges his readers to try to "understand a pathology that all of us acknowledge (at the level of the institution) without assuming a pathology that few could fairly believe (at the level of the individual)."[53] Politicians face a simple choice: play the game by the established rules, distasteful as they may be, or get out of the game altogether. Actually, politicians who believe they can make a difference in public office do not have a choice; they must play the game.

I believe Lessig overstates the amount of corruption caused by campaign finance.[54] But even if one were to think that the system is shot through with malfeasance, Lessig makes clear that this is not the result of a character flaw in elected officials. The system needs to be changed, not the individuals in the system.

As with many of the other forms of bad behavior I have discussed in this chapter, there is a strong disincentive for politicians to engage in public corruption or financial impropriety. That disincentive is public attention. "Sunlight," as former Supreme Court Justice Louis Brandeis wrote, "is said to be the best of disinfectants."[55] Does the spotlight prevent every act of dishonesty? Certainly not. But is there an enormous amount of dishonesty taking place out of public view? It is highly unlikely.

Politicians, then, are not inherently any worse than any other group of citizens. Nor are they inherently any better. Nevertheless, fervent partisanship, wherein one's opponents are constantly on the lookout for misbehavior, and intense public scrutiny may force politicians to behave better than they—or any other group of people—otherwise might. Rather than corrupting, politics may actually constrain human nature, thereby improving it (if ever so slightly). But one does not have to go that far to conclude that politicians are not the thoroughly rotten group of people they are often made out to be. They are, for better or worse, just like the rest of us.

Chapter 8

Rebuilding Trust in Politicians

The expectations trap that we set for politicians, and the resulting anti-politician sentiment it engenders, may seem innocent enough. In fact, one might be tempted to argue that it serves democracy well by keeping politicians in their place. On the contrary, my closing argument is that the way we think about politicians threatens democracy by rendering it unworkable.

I begin this chapter with a brief review of the expectations trap and various other factors that are contributing to widespread animosity toward politicians. Next, I examine the importance of trust, and the corrosive nature of cynicism, for the legitimacy of a democratic system of government. Finally, I make a plea for the public to develop a more realistic view of politics and a more reasonable set of expectations for politicians as well as a more active role in governing.

Why Americans Hate Politicians . . . and Do So Now More Than Ever

Earlier in this book, I argued that Americans have always held negative attitudes about politicians. Some of this stems from a "leveling spirit" that lies at the core of democratic values; some of it emerges out of the unique history and political culture of "the first new nation" (to use Lipset's phrase). The operation of our system of government and politics also contributes to anti-politician sentiment. Democracy is messy and confusing and it generates a great deal of disagreement and conflict. People blame politicians for that conflict, though politicians are only the most visible actors in the struggle and are not solely responsible for the discord.

Though Americans have long disliked politicians, their level of contempt has risen in recent decades. Why this should be the case is not entirely clear but it is worth considering if we hope to reverse the trend. One explanation for the growth in anti-politician attitudes is the roughly simultaneous rise in anti-government rhetoric.[1] This rhetoric has been propagated, in the main, by one of the two political parties in the United States. Though Barry Goldwater's 1964 presidential bid was the first mainstream campaign to introduce anti-government ideas into wider public discourse, it was the success of Ronald Reagan that made such views acceptable.[2] If, as Reagan claimed in his First Inaugural Address, government is not the solution to our problems but is itself the problem,[3] then anything and anyone associated with government is also problematic. That would include, perhaps especially, politicians.

More fundamentally, the anti-government rhetoric of the Republican Party has become something of a self-fulfilling prophecy. Governing in an increasingly complex and interconnected world is difficult enough. When national leaders insist that it cannot be done well, and when they exploit any failure of government—real or perceived—to support their claims (and their electoral prospects), governing becomes even more difficult.[4] In fact, when public policy solutions are said to be doomed to failure before they are even attempted, governing becomes an exercise in futility. Once enfeebled, government will inevitably fail to solve the nation's problems, a fact used to further weaken the government. In this environment, politics—as the quest for control of government—is pointless and those who practice it are fools.

If those on the right have disparaged government, it should be said that some elements within American liberalism have done the same to politics. This is not a particularly new trend as anti-politics on the left can be traced at least as far back as the Progressive movement (see Chapter 2). Nevertheless, many on the left view politics as a diversion, a way for the wealthy and powerful to divide and conquer the rest of us. This is the logic behind the Occupy Wall Street movement and its claim to act on behalf of the "99 percent." Since the vast majority of people are not wealthy or powerful, the implicit (though at times not so implicit) assumption is that the "real" interests of the people are aligned. Any disagreements, therefore, are simply the artifacts of politics. In the pursuit of social harmony and the common good, many on the left believe politics is something to avoid.

This aversion to politics explains why the Occupy movement has had no influence on the Democratic Party; the movement never sought, and might not even want, such influence. The Tea Party movement, on the other hand, had a significant impact on the Republican Party almost from its inception.[5] So, on the right, we see a willingness to engage in politics for the purpose of undermining government, thereby turning politics into a Machiavellian game. On the left, where there is a genuine desire to use government for beneficial ends, there is an idealistic opposition to the means of achieving the control of government. Politics is a nasty business that must be transcended. Neither side puts politics in a particularly attractive light and both diminish our capacity to view politicians as public servants.

To be clear, anti-government rhetoric on the right is a better explanation of the relatively recent uptick in anti-politician sentiment than is anti-politics on the left. To begin with, the former developed (at least in its resurgent form following the 1960s) at roughly the same time as attitudes toward politicians began to noticeably decline. In addition, anti-government attitudes are far more widely held on the right, including throughout the Republican Party, than is anti-politics on the left. Nevertheless, considering the two together reminds us that politics and politicians are savaged on both sides of the ideological spectrum in the United States.

Recall that the most basic explanation for anti-politician sentiment in the United States is our commitment to democratic values and, yet, our distaste for the operation of democracy. Changes in both of these factors may also explain recent trends in opinions about politicians. The 1960s were a time of tremendous expansion of democratic values in the United States. The "rights revolution," as it is often called, further reinforced a belief in the equality of all Americans. This, in turn, may well have bolstered the leveling spirit in the United States.

With respect to the operation of democracy, technological changes beginning in the late 1970s gave rise to ubiquitous media. In particular, cable television news channels, with a 24-hour newshole to fill, began covering politics from morning to night. Eventually, some of these channels would enter the fray on one side of the partisan divide or the other. This unprecedented ability to observe the inner workings of democracy, and the relentless bombardment of partisan talking points, is likely to have soured attitudes about the political process and the politicians who participate in it.

It is probably worth mentioning that citizens around the world have become increasingly critical of their leaders. Though the trends in public support for, and trust in, political systems are not consistent from country to country, Pippa Norris has recently shown that "in many countries, satisfaction with the performance of democracy diverges from public aspirations" for it.[6] Norris refers to this as a "democratic deficit" and notes, "The most plausible potential explanations for the democratic deficit suggest that this phenomenon arises from some combination of growing public expectations, negative news, and/or failing government performance."[7]

We cannot ignore the role played by that last factor—malfunctioning governance—in Americans' condemnation of politicians. Norris finds that both process and policy performance influence the attitudes people have toward their governments. The sharp increase in partisan polarization and the U.S. government's inability to ensure economic security for many Americans during the last three or four decades have certainly eroded faith not only in the government but also elected officials (and, by extension, those wanting to become elected officials). If I have underemphasized government performance throughout this book, it is because it receives more than its share of attention from other sources. It is also because, as I tried to show in Chapters 3 and 4, much of what we think of as the "failure" of governance is primarily structural and is not the result of flaws in the individuals who govern.

At any rate, the public's disdain for politicians is not only the result of poor government performance. It is also, according to the concept of the democratic deficit, a product of citizens' expectations (not to mention negative media coverage of government and politics). Those expectations are rarely, if ever, examined in contemporary political commentary. This is the justification, in part, for making them the centerpiece of my argument in this book.

In Chapter 1, I described what I call the "expectations trap" that the American people set for politicians. Fundamentally, the public creates the trap by expecting politicians to satisfy demands that are unrealistic and often contradictory. I have identified three prevalent variations of the expectations trap. First, people want politicians to be leaders and, at the same time, followers. That is, they want elected officials to be willing to ignore public opinion and do what they think is best for the city, state, or country. However, voters punish elected officials who have not hewed closely enough to the public's wishes. Second, the public expects politicians to be principled but also pragmatic. Of course, politicians cannot simultaneously stick to principles and compromise. But striking a perfect balance between the two is nearly impossible. Being too obvious in one's willingness to compromise undermines his or her ability to advocate for principles; but being too committed to principle precludes the possibility of compromise. Finally, American politicians are expected to be ordinary and yet exceptional. They must be "just like the rest of us," but they must also be better than us, at least in certain important—and not always clearly specified—ways.

The expectations trap puts politicians in a no-win situation. Because they cannot fulfill contradictory expectations simultaneously, politicians will inevitably and constantly disappoint the public. Though I did not always identify them as such, numerous examples throughout the book illustrate the various aspects of the expectations trap. For instance, during the debt ceiling debate (which I describe in some detail in Chapter 5), politicians were asked to lead but also to be responsive to the will of the people. The public wanted elected officials to "do the right thing" and they opposed raising the debt ceiling. If raising the debt limit was the right thing to do, as so many knowledgeable analysts concluded it was, politicians were trapped. In the end, they chose to lead, and not simply satisfy the public, by doing what they thought was best. They did not, of course, get credit for having done so.

Perhaps the most serious consequence of these unrealistic expectations is an erosion of trust in our elected officials. This loss of trust creates a deep-seated cynicism that, ultimately, threatens to undermine the legitimacy of our government. Citizens in a representative democracy must have a certain level of faith in their elected officials or that system of government cannot function properly. The next section discusses the important role played by trust in a republican form of government and the danger posed by cynicism.

Trust and Cynicism in a Representative Democracy

Modern democracies are too large and complex to allow for direct rule by the people. As a result, citizens in modern democracies elect representatives to conduct their collective business. This does not mean that the people's role is limited to voting, though many citizens behave as though it does (and many others do not even fulfill the most basic obligation to cast a ballot). Indeed, political theorists have come to believe that representation works best when the citizenry is actively involved in deliberations about the direction their city, state, or nation should take. As the co-authors of a recent review of scholarship on representation note:

> we should think of representative democracy not as a pragmatic alternative to something we modern citizens can no longer have, namely direct democracy, but as an intrinsically modern way of intertwining participation, political judgment, and the constitution of demoi capable of self-rule. Understood in this way, elections are

not an alternative to deliberation and participation, but rather structure and constitute both.[8]

The people, in other words, have a significant role to play even in a *representative* democracy. For most Americans, however, governing is the responsibility of someone else. This distinction between those who govern and those who are governed likely contributes to the "us versus them" attitude that so many people have toward politicians.

It would be far more beneficial to the efficacy of our system of government to view elected officials as our partners in governing. In any healthy partnership, there should be robust dialogue between partners. One does not simply give marching orders to the other; the preferences and opinions of both sides of the partnership should be expressed and, ideally, modified after several rounds of back-and-forth.

This book is not the place for an extended discussion of alternative visions of representative democracy.[9] However, it is necessary to recognize that whether one views elected officials strictly as agents of the people or as partners in governing, trust is an indispensible feature of representation. Indeed, trust is critical to democracy generally.

That trust is important to democracy may not be immediately obvious. Democracy, after all, assumes that authorities need to be watched closely and held accountable for their actions. Its very design—elections, the protection of civil liberties, etc.—is premised on a certain level of skepticism about the intentions of those in power. Furthermore, democracy is a *political* system and, as such, is a system for managing conflicts of interest. Trust is likely to be increasingly difficult to maintain as the clash of interests becomes more intense.[10]

Yet it is precisely because of these disagreements over interests, not to mention values, that trust is essential in a democracy. Mark Warren, a political theorist who has explored the connections between democracy and trust as much as anyone, notes that the very meaning of the term "trust" implies a willingness "to accept vulnerability to the potential ill will of others by granting them discretionary power over some good. When one trusts, one accepts some amount of risk for potential harm in exchange for the benefits of cooperation."[11] Trust is needed precisely when others are in a position to influence our lives and when we are not necessarily of like mind with them.

Most fundamentally, democracy requires trust between citizens. In fact, as Robert Putnam has famously demonstrated, society itself is dependent on trust. In *Bowling Alone*, Putnam found that communities with little cooperation, reciprocity, and trust are worse off in numerous ways than those in which reasonable levels of social capital exist.[12] In a democracy, we agree to solve social problems collectively. Though we can—and do—disagree with one another on the best solutions, we have to assume that our fellow citizens want what is best for the country (or state or city) and not just what is best for themselves. If we believed otherwise, why would we consent to a system that allowed for the possibility that others would get what they want at the expense of our own needs? Perhaps we would do so because, in the long run, we think the benefits of such a system will balance out. If, in fact, the distribution of benefits is perceived to be fair, democracy may survive a lack of interpersonal trust, but it will be a thin and fragile democracy in which everyone is concerned only with his or her own well-being. If, however, we come to believe that the benefits of the system are not distributed fairly, political instability is the likely result.[13]

If trust among citizens is critical to the health of democracy, is trust in politicians also necessary? I would argue that it is. Admittedly, though, trust in politicians is difficult to maintain. That difficulty has little to do with politicians' supposed lack of trustworthiness. Instead, the nature of politics makes trust in politicians extremely complicated. As noted earlier, politics puts conflict center stage. Issues only become political when easy resolution is unattainable. Thus, the contentiousness of politics will mean that roughly half the population is likely to distrust any given elected official. Furthermore, campaigning may establish a superficial sense of trust in candidates that will only be dashed when, as elected officials, those politicians are forced to make choices that alienate at least some of their earlier supporters. As Warren puts it, "representatives are caught between the promise of politics to look toward collective futures—an element of every campaign—and the fact of conflicting interests/identities and competing powers."[14] (This, once again, points to the importance of establishing reasonable expectations.)

Finally, trust requires a certain level of knowledge of the motivations of other people. As Russell Hardin writes, "To say 'I trust you' means that I know or think I know relevant things about you, especially about your motivations toward me."[15] This knowledge, according to Hardin, is nearly impossible to possess "with respect to most government officials or with respect to government generally."[16] But elected officials—those government officials whom I have been referring to when I have used the term "politicians" in this book—are not most government officials. Indeed, they make up a small subsection of all government officials.

Can we know the motivations of elected officials? Not perfectly, of course, but one of the primary purposes of election campaigns is to gain as much knowledge of the candidates' motivations as possible. During a campaign, we are asking, essentially, what are the candidates' intentions and can we be reasonably assured that they will act in accordance with those intentions if elected? We are concerned with policy positions, to be sure, but also with character traits. Many political scientists argue, and have demonstrated, that campaigns are effective at conveying important information about candidates and issues.[17]

But is the information voters obtain from campaigns, or from following the news for that matter, sufficient for establishing trust in politicians? Hardin would argue that it is not. For him, trust amounts to "expectations grounded in encapsulated interest."[18] That is, "To say that I trust you with respect to some matter means that I have reason to expect *you to act in my interest* with respect to that matter because you have good reasons to do so, *reasons that are grounded in my interest.*"[19] It certainly seems as though it is in the interest of an elected official to act in the voters' interests; that is the very basis of his or her re-election. Politicians' interests, in other words, encapsulate the voters' interests. According to Hardin, however, the expectation that representatives will behave responsibly is not enough. If we are to have trust in them, we must know that they will behave responsibly. But, as Hardin claims, "trust requires too rich an understanding of the other's incentives for it to come easily to many people."[20] Given the scale of the American government, trust in political institutions and politicians is "epistemologically virtually impossible."[21]

There are several important implications of Hardin's argument. The first is that, according to his criteria, we are unlikely to be able to trust any strangers or large-scale institutions in society. Yet we appear to place sufficient trust in banks, and individual bank tellers, to hand over our money to them.[22] Parents appear to trust daycares and schools, as well as individual teachers, because they leave their children with them. Hardin's response to this would likely be that we have well-founded expectations that these institutions will function as they should, but that these expectations do not, in and of themselves, amount to trust. As a philosophical argument, this response may or may not be persuasive, but in practical terms, there seems to be little difference in the behavior generated by trust (as Hardin conceptualizes it) and by expectations alone.

For our present purposes, perhaps a more relevant implication of Hardin's argument is that a lack of trust in government and politicians does not necessarily imply distrust. Without much knowledge of a politician's motivations, we can neither trust nor distrust that politician. At times, Hardin seems to acknowledge this. He notes, for example, that "for most people there might be neither trust nor distrust of a reliable government or agency."[23] In fact, Hardin suggests that governments can be stable even if they are not legitimate (in the sense that they lack the citizens' trust). "It may suffice," he writes, "that government not be generally distrusted."[24] I will have more to say about trust and legitimacy later. For now, the point is that a paucity of trust in politicians does not necessarily have to produce an abundance of distrust.

At the same time, Hardin suggests, "Inductive expectations that government will be capricious might be sufficient to ground distrust."[25] Why expectations are enough to ground distrust but not trust is unclear. Nevertheless, this claim seems to nicely capture the logic of the American public's mistrust of politicians. They see (fairly and accurately or not) politicians behaving badly and a government supposedly incapable of solving problems, they come to expect such results, and they develop a generalized distrust of politicians and government.

The generalized distrust Americans have of their politicians is problematic in several ways. The first is that it is simply poor reasoning. Drawing conclusions about all politicians based on the actions of several, or even many, specific politicians is an example of the logical fallacy called "hasty generalization."[26] It seems obvious, but it is worth reminding ourselves that unless we have evidence that *every* politician is untrustworthy, we cannot logically conclude that they all are.

The second problem with generalized distrust is that it is unwarranted. Perhaps some would argue, contrary to my previous point, that they do have evidence that every single politician is untrustworthy. One of the primary purposes of this book, however, has been to challenge such a claim and I believe I have provided ample counter-evidence. Despite conventional wisdom, for example, elected officials rarely break campaign promises. Furthermore, while the collective behavior of politicians may appear—and may even be—dysfunctional, it is the product of the perfectly rational and, indeed, desirable behavior of individual politicians. When elected officials represent the interests of their districts and states, not to mention the partisan and ideological viewpoints of their supporters, interests will conflict and gridlock will result. Any policies that happen to emerge from the process will be based on concessions and compromises that are unlikely to make those policies completely satisfactory to anyone. As I argued in Chapter 3, most of what we dislike in American government and politics is the result of the design of the system itself.

This is not to say that individual politicians never violate citizens' trust. When they do, they should be roundly criticized and, indeed, punished for doing so. That, in part, is the reason we hold elections. But my purpose in writing this book was to make the case that the vast majority of politicians, and most of what they do, are (and is) perfectly trustworthy.

Generalized distrust should be avoided not only because it is illogical and unwarranted. More importantly, we should refrain from it because it produces cynicism. Indeed, generalized distrust could well serve as the definition of cynicism. The sociologist Jeffrey Goldfarb, who has long been a student (and critic) of cynicism, has referred to its modern form as "a legitimation of disbelief."[27] Because cynics feel that their distrust is warranted—it is legitimate—they see no need to gather further evidence. The cynic *knows* what is really going on, which is that all politicians are up to no good. "Cynicism," writes Goldfarb, "is confused for wisdom."[28] But such smug certainty is unexamined and, therefore, ultimately unjustified.

The cynic's knowing disdain for all things political appears to be hard-nosed realism. In truth, it is naivety. The cynic's view of politics is simplistic and betrays a lack of understanding of the complex dynamics of politics and the intense and conflicting demands of governing. But because cynics are convinced that they know the truth about politics, they are uninterested in learning more about it.

It is often argued that one of the by-products of cynicism is apathy. That is not the claim being made here. Though it makes sense to suppose that those who are least trusting of politicians would be most turned off by politics, one can also hypothesize that distrust would stimulate political activism, even if of an unconventional sort. Indeed, scholarship on the link between trust and participation has "generated a profusion of complex hypotheses" and mixed results.[29] Certainly, voter turnout has been relatively strong in recent years while cynicism has also been widespread.

The more worrisome effect of cynicism, to my mind, is the negative impact it has on one's ability (or, perhaps, willingness) to think critically. Goldfarb explains that while an ancient form of cynicism (that of Diogenes) was critical, contemporary cynicism is merely "mocking" and, as such, "expresses resignation, if not support, for the way things are."[30] When one assumes that the intentions of all politicians are ruinous, it is impossible to distinguish truly harmful intentions from those that are not. If nothing a politician says is worth listening to, dangerous pronouncements get ignored along with those that are merely worthless (not to mention those that might be edifying).

It is tempting to attribute this lack of critical thinking to laziness. It is, after all, hard work to discern beneficial ideas and actions from those that are not as useful, or even detrimental. To do so, one must pay close attention and analyze competing proposals.[31] But the cynic cannot be bothered; he or she is sure that it is all garbage.

In fact, cynicism is more pernicious than laziness. It is an active withdrawal from the work of democracy. Without a willingness to take seriously the claims and counterclaims made by those involved in the political process, deliberation is impossible. A politician, or a fellow citizen, cannot communicate with a cynic because there is no point to the conversation. But democracy is a system of government based on communication. As the political theorist Steven Bilakovics points out, "the politics of democracy is premised upon the possibility of replacing force with persuasion" and, thus, "argument serves as the very medium of democratic politics."[32] There is no persuading a cynic, no point arguing that one policy, one party, one politician is better than another. The cynic rejects them all and, in so doing, rejects democracy itself even as he or she would likely praise democracy as the best form of government.[33]

Because the public's distaste for politicians, and politics generally, leads so easily to cynicism, I would argue that it also threatens the legitimacy of American government. Democratic stability, according to Seymour Martin Lipset, depends upon both the effectiveness and the legitimacy of the government.[34] "Legitimacy," writes Lipset, "involves the capacity of a political system to engender and maintain the belief that existing political institutions are the most appropriate or proper ones for the society."[35] But belief such as this is precisely what cynicism lacks. Indeed, one scholar defines cynicism as "the condition of lost belief."[36]

This does not mean that blind trust in government is necessary for legitimacy. Healthy skepticism, even a distrust of particular policies, parties, and politicians, is vital to a successful democracy. But skepticism must strike a balance with trust. Without skepticism, we are unduly deferential; without trust, we cannot cooperate. Cynicism not only upsets this balance, it tosses both skepticism and trust off the scales.

To this point, I have admittedly been blurring the distinction between individuals and institutions as the target of cynicism. One might argue that support for a political system, including the rules and the institutions that constitute it, can retain legitimacy even when those who inhabit positions of power within a system—individual authorities or politicians—are universally distrusted. Indeed, the "democratic deficit," which I discussed a bit earlier in this chapter, is the result of high levels of support for democracy as a system of government and, at the same time, considerable dissatisfaction with the performance of those running the government.

Perhaps this distinction between the system and its inhabitants, and the respective trust and distrust of each, can be maintained indefinitely. I have my doubts. As the eminent political scientist David Easton concluded, "If no system is able to persist without assuring itself of a minimal flow of support toward the regime, including the structure of authorities, there is equally little likelihood that a system could survive if it failed to support occupants for these authority roles."[37] Individual politicians, even entire parties, can lose support and can be replaced in a system. That, indeed, is the wonderful benefit of democracy. But when the positions of authority lose support generally, because *any* occupant will lack support, the system itself is effectively illegitimate. It is worth quoting Easton at length on this. "If [citizens] lose confidence in the ability of any authorities at all to cope with the problems of the day," writes Easton,

> the effect on support to other levels of the system may be very serious, at least for the persistence of that kind of system. But if no authorities are seen as being equal to the tasks of managing the affairs of state and confidence in any set of authorities or any government is completely undermined—historically a most unusual but possible condition—the result is that no set of persons will be able to mobilize enough support behind them to make and put into effect the necessary day-to-day decisions. Clearly, the system would be paralyzed; it would lose its capacity to act as a collectivity.[38]

Note these words carefully: The system would be paralyzed. Paralysis is precisely how many observers describe the current state of American politics. It would be a gross exaggeration to conclude, on the basis of that description, that American government is therefore illegitimate. But, at the risk of sounding alarmist, one must wonder if it is just a matter of time.

Were the government to lose legitimacy, the results would be disastrous. A belief that the government does not have legitimate authority threatens the rule of law.[39] As Norris found after her empirical examination of legitimacy theory, "the net effect of the democratic deficit was to reduce voluntary compliance with the law significantly."[40] Deep and widespread distrust of those in positions of power threatens the stability of the system so many Americans claim to revere.

In addition, generalized distrust makes it impossible to deal with serious long-term problems. Without trust in elected officials, the public is not likely to believe that certain problems exist in the first place. Even if we were all to agree on the problems, the public must have faith that the solutions policymakers offer are sincere attempts to solve them. Regardless of how far along the road to illegitimacy the United States government might currently be, it seems clear that we must rebuild trust in our politicians if they are to have the capacity to address the problems we say we want solved.

A Plea

We cannot begin trusting politicians simply by willing ourselves to do so. As American citizens, anti-politician sentiment is part of our political DNA. But our cynicism has grown in recent decades, suggesting that our attitudes about politicians are at least somewhat malleable. If that is the case, then our cynicism can be reversed.

Many will no doubt argue that the responsibility for rebuilding trust lies with the politicians. If they would only behave better, we would trust them more. There is no doubt that politicians have given at least some ammunition to those who would vilify them. Individual politicians have had their share of personal problems. And sometimes they act in ways that appear blatantly and shamelessly intended for partisan or self-interested gain.

As I have tried to make clear throughout this book, however, claims about the amount of misconduct politicians engage in are greatly exaggerated. We tend to remember objectionable behavior and forget all of the times when politicians behave respectably. Lies and scandals are newsworthy because they are aberrant. "Politician Tells Truth," though it sounds like a headline from the satirical newspaper *The Onion*, is not news because it is commonplace. A politician acting ethically is as newsworthy as an airplane landing safely.

Nevertheless, politicians do misbehave. They do so because they are human. It seems silly to have to remind ourselves of this, but it is easy to caricature and demonize people we do not know personally. As human beings, politicians share the range of foibles all humans possess. That fact does not excuse individual instances of misbehavior, but it should put them in perspective. Any group of people will include a few who make bad decisions. Why should politicians be any different?

Another claim I have made in this book is that much of what passes for misconduct by politicians is perfectly reasonable behavior given the design of our system of government. Citizens are clearly unhappy with the way government is currently functioning. Who, or what, is to blame for the perceived dysfunction? My argument has been that the system itself is more blameworthy than the participants in that system. As constitutional scholar Sanford Levinson recently wrote in an opinion piece for the *New York Times*, "critics across the spectrum call the American political system dysfunctional, even pathological. What they do not mention, though, is the role of the Constitution itself in generating the pathology."[41] Levinson went on to identify several sources of dysfunction in our system of government, some of which I pointed to in Chapter 3, including the separation of powers and checks and balances.

This argument, I realize, does not sit well with most Americans. Take, for example, the claim made in a letter to the editor in response to Levinson's essay. "Our system of checks and balances," wrote the author, "cannot eradicate the politics that often makes our government ineffective; the power to do that rests squarely on the shoulders of the politicians we elect. Blaming the Constitution for the ineffectiveness of our politics removes accountability from those most responsible."[42] With all due respect to this letter writer, blaming the Constitution for the ineffectiveness of our government does not remove accountability from elected officials. There is plenty of accountability in the current system. Members of the House of Representatives are certainly accountable to their constituencies, just as senators and members of state legislatures are. The president is accountable to the American people for the direction of the country (though the presidential term limit eliminates accountability from the second term). The real problem is that no one elected official or group of politicians is responsible for effective government and so no one can be held accountable for ineffective governance. It cannot be the president, who must rely on Congress to pass legislation. It cannot be Congress, which consists of both the House (with members elected from local districts) and the Senate (with members elected statewide). It cannot be the Democratic Party because, as I write this, they do not control the House and cannot, by themselves, override filibusters in the Senate. Nor can it be the Republican Party because they are the minority in the Senate and do not control the White House.

The Framers of the Constitution made trade-offs. They preferred a system that prevented any one group of Americans from imposing its will on the rest of us. But that benefit is achieved at the expense of having any one group responsible for governing. A parliamentary system would have reversed this trade-off. When fully educated about the alternatives, not just to the separation of powers and checks and balances, but to every aspect of the Constitution, the American people may still prefer the Framers' arrangement. If they do, then they must accept that the lion's share of the current dysfunction is the result of our constitutional design.

Frankly, however, I am not convinced that the public currently understands the structure of American government, and alternatives to it, well enough to reach a conclusion about its desirability. Instead, Americans revere the Constitution blindly and assume that any malfunctioning is the result of the people elected to operate the system, not the system itself. Some of the responsibility for educating the public about these matters obviously lies with schools in the United States. But they are currently not doing a particularly good job of it. Indeed, former Supreme Court Justice Sandra Day O'Connor said recently that American civics education is in "crisis."[43] The media also has a role to play in the educational process. Journalists might consider spending more time explaining the basic design of the American constitutional system rather than obsessively focusing on the strategy and tactics that are an inevitable part of politics.

American politics are also the result of a conscious design. The Electoral College, for example, produces a different kind of presidential politics than would a national popular vote using instant run-off voting to ensure a majority winner. And the two-party system is the result, largely, of electing representatives by plurality vote in single-member districts. Proportional representation would likely produce at least one additional viable party. If Americans want more than two parties to choose from at election time, they should not blame the major parties but should reject the "first-past-the-post" electoral system we currently use.

Ultimately, however, politics are a natural part of a free society. Perhaps more than anything else we might do to rebuild trust in politicians is teach the American public to accept and appreciate the value of politics. As Bernard Crick argues in his classic In Defense of Politics, a book from which the present one draws its inspiration and its title, politics "is a way of ruling in divided societies without undue violence."[44] "Politics," he continues, "is not just a necessary evil; it is a realistic good."[45] Crick comes to this conclusion after considering the alternatives. For instance, there are no politics, at least as defined by Crick, in totalitarian regimes. Interests do not compete under totalitarianism, because the state embodies the one true ideology. As such, there is no room for disagreement. Nationalism and "scientism" (or rule by experts) also preclude politics.[46] Only where diverse interests are free to compete for finite resources is politics not only possible, but necessary. Despising politics, by Crick's formulation, is tantamount to spurning freedom.

Politics resolves conflict peacefully and, if for no other reason, should be considered a noble activity. Those who devote themselves to this "conciliatory vocation" have chosen an honorable profession. They deserve our gratitude, not our contempt. As Crick maintained, "Politics as a vocation is a most precarious thing, so we should not grudge the politician any of the incidental rewards he [sic] can pick up."[47] But Americans do begrudge politicians "incidental rewards," including basic respect. Some have even recently argued that, once out of office, elected officials should cease using their former titles. In an article for Slate.com, Emily Yoffe called the practice "not only pretentious and incorrect, it is un-American."[48] Though acknowledging that those in elected office "deserve a bit of deference," Yoffe objected to politicians who "take the deference personally" and argued, "our country was founded on the notion that certain people don't get to lord it over the rest of us just because of the title they carry."[49] This is the silliness of the cynical attitude taken toward politicians. A show of respect and appreciation for one's service to the country is expected to give way to a fear of somehow being lorded over by those no longer in positions of power.

In addition to accepting and appreciating politics and those who engage in it, Americans should give serious thought to the contradictory expectations we hold for politicians. Ideally, we would decide whether we want politicians to be leaders or followers; whether we would prefer them to be principled or pragmatic; and whether we want elected officials to be like ordinary Americans or to be exceptional. Once we had derived a set of expectations, we would then apply those expectations consistently.

If we decided to elect leaders, as opposed to followers, we would give them room to lead. We could not then demand that they follow public opinion. If we are unhappy with their leadership, or with the direction they had taken the country, we would reject them at the next election. But we would give them latitude to do what they think is best for the country (or city or state). If, on the other hand, we want elected officials to hew closely to the public's will, we would not be able to accuse them of pandering. We would expect them to read polls and act accordingly. If they had to change positions on an issue in order to fall in line with public opinion, we would welcome that and not accuse them of flip-flopping.

Do we want principled or pragmatic politicians? If we prefer them to be principled, we cannot constantly harp on about compromise. Reaching compromise might eventually be necessary if we are to address current problems. But if we want politicians to be principled, then we must allow them to fight for their principles as they see fit. Occasionally, that would mean that compromise is sacrificed for the vigorous defense of principle. On the other hand, if we want pragmatic politicians, we cannot accuse them of selling out. The charge that politicians do not stand for anything, that they are opportunists or empty suits, would have to be discarded because we would have decided that politicians' values are less important than their willingness to find common ground with other politicians. We could, of course, be interested in the preferences of politicians. But we would not allow them to become attached to those preferences.

If we decide we want politicians to be just like the rest of us, then we would have to accept the fact that those in leadership positions might not be particularly refined. Our presidents, for example, would not be broadly educated. They might embarrass us on the world stage. Their speeches might not be as eloquent and would, in all likelihood, be less inspirational. But if we want to elect the best among us, we would have to tolerate their cosmopolitan tastes. We would not mock them for being smarter than us. And we would not expect them to be able to milk a cow or bowl a strike.

In reality, politics may be too complicated to make such clear-cut determinations. Though it should be easy to decide whether we want elected officials to be ordinary or exceptional, the other expectations may depend on circumstances. In some situations, we might need leaders and in others we will want followers. Sometimes we would prefer elected officials to stick to principle and at other times pragmatism will be necessary. Still, we should try hard to decide when we want one and when the other. If we do not devote time to thinking about these expectations, we will apply them inconsistently. The result will be the problem we currently face, namely, that politicians will never know how we would like them to behave. Violating some of our expectations all of the time, they will be unable to gain our trust.

Of course, even if each of us is able to settle on our own individual expectations, it is unlikely that we would reach a consensus collectively. Some of us, for example, will want ordinary folks to hold office and others will want the best and the brightest in positions of authority; some will want leaders and others followers. Perhaps the most we can hope to achieve, then, is the dual recognition that (a) in a democracy, politics is not only unavoidable but is extremely messy; and (b) politicians are doing the best they can in complicated circumstances.

It would be even more beneficial, however, for the public to embrace politics as a public good worth cultivating. Rather than view politics as something only "they" (i.e., politicians) do, citizens must begin taking a more active role in governing. Since at least 1863, when Lincoln delivered his Gettysburg Address, we have thought of democracy as government "of the people, by the people, and for the people." In practice, however, we want democracy to be *for* us without being *of*, and certainly not *by*, us. We expect politicians to fix problems like the national debt, but we offer no help in finding solutions.

Ironically, when the people leave governing solely to elected officials, they are endorsing an elitist view of representative democracy that they would surely reject if asked to make a conscious choice in the matter. "In this view," writes the political theorist Nadia Urbinati, "representation is founded on the principle of the division of labor and a functional selection of expertise."[50] That is, citizens give consent and elected officials, being more competent than the people at large, govern. A competing view of representation is more democratic. It sees elections "as the expression of the right to participate at some level in lawmaking, not as a method for transferring people's idiosyncratic preferences to selected political professionals."[51] Representation is only part of a system of popular sovereignty. Citizens, too, have responsibility for governing.

If citizens are to meet their responsibility, they will have to engage in political activity. When they do, politics is likely to be transformed. As Urbinati notes, when the more democratic of the two views of representative democracy is adopted, "It marks the end of a yes/no politics and the beginning of politics as an open arena of contestable opinions and ever-revisable decisions."[52] The give-and-take of this kind of politics will require the average citizen to develop democratic skills—particularly the ability to debate—and a tolerance for the noise of politics. Once actively involved, the public might come to realize that the demands of politics are taxing.

While we build the skills necessary to take a more active role in politics and governing, Americans might also strive for a bit more humility with regard to politicians. I have been concerned in this chapter with the public's trust in elected officials (and those who would become elected officials). But we might also consider whether elected officials can trust us. For instance, when we express our collective opinions about public policy, can politicians be certain that we have considered the options and are expressing true preferences? I noted in Chapter 5 that the public is of two minds about how to reduce the nation's debt. We want the debt reduced and our annual budget balanced, but we do not want to raise taxes (except, perhaps, on the wealthy) or cut spending on the most expensive budget items. When there are hard truths that we need to be told but do not want to hear, how will we respond to the politician who tells us those truths? My hunch is that it will not be pretty for that politician. The result is not that politicians will lie to us, but that hard truths will simply be avoided.

The American public deserves at least as much blame as our politicians for the political dysfunction we face. Until people become less naive about politics, more educated about the system, more active in the process, and a bit more humble in their judgment of politicians, the trust so necessary for a stable and healthy democracy will continue to evaporate. And we are likely to get exactly the kinds of politicians we so despise. When we treat all politicians like scoundrels, only scoundrels will enter politics.

Let us not forget to lay most of the blame for the dysfunction we see in government on our constitutional design. Though it is beyond the scope of this book to consider them, there are many ways to alter that design to bring our politics in line with our institutions. None of them will be easy to achieve and all of them will require a significant amount of study and deliberation. Without the active participation of the public, however, such reforms are likely to be unsuccessful because they will have been imposed from on high. If we are serious about fixing, or even maintaining, our democracy, we can no longer act as innocent bystanders in the political process.

If after having read this book the reader is still convinced that the way to fix our politics and, by extension, our government is to elect better people to office, then I have failed. Better politicians are not the solution to our problems. Changes to our system of government and politics, and a citizenry more active in both, may well be.

Notes

Preface

1. See the ad at www.youtube.com/watch?v=6WaUPTHJsrM (accessed June 13, 2012).
2. As quoted in Christopher Hitchens. 2010. "In Search of the Washington Novel: A Colorful Genre Awaits its Masterpiece." *City Journal* 20 (4), www.city-journal.org/2010/20_4_urb-the-washington-novel.html (accessed January 3, 2011).
3. Tony Blair. 2007. Statement to the House of Commons, June 27. House of Commons Hansard Debates, column 334, www.publications.parliament.uk/pa/cm200607/cmhansrd/cm070627/debtext/70627-0003.htm#07062782003584 (accessed June 19, 2009).
4. Bernard Crick. 2005. *In Defense of Politics*, 5th ed. New York: Continuum.
5. Louis Alvarez, Andrew Kolker, and Paul Stekler. 1996. *Vote For Me: Politics in America.* New York: The Center for New American Media.

1 The Problem

1. As quoted in Richard Carwardine. 2007. *Lincoln: A Life of Purpose and Power.* New York: Vintage Books, 61. The details of this anecdote are taken from same.
2. Ibid., 64.
3. Chester Maxey. 1948. "A Plea for the Politician." *The Western Political Quarterly* 1: 275–6.
4. To be fair to at least some politicians, local office-holders ranked slightly higher, with 20 percent saying their honesty and ethical standards were very high or high. See Gallup, "Honesty/Ethics in Professions: Selected Trend," November 7–9, 2008, http://www.gallup.com/poll/1654/honesty-ethics-professions.aspx (accessed October 1, 2009).
5. 2008 American National Election Study (variable 085150 – M1d), Survey Documentation and Analysis, University of California, Berkeley, http://sda.berkeley.edu/cgi-bin/hsda?harcsda+nes08new (accessed July 25, 2010).

6. Gallup, "Blagojevich Scandal Feeds Into Public Skepticism," December 12, 2008, www.gallup.com/poll/113308/blagojevich-scandal-feeds-into-public-skepticism.aspx (accessed October 1, 2009).

7. John R. Hibbing and Elizabeth Theiss-Morse. 1995. *Congress as Public Enemy: Public Attitudes Toward American Political Institutions*. New York: Cambridge University Press, 94.

8. John R. Hibbing and Elizabeth Theiss-Morse. 2002. *Stealth Democracy: Americans' Beliefs about How Government Should Work*. New York: Cambridge University Press, 110.

9. Ibid., 127.

10. Ibid., 128.

11. Hibbing and Theiss-Morse, *Congress as Public Enemy*, 106–8.

12. It is also due in large part to the fact that congressional districts tend to be quite homogeneous in terms of partisanship and ideology. Thus, most people are likely to agree with their Member of Congress on most policy matters.

13. Jody Baumgartner and Jonathan S. Morris. 2006. "*The Daily Show* Effect: Candidates Evaluations, Efficacy, and American Youth." *American Politics Research* 34: 341–67.

14. Roderick P. Hart and E. Johanna Hartelius. 2007. "The Political Sins of Jon Stewart." *Critical Studies in Media Communication* 24: 263, 264. For a defense of Stewart, see Robert Hariman. 2007. "In Defense of Jon Stewart." *Critical Studies in Media Communication* 24: 273–7; and W. Lance Bennett. 2007. "Relief in Hard Times: A Defense of Jon Stewart's Comedy in an Age of Cynicism." *Critical Studies in Media Communication* 24: 278–83.

15. Russell L. Peterson. 2008. *Strange Bedfellows: How Late-Night Comedy Turns Democracy into a Joke*. New Brunswick: Rutgers University Press, 14. In fact, Peterson distinguishes "the late-night mainstream" like Jay Leno and David Letterman, which aims for partisan balance in their targets but do not take politics seriously, from Jon Stewart and Stephen Colbert, whom he believes are "engaging with the subject" and not "merely dismissing it," thereby offering arguments about politics and "a form of debate, not just entertainment" (p. 20).

16. There were no statistically significant differences between responses in the two conditions.

17. Stephen Earl Bennett. 2001. "Were the Halcyon Days Really Golden? An Analysis of Americans' Attitudes about the Political System, 1945–1965," in *What is it About Government that Americans Dislike?*, eds. John R. Hibbing and Elizabeth Theiss-Morse. New York: Cambridge University Press, 53.

18. William C. Mitchell. 1959. "The Ambivalent Social Status of the American Politician," *The Western Political Quarterly* 12: 688.

19. Ibid., 689.

20. Ibid., 690–1.

21. Ibid., 691.

22. Ibid.

23. Paul Hollis. 2008. "Second 'Great Malaise' Gripping U.S. as Lack of Leadership Continues to Prevail," *Southeast Farm Press*, May 7, http://southeastfarmpress.com/second-great-malaise-gripping-us-lack-leadership-continues-prevail (accessed June 10, 2011).

24. Murray Evans. 2008. "Retired General Says Politicians Need to Provide Leadership," *Associated Press*, June 3. LexisNexis Academic (accessed June 10, 2011).
25. Robert Guttman. 2010. "Lack of Leadership Is the Problem: Not the System." *Huffington Post*, March 3, www.huffingtonpost.com/robert-guttman/lack-of-leadership-is-the_b_483660.html (accessed June 7, 2011).
26. That is, 435 members of the House of Representatives, 100 senators, and the president.
27. Kari Huus. 2008. "Pro or Con, Readers Decry Lack of Leadership," MSNBC.com, September 30, www.msnbc.msn.com/id/26948830/ns/us_news-gut_check/t/pro-or-con-readers-decry-lack-leadership/ (accessed June 9, 2011).
28. See Bartleby.com, www.bartleby.com/73/1021.html (accessed June 7, 2011).
29. Frank Newport. 2005. "Americans Want Leaders to Pay Attention to Public Opinion," Gallup.com, October 12, www.gallup.com/poll/19138/americans-want-leaders-pay-attention-public-opinion.aspx (accessed June 10, 2011).
30. Pew Research Center for the People & the Press. 2007. "Broad Support for Political Compromise in Washington; But Many Are Hesitant to Yield on Contentious Issues," January 22, http://people-press.org/2007/01/22/broad-support-for-political-compromise-in-washington/ (accessed June 13, 2011).
31. There is much empirical evidence for this conclusion. For classic examples, see James W. Prothro and Charles M. Grigg. 1960. "Fundamental Principles of Democracy: Bases of Agreement and Disagreement," *The Journal of Politics* 22: 276–94; and Herbert McClosky. 1964. "Consensus and Ideology in American Politics," *American Political Science Review* 58: 361–82.
32. Pew Research Center for the People & the Press, "Broad Support for Political Compromise in Washington."
33. Kathleen Knight. 2006. "Transformations of the Concept of Ideology in the Twentieth Century," *American Political Science Review* 100: 619–26.
34. Pew Research Center for the People & the Press, "Broad Support for Political Compromise in Washington."
35. Ibid.
36. Ibid.
37. Pollingreport.com. 2010. "Congress: Misc. Questions," McClatchy-Marist Poll, November 15–18, www.pollingreport.com/congress.htm (accessed June 15, 2011).
38. Pew Research Center for the People & the Press. 2010. "Little Compromise on Compromising," September 20, http://pewresearch.org/pubs/1735/political-compromise-unpopular-neither-party-favored-on-economy-four-in-ten-say-cutting-tax-cuts-for-wealthy-hurts-economy (accessed June 15, 2011).
39. Pew Research Center for the People & the Press, "Broad Support for Political Compromise in Washington."
40. Ibid.
41. Philip E. Tetlock. 1981. "Pre- to Postelection Shifts in Presidential Rhetoric: Impression Management or Cognitive Adjustment?" *Journal of Personality and Social Psychology* 41: 211.

42. Ros Krasny. 2010. "New U.S. Senator Drives Pick-up Truck to Victory," Reuters.com, January 20, www.reuters.com/article/2010/01/20/usa-politics-brown-idUSN1911214820100120 (accessed July 1, 2011).
43. Joseph B. White. 2010. "Pickup Truck Politics in Massachusetts Senate Race," Washington Wire, The Wall Street Journal, January 19, http://blogs.wsj.com/washwire/2010/01/19/pickup-truck-politics-in-massachusetts-senate-race/ (accessed July 1, 2011).
44. Ian McAllister. 2007. "The Personalization of Politics," in The Oxford Handbook of Political Behavior, eds. Russell J. Dalton and Hans-Dieter Klingemann. New York: Oxford University Press.
45. Whether politics is more personalized now than in the past is certainly debatable. (See, for example, Danny Hayes. 2009. "Has Television Personalized Voting Behavior?" Political Behavior 31: 231–60.) What is not, as we'll see in a moment, is that personal characteristics of politicians are important components in the voters' process of evaluating candidates.
46. Roderick P. Hart. 2000. Campaign Talk: Why Elections Are Good for Us. Princeton: Princeton University Press, 60–6.
47. CNN. 2011. "Republican Debate," CNN.com, June 13, http://archives.cnn.com/TRANSCRIPTS/1106/13/se.02.html (accessed July 1, 2011).
48. David M. Stoloff. 1999. " 'Boxers or Briefs' Girl Recalls Fleeting Fame; Question to President Now Seems Tame," The Washington Times, January 17, LexisNexis Academic (accessed July 1, 2011).
49. As quoted in Anna Fifield. 2010. "Everyman Charm Delivers Republican Triumph," FT.com, January 20, www.ft.com/cms/s/0/b6b0842a-05d1-11df-88ee-00144feabdc0.html#axzz1R95p5QeL (accessed July 4, 2011).
50. Carolyn L. Funk. 1999. "Bringing the Candidate into Models of Candidate Evaluation," The Journal of Politics 61: 700–20; and Kim L. Fridkin and Patrick J. Kenney. 2011. "The Role of Candidate Traits in Campaigns," The Journal of Politics 73: 61–73.
51. Arthur H. Miller, Martin P. Wattenberg, and Oksana Malanchuk. 1986. "Schematic Assessments of Presidential Candidates," American Political Science Review 80: 521–40.
52. Samuel L. Popkin. 1994. The Reasoning Voter: Communication and Persuasion in Presidential Campaigns, 2nd ed. Chicago: University of Chicago Press, 97.
53. The five "master variables" are Certainty, Optimism, Activity, Realism, and Commonality; Hart, Campaign Talk, 37.
54. Ibid., 96.
55. Cecil A. Gibb. 1969. "Leadership," in The Handbook of Social Psychology, 2nd ed., Vol. 4, eds. Gardner Lindzey and Elliot Aronson. Reading, MA: Addison-Wesley Publishing Company, 218.
56. Dean Keith Simonton. 1993. "Putting the Best Leaders in the White House: Personality, Policy, and Performance," Political Psychology 14: 543.
57. Richard A. Posner. 2001. Breaking the Deadlock: The 2000 Election, the Constitution, and the Courts. Princeton: Princeton University Press, 15.
58. Ibid., 16.
59. See Carolyn L. Funk. 1996. "Understanding Trait Inferences in Candidate Images," in Research in Micropolitics: Rethinking Rationality, Vol. 5, eds. Michael X. Delli Carpini, Leonie Huddy, and Robert Y. Shapiro. Greenwich: JAI.

60. Pew Research Center. 2010. "Millennials: Confident. Connected. Open to Change," February, http://pewsocialtrends.org/files/2010/10/millennials-confident-connected-open-to-change.pdf (accessed July 6, 2011), 23.
61. John L. Sullivan, John H. Aldrich, Eugene Borgida, and Wendy Rahn. 1990. "Candidate Appraisal and Human Nature: Man and Superman in the 1984 Election," *Political Psychology* 11: 474.
62. Ibid.
63. Funk, "Bringing the Candidate into Models of Candidate Evaluation," 714.

2 The Sources of Anti-Politician Sentiment

1. See *Notes on the Debates in the Federal Convention*, June 26, 1787, http://avalon.law.yale.edu/18th_century/debates_626.asp (accessed January 5, 2011).
2. Alexis de Tocqueville. 1835 [2000]. *Democracy in America*. Translated and edited by Harvey C. Mansfield and Delba Winthrop. Chicago: University of Chicago Press, 52.
3. Robert A. Dahl. 2006. *On Political Equality*. New Haven: Yale University Press, 1.
4. Robert A. Dahl. 1998. *On Democracy*. New Haven: Yale University Press, 37. See also Paul Woodruff, who writes, "Democracy rests on the idea that the poor should be equal to the rich or well born – at least for sharing governance." Paul Woodruff. 2005. *First Democracy: The Challenge of an Ancient Idea*. New York: Oxford University Press, 132.
5. S. de Madariaga. 1937. *Anarchy or Hierarchy*. New York: The Macmillan Company, 33–4.
6. Ibid., 34.
7. Ibid., 35.
8. Ibid., 34.
9. Steven Bilakovics makes a similar argument with respect to what he calls "democratic openness," which he describes as "the type of freedom that comes to the fore in the context of democratic equality." "Framed by the freedom of openness," Bilakovics contends, "by the impossible promise of possibility without limits, democratic society harbors a tendency toward idealism as extreme as its concomitant tendency toward cynicism." Steven Bilakovics. 2012. *Democracy without Politics*. Cambridge, MA: Harvard University Press, 11.
10. By "jokes," I mean not only those shared person-to-person, but the entire category of political humor including the sketch comedy of *Saturday Night Live* and the satire of Stewart and Colbert. The sociologist Christie Davies, who has studied jokes extensively, finds that traditional political jokes, with what we might call "grassroots" origins, are not particularly common in democracies. This is due in large part to the widespread existence of (professional) political satire in free societies. (Christie Davies, personal e-mail correspondence, March 5, 2011.)
11. In e-mail correspondence with Professor Davies, he noted that jokes in non-democracies differ by regime type. In totalitarian regimes, "jokes about the system flourish" (though they do not entirely displace jokes

about leaders); in authoritarian regimes, "jokes about the dictator proliferate." (Christie Davies, personal e-mail correspondence, March 5, 2011.) This is an important distinction. Nevertheless, I suspect that a case could be made that jokes in authoritarian regimes are ultimately about the system given that the dictator is, at least symbolically, synonymous with the state.

12. Russell J. Dalton. 2004. *Democratic Challenges, Democratic Choices: The Erosion of Political Support in Advanced Industrial Democracies.* New York: Oxford University Press, 29–30.

13. For a discussion of various theories explaining trends in political trust and support for politicians and governments throughout the world, see Susan J. Pharr and Robert D. Putnam, eds. 2000. *Disaffected Democracies: What's Troubling the Trilateral Countries?* Princeton: Princeton University Press; Pippa Norris, ed. 1999. *Critical Citizens: Global Support for Democratic Governance.* New York: Oxford University Press; and Dalton, *Democratic Challenges, Democratic Choices.*

14. Robert D. Putnam, Susan J. Pharr, and Russell J. Dalton. 2000. "Introduction: What's Troubling the Trilateral Democracies," in *Disaffected Democracies: What's Troubling the Trilateral Countries?*, eds. Susan J. Pharr and Robert D. Putnam. Princeton: Princeton University Press, 8.

15. Anthony King. 2000. "Distrust of Government: Explaining American Exceptionalism," in *Disaffected Democracies: What's Troubling the Trilateral Countries?*, eds. Susan J. Pharr and Robert D. Putnam. Princeton: Princeton University Press, 79.

16. Seymour Martin Lipset. 1979. *The First New Nation: The United States in Historical and Comparative Perspective.* New York: W. W. Norton and Company, 15.

17. King, "Distrust of Government," 79. See also Adam Sheingate. 2009. "Why Can't Americans See the State?" *The Forum* 7 (4), Article 1, www.bepress.com/forum/vol7/iss4/art1 (accessed July 16, 2011).

18. King, "Distrust of Government," 79.

19. James A. Morone. 1990. *The Democratic Wish: Popular Participation and the Limits of American Government.* New York: Basic Books, 1.

20. Morone, *The Democratic Wish,* 5.

21. Incidentally, this is not an entirely unjustified faith, though the relative wisdom of the people versus elected officials is, ultimately, an empirical matter. On the value of collective judgment, see James Surowiecki. 2004. *The Wisdom of Crowds: Why the Many Are Smarter than the Few and How Collective Wisdom Shapes Business, Economies, Societies, and Nations.* New York: Doubleday. For an assessment of the rationality of aggregate public opinion, see Benjamin I. Page and Robert Y. Shapiro. 1992. *The Rational Public: Fifty Years of Trends in Americans' Policy Preferences.* Chicago: University of Chicago Press.

22. Seymour Martin Lipset. 1963. "The Value Patterns of Democracy: A Case Study in Comparative Analysis," *American Sociological Review* 28: 516.

23. On the other hand, prior to the Founding Era there were strenuous efforts by colonial elites to spread a fear of leveling and to maintain hierarchies of all sorts. See Thomas N. Ingersoll. 1999. " 'Riches and Honour Were Rejected by Them as Loathsome Vomit': The Fear of Leveling in New England," in

Inequality in Early America, eds. Carla Gardina Pestana and Sharon V. Salinger. Hanover: University Press of New England.

24. Gordon S. Wood. 1993. *The Radicalism of the American Revolution*. New York: Vintage Books, 232.

25. Joyce Appleby. 1992. "Recovering America's Historic Diversity: Beyond Exceptionalism," *The Journal of American History* 79: 424.

26. See Carla Gardina Pestana and Sharon V. Salinger, eds. 1999. *Inequality in Early America*. Hanover: University Press of New England.

27. J. Hector St. John Crevecoeur. 1782. *Letters from an American Farmer*, http://xroads.virginia.edu/~HYPER/CREV/letter03.html (accessed March 18, 2011).

28. Tocqueville, *Democracy in America*, 52.

29. Ibid., 53.

30. It must be noted, however, that anti-egalitarian thinking has always played, indeed continues to play, a significant role in American political culture. See Rogers M. Smith. 1993. "Beyond Tocqueville, Myrdal, and Hartz: The Multiple Traditions in America," *American Political Science Review* 87: 549–66.

31. There are several versions of the saying, the origins of which are disputed. The most common is attributed to Otto von Bismarck – "Laws are like sausages. It is better not to see them being made." Lewis D. Eigen and Jonathan P. Siegel. 1993. *The Macmillan Dictionary of Political Quotations*. New York: Macmillan Publishing Company. Another, supposedly said by an Illinois state legislator in the 1870s, is that "the making of laws is like the making of sausages – the less you know about the process the more you respect the result." Wikiquote, "Talk:Otto von Bismarck," http://en.wikiquote.org/wiki/Talk:Otto_von_Bismarck (accessed June 18, 2012).

32. Glenn C. Altschuler and Stuart M. Blumin. 2000. *Rude Republic: Americans and Their Politics in the Nineteenth Century*. Princeton: Princeton University Press, 8.

33. William L. Riordon. 1905 [1963]. *Plunkitt of Tammany Hall*. New York: E. P. Dutton & Co., 45.

34. Elmer E. Cornwell, Jr. 1964. "Bosses, Machines, and Ethnic Groups," *Annals of the American Academy of Political and Social Science* 353: 28.

35. Altschuler and Blumin, *Rude Republic*, 196.

36. Riordon, *Plunkitt of Tammany Hall*, 3.

37. Shelton Stromquist. 2006. *Reinventing "The People": The Progressive Movement, The Class Problem, and the Origins of Modern Liberalism*. Urbana: University of Illinois Press, Chapter 3.

38. Michael E. McGerr. 1986. *The Decline of Popular Politics: The American North, 1865–1928*. New York: Oxford University Press, 53.

39. See Stromquist, *Reinventing "The People,"* 59–63.

40. Quoted in ibid., 55.

41. Alexander Keyssar. 2000. *The Right to Vote: The Contested History of Democracy in the United States*. New York: Basic Books, 151–9.

42. Stromquist, *Reinventing "The People,"* 68–9.

43. Michael McGerr. 2003. *A Fierce Discontent: The Rise and Fall of the Progressive Movement in America, 1870–1920*. New York: Free Press, 216.

44. Michael Schudson. 1998. *The Good Citizen: A History of American Civic Life*. New York: Martin Kessler Books, 184.

45. Bernard Crick. 1972. *In Defense of Politics*, 2nd ed. Chicago: University of Chicago Press, 68.
46. James Madison, "The Federalist No. 10," November 22, 1787, www.constitution.org/fed/federa10.htm (accessed March 5, 2011).
47. As I'll discuss in more detail in the final chapter of this book, my contention here owes a great deal to Bernard Crick's argument in *In Defense of Politics*. However, Crick pits democracy *against* politics in his classic book because he treats "democracy" as something akin to majoritarianism; that is, it is a form of government in which "the people," as an entity, are sovereign. (Having said that, he does acknowledge the existence of what he calls "political democracy"; Crick, *In Defense of Politics*, 67.) Here, I use democracy in the more general sense of a free system of government that enables majorities to rule while preserving minority rights.
48. Nina Eliasoph. 1998. *Avoiding Politics: How Americans Produce Apathy in Everyday Life*. New York: Cambridge University Press, 14–16.
49. An earlier study of democratic practices in intimate groups (i.e., a town hall meeting and an urban crisis center) by Jane Mansbridge found a similar fear of conflict. For Mansbridge's subjects, however, this fear appeared to be based largely on the fact that they had to live with (or, at least, near) their would-be adversaries. The social "sanctions their neighbors can wield" is what caused individuals to avoid conflict. Jane Mansbridge. 1983. *Beyond Adversary Democracy*. Chicago: University of Chicago Press, 283.
50. John R. Hibbing and Elizabeth Theiss-Morse. 2002. *Stealth Democracy: American's Beliefs about How Government Should Work*. New York: Cambridge University Press, 135.
51. Also of interest is the fact that those who themselves avoid arguing reported the same levels of anger and disgust with the congressional debate whether or not it included animosity. In other words, some portion of the population in Funk's experiment (i.e., those with a tendency to avoid arguing) simply recoil from disagreement of *any* sort. Carolyn L. Funk. 2001. "Process Performance: Public Reaction to Legislative Policy Debate," in *What is it About Government that Americans Dislike?*, eds. John R. Hibbing and Elizabeth Theiss-Morse. New York: Cambridge University Press, 199–200, 202.
52. Ibid., 204.
53. Eliasoph, *Avoiding Politics*, 47.
54. Ibid., 46; see also 21–2.
55. Ibid., 31.
56. Ibid., 37, 69.
57. Hibbing and Theiss-Morse, *Stealth Democracy*, 132–3.
58. E. J. Dionne, Jr. 1991. *Why Americans Hate Politics*. New York: Simon & Schuster, 11–18.
59. Ibid., 14.
60. Morris P. Fiorina with Samuel J. Abrams and Jeremy C. Pope. 2011. *Culture War? The Myth of a Polarized America*, 3rd ed. Boston: Longman, 55.
61. Barack Obama. July 27, 2004. "Keynote Address to the Democratic National Convention," www.washingtonpost.com/wp-dyn/articles/A19751-2004Jul27.html (accessed January 6, 2011).
62. Alan I. Abramowitz. 2010. *The Disappearing Center: Engaged Citizens, Polarization, and American Democracy*. New Haven: Yale University Press,

37. See also Alan I. Abramowitz and Kyle L. Saunders. 2008. "Is Polarization a Myth?" *The Journal of Politics* 70: 542–55.

63. Abramowitz, *The Disappearing Center*, 48, 43.

64. Ibid., 57.

65. Matthew Levendusky. 2009. *The Partisan Sort: How Liberals Became Democrats and Conservatives Became Republicans*. Chicago: University of Chicago Press.

66. Ibid., 4–7.

67. On the effect of sorting on voting behavior, see Joseph Bafumi and Robert Y. Shapiro. 2009. "A New Partisan Voter," *The Journal of Politics* 71: 1–24; on its effect on political evaluations, see Larry M. Bartels. 2002. "Beyond the Running Tally: Partisan Bias in Political Perceptions," *Political Behavior* 24: 117–50.

68. Gary C. Jacobson. 2007. *A Divider, Not a Uniter: George W. Bush and the American People*. New York: Pearson Longman; and Gregory E. McAvoy and Peter K. Enns. 2010. "Using Approval of the President's Handling of the Economy to Understand Who Polarizes and Why," *Presidential Studies Quarterly* 40: 545–58.

69. Marc J. Hetherington and Jonathan D. Weiler. 2009. *Authoritarianism & Polarization in American Politics*. New York: Cambridge University Press, 5.

70. Ibid., Chapter 7.

71. Unfortunately, as Hetherington and Weiler acknowledge, the term "authoritarian" carries considerable baggage and, to some, this may make their analysis seem biased. But they continue to use the term for lack of a better one that captures the worldview they are interested in examining. That worldview contains two core features, according to Hetherington and Weiler. One is a tremendous need for order and a consequent aversion to ambiguity; the other is "a propensity to rely on established authorities to provide that order." Such authorities include texts, institutions, traditional social norms, and like-minded leaders. Ibid., 34.

72. Ibid., 146–9.

73. See Mark E. Neely, Jr. 2002. *The Union Divided: Party Conflict in the Civil War North*. Cambridge, MA: Harvard University Press.

74. Paul H. Smith. 1968. "The American Loyalists: Notes on Their Organization and Numerical Strength," *The William and Mary Quarterly* 25: 269.

75. Arthur M. Schlesinger. 1955. "Political Mobs and the American Revolution, 1765–1776," *Proceedings of the American Philosophical Society* 99: 244–50.

76. Madison, "The Federalist No. 10."

77. Brutus, "No. 1," October 18, 1787, www.constitution.org/afp/brutus01.htm (accessed March 4, 2011).

78. Madison, "The Federalist No. 10."

79. Hibbing and Theiss-Morse, *Stealth Democracy*, 134.

80. It is important to note that 'equality' is used here to mean equality of status, not condition. There has never been much of a commitment in the United States, or at least not as much as in many European democracies, to equalizing the material conditions of all citizens. See, for instance, Seymour Martin Lipset and Gary Marks. 2000. *It Didn't Happen Here: Why Socialism Failed in the United States*. New York: W. W. Norton and Company.

81. Crick, *In Defense of Politics*, 66.

3 The Public Lives of Politicians: Do Politicians Pander?

1. This section will describe politics at the national level, though many of the ingredients are present in state and even local politics, though perhaps to a smaller degree.
2. George Washington. 1796. "Farewell Address," The Avalon Project, http://avalon.law.yale.edu/18th_century/washing.asp (accessed July 22, 2011).
3. See William Nisbet Chambers. 1963. *Political Parties in a New Nation: The American Experience, 1776–1809*. New York: Oxford University Press.
4. E. E. Schattschneider. 1942. *Party Government*. New York: Rinehart & Company, 1.
5. For a classic study of the origin of parties in the United States, see John H. Aldrich. 1995. *Why Parties? The Origin and Transformation of Political Parties in America*. Chicago: University of Chicago Press. While Aldrich doesn't quite argue that parties are inevitable, he notes that there are powerful incentives for politicians to form parties. "The situations that give rise to incentives for turning to parties," writes Aldrich, "are problems endemic to republican government" (29).
6. See Steven S. Smith. 2007. *Party Influence in Congress*. New York: Cambridge University Press.
7. Alan Ware. 2002. *The American Direct Primary: Party Institutionalization and Transformation in the North*. New York: Cambridge University Press, 117.
8. Ibid., 242–6.
9. David W. Brady, Hahrie Han, and Jeremy C. Pope. 2007. "Primary Elections and Candidate Ideology: Out of Step with the Primary Electorate?" *Legislative Studies Quarterly* 32: 79–105.
10. Of course, attempts to measure public opinion have been around for a very long time. But statistically reliable measures were not developed until, roughly, the 1940s. See Susan Herbst. 1993. *Numbered Voices: How Opinion Polling Has Shaped American Politics*. Chicago: University of Chicago Press.
11. Jeffrey M. Berry and Clyde Wilcox. 2007. *The Interest Group Society*, 4th ed. New York: Pearson Longman, 16.
12. Ken Kollman. 1998. *Outside Lobbying: Public Opinion & Interest Group Strategies*. Princeton: Princeton University Press.
13. Ibid., 56.
14. Thomas E. Patterson. 2000. "Doing Well and Doing Good: How Soft News and Critical Journalism Are Shrinking the News Audience and Weakening Democracy – And What News Outlets Can Do About It." The Joan Shorenstein Center on the Press, Politics and Public Policy, Harvard Kennedy School, www.hks.harvard.edu/presspol/publications/reports/soft_news_and_critical_journalism_2000.pdf (accessed July 25, 2011).
15. Markus Prior. 2003. "Any Good News in Soft News? The Impact of Soft News Preference on Political Knowledge," *Political Communication* 20: 149–71.
16. Cass R. Sunstein. 2009. *Republic.com 2.0*. Princeton: Princeton University Press.
17. Hanna Fenichel Pitkin. 1967. *The Concept of Representation*. Berkeley: University of California Press, 145.

18. Ibid., 145–6.
19. Edmund Burke. 1774. "Speech to the Electors of Bristol," The Online Library of Liberty, http://oll.libertyfund.org/?option=com_staticxt&staticfile=show.php%3Ftitle=659&chapter=20392&layout=html&Itemid=27 (accessed May 24, 2011).
20. Ibid.
21. Hadley Cantril. 1951. Public Opinion 1935–1946. Princeton: Princeton University Press, 133. In the fourth poll, only 37.4 percent favored the delegate model. But that question differed in one key way from the questions in the other three polls. In the polls with over 60 percent support for representatives-as-delegates, that option was presented as either representatives voting "according to the way the people in their districts feel" or "according to the way the majority of his district feels." In the poll that seemed to favor the trustee model, the delegate view was expressed as voting "as the majority of his constituents desire" (ibid.).

    Given that most research indicates a preference on the part of the public for the delegate model, we can safely assume that the wording in the outlying poll caused the discrepant result. The culprit is likely to be the term "constituents," the meaning of which may well have been unclear to many respondents.
22. Carl D. McMurray and Malcolm B. Parsons. 1965. "Public Attitudes Toward the Representational Roles of Legislators and Judges," Midwest Journal of Political Science 9: 167–85. The questions were worded as follows: "An elected legislator should find out what his district wants and always vote accordingly" (delegate); "An elected legislator should decide what he thinks is best, and always vote accordingly, even if it is not what his district wants" (trustee).
23. Ibid., 169, 170.
24. Ibid., 185. See also Table 2, p. 177.
25. Ibid.
26. Ibid., 169.
27. As we might expect, such support varies according to an individual's level of political efficacy and trust in government, age, race, sex, and education level, among other predictors. See Christopher Jan Carman. 2007. "Assessing Preferences for Political Representation in the US," Journal of Elections, Public Opinion and Parties 17: 1–19.
28. Potentially contradictory results can be found in Glenn R. Parker. 1974. Political Beliefs about the Structure of Government: Congress and the Presidency. Beverly Hills: Sage; and Samuel C. Patterson, Ronald D. Hedlund, and G. Robert Boynton. 1975. Representatives and Represented: Bases of Public Support for the American Legislatures. New York: John Wiley & Sons. Based on a survey of Iowans, Patterson and colleagues found that the public wanted state legislators to value their own conscience more highly than five other referents, including their district constituents, the statewide constituency, the governor, their political parties, and interest groups (pp. 139–49).
29. American National Election Study. 1978. "Codebook Variable Documentation, 1978 Post-Election Study," VAR 780246, ftp://ftp.electionstudies.org/ftp/nes/studypages/1978post/nes1978.txt (accessed June 2, 2011).
30. Roger H. Davidson. 1970. "Public Prescriptions for the Job of Congressman," Midwest Journal of Political Science 14: 652.

31. Ibid., 653.
32. Lee Sigelman, Carol K. Sigelman, and Barbara J. Walkosz. 1992. "The Public and the Paradox of Leadership: An Experimental Analysis," *American Journal of Political Science* 36: 380.
33. Ibid., 374.
34. Ibid., 376.
35. Ibid.
36. Ibid., 379.
37. Paul J. Quirk. 2009. "Politicians Do Pander: Mass Opinion, Polarization, and Law Making," *The Forum* 7 (1), www.bepress.com/forum/vol7/iss4/art10.
38. Ibid., 7.
39. Ibid., 6.
40. Ibid.
41. Paul J. Quirk. 2011. "Polarized Populism: Masses, Elites, and Partisan Conflict," *The Forum* 9 (5), http://www.bepress.com/forum/vol9/iss1/art5.
42. Ibid., 4.
43. Matthew Levendusky. 2009. *The Partisan Sort: How Liberals Became Democrats and Conservatives Became Republicans.* Chicago: University of Chicago Press.
44. Lawrence R. Jacobs and Robert Y. Shapiro. 2000. *Politicians Don't Pander: Political Manipulation and the Loss of Democratic Responsiveness.* Chicago: University of Chicago Press.
45. Ibid., 27.
46. Ibid., 44.
47. Jacobs and Shapiro use the tug-of-war metaphor in a recent version of their argument. See Robert Y. Shapiro and Lawrence Jacobs. 2010. "Simulating Representation: Elite Mobilization and Political Power in Health Care Reform," *The Forum* 8 (9), www.bepress.com/forum/vol8/iss1/art4.
48. Jacobs and Shapiro, *Politicians Don't Pander*, xiii.
49. Steven M. Gillon. 1987. *Politics and Vision: The ADA and American Liberalism, 1947–1985.* New York: Oxford University Press.
50. James Q. Wilson. 1966. *The Amateur Democrat: Club Politics in Three Cities.* Chicago: University of Chicago Press, vii–viii.
51. Ibid., 340.
52. Ibid., 4.
53. Marty Cohen, David Karol, Hans Noel, and John Zaller. 2008. *The Party Decides: Presidential Nominations Before and After Reform.* Chicago: University of Chicago Press, 30–1.
54. See Gregory Koger, Seth Masket, and Hans Noel. 2009. "Partisan Webs: Information Exchange and Party Networks," *British Journal of Political Science* 39: 633–53.
55. Cohen et al., *The Party Decides*, 310–11.
56. Geoffrey C. Layman, Thomas M. Carsey, and Juliana Menasce Horowitz. 2006. "Party Polarization in American Politics: Characteristics, Causes, and Consequences," *Annual Review of Political Science* 9: 96–100.
57. See Alan I. Abramowitz. 2010. *The Disappearing Center: Engaged Citizens, Polarization and American Democracy.* New Haven: Yale University Press.

4 The Public Lives of Politicians: Election (or Ideology, or Party) Above All Else?

1. Joseph A. Schlesinger. 1966. *Ambition and Politics: Political Careers in the United States.* Chicago: Rand McNally & Company, 6.
2. Patricia A. Hurley. 2001. "David Mayhew's *Congress: The Electoral Connection* after 25 Years," *PS: Political Science and Politics* 34: 259.
3. John W. Kingdon. 1993. "Politicians, Self-Interest, and Ideas," in *Reconsidering the Democratic Public*, eds. George E. Marcus and Russell L. Hanson. University Park: Pennsylvania State University Press, 74.
4. Ibid., 83–6.
5. Ibid., 84 (emphasis in original).
6. Mark N. Franklin. 2004. *Voter Turnout and the Dynamics of Electoral Competition in Established Democracies Since 1945.* New York: Cambridge University Press, 98.
7. As quoted in James Madison. 1787 [1987]. *Notes of Debates in the Federal Convention of 1787, Reported by James Madison.* New York: W. W. Norton & Company, 107.
8. Ibid., 170.
9. Ibid., 106.
10. Ibid., 170.
11. Alan Ware. 2002. *The American Direct Primary: Party Institutionalization and Transformation in the North.* New York: Cambridge University Press.
12. Ibid., 215.
13. Ibid., 63–77.
14. Ibid., 199.
15. Ibid., 262–4.
16. For a brief history of anti-partyism in the United States, see Sean Wilentz. 2011. "The Mirage: The Long and Tragical History of Post-Partisanship, from Washington to Obama," *The New Republic*, November 17. A more comprehensive treatment can be found in Nancy L. Rosenblum. 2008. *On the Side of the Angels: An Appreciation of Parties and Partisanship.* Princeton: Princeton University Press.
17. Campaign Finance Institute. 2010. "Non-Party Spending Doubled in 2010 But Did Not Dictate Results," November 5, www.cfinst.org/Press/PReleases/10-11-05/Non-Party_Spending_Doubled_But_Did_Not_Dictate_Results.aspx (accessed January 4, 2012), Table 3.
18. Author's calculation based on median receipts of nearly $6 million for 2010 Senate winners. Ibid.
19. Stephen Ansolabehere, John M. de Figueiredo, and James M. Snyder, Jr. 2003. "Why Is There So Little Money in Politics?" *The Journal of Economic Perspectives* 17: 114.
20. Douglas D. Roscoe and Shannon Jenkins. 2005. "A Meta-Analysis of Campaign Contributions' Impact on Roll Call Voting," *Social Science Quarterly* 86: 52–68.
21. See Nolan McCarty, Keith T. Poole, and Howard Rosenthal. 2006. *Polarized America: The Dance of Ideology and Unequal Riches.* Cambridge, MA: The MIT Press, 9.

22. David W. Brady and Charles S. Bullock, III. 1980. "Is There a Conservative Coalition in the House?" *The Journal of Politics* 42: 549–59.
23. Ibid., 551.
24. Jules Witcover. 2003. *Party of the People: A History of the Democrats.* New York: Random House, 429–31.
25. Committee on Political Parties. 1950. *Toward a More Responsible Two-Party System.* New York: Rinehart & Company, 19.
26. Ibid., 20.
27. Nicol C. Rae. 2007. "Be Careful What You Wish For: The Rise of Responsible Parties in American National Politics," *Annual Review of Political Science* 10: 188.
28. Alan I. Abramowitz. 2010. *The Disappearing Center: Engaged Citizens, Polarization, and American Democracy.* New Haven: Yale University Press, 26.
29. Charles S. Taber and Milton Lodge. 2006. "Motivated Skepticism in the Evaluation of Political Beliefs," *American Journal of Political Science* 50: 755–69.
30. Cass R. Sunstein. 2007. "Ideological Amplification," *Constellations* 14: 273–9. See also Cass R. Sunstein. 2009. *Going to Extremes: How Like Minds Unite and Divide.* New York: Oxford University Press.
31. Sander L. Koole, Wander Jager, Agnes E. van den Berg, Charles A. J. Vlek, and Willem K. B. Hofstee. 2001. "On the Social Nature of Personality: Effects of Extraversion, Agreeableness, and Feedback About Collective Resource Use on Cooperation in a Resource Dilemma," *Personality and Social Psychology Bulletin* 27: 289–301.
32. Daniel Druckman, Benjamin J. Broome, and Susan H. Korper. 1988. "Value Differences and Conflict Resolution: Facilitation or Delinking?" *The Journal of Conflict Resolution* 32: 489–510.
33. Frances E. Lee. 2009. *Beyond Ideology: Politics, Principles, and Partisanship in the U.S. Senate.* Chicago: University of Chicago Press, 65.
34. Ibid., 18.
35. Ibid., 106.
36. See Alexander Keyssar. 2000. *The Right to Vote: The Contested History of Democracy in the United States.* New York: Basic Books.
37. Charlene Carter. 2011. "House Votes to End Presidential Campaign Fund," *Roll Call,* December 1, www.rollcall.com/news/house_votes_to_end_presidential_campaign_fund-210706-1.html (accessed January 10, 2012).
38. Lee, *Beyond Ideology,* 19.
39. See "Table 5-9 Party Unity and Polarization in Congressional Voting, 1953–2008 (percent)" in Harold W. Stanley and Richard G. Niemi. 2009. *Vital Statistics on American Politics 2009–2010.* Washington, DC: CQ Press, http://library.cqpress.com/vsap/vsap09_tab5-9 (accessed January 10, 2012), 202.
40. Thomas E. Patterson. 1993. *Out of Order.* New York: Knopf; and Kathleen Hall Jamieson. 1992. *Dirty Politics: Deception, Distraction, and Democracy.* New York: Oxford University Press.
41. Regina G. Lawrence. 2000. "Game-Framing the Issues: Tracking the Strategy Frame in Public Policy News," *Political Communication* 17: 93–114.
42. Nicholas A. Valentino, Thomas A. Buhr, and Matthew N. Beckmann. 2001. "When the Frame is the Game: Revisiting the Impact of 'Strategic'

Campaign Coverage on Citizens' Information Retention," *Journalism & Mass Communication Quarterly* 78: 93–112.

43. See, for example, Joseph N. Cappella and Kathleen Hall Jamieson. 1997. *The Spiral of Cynicism: The Press and the Public Good.* New York: Oxford.

44. Clause H. de Vreese and Matthijs Elenbaas. 2008. "Media in the Game of Politics: Effects of Strategic Metacoverage on Political Cynicism," *The International Journal of Press/Politics* 13: 299.

45. William Safire. 2008. *Safire's Political Dictionary*, updated and expanded ed. New York: Oxford University Press, 688.

46. Lawrence R. Jacobs and Robert Y. Shapiro. 2000. *Politicians Don't Pander: Political Manipulation and the Loss of Democratic Responsiveness.* Chicago: University of Chicago Press, 27.

47. I devote a few pages to this topic in an earlier book. See Stephen K. Medvic. 2001. *Political Consultants in U.S. Congressional Elections.* Columbus: Ohio State University Press, 150–2. See also Wayne Le Cheminant and John Parrish, eds. 2011. *Manipulating Democracy: Democratic Theory, Political Psychology, and Mass Media.* New York: Routledge; and Nathaniel J. Klemp. 2012. *The Morality of Spin: Virtue and Vice in Political Rhetoric and the Christian Right.* Lanham: Rowman & Littlefield, especially Chapter 2.

48. See Richard Dawkins and John R. Krebs. 1978. "Animal Signals: Information or Manipulation?" in *Behavioural Ecology*, eds. John R. Krebs and Nicholas B. Davies. Oxford: Blackwell Scientific.

49. Most of what follows in this paragraph is based on the discussion in Rom Harré. 1985. "Persuasion and Manipulation," in *Discourse and Communication: New Approaches to the Analysis of Mass Media Discourse and Communication*, ed. Teun A. van Dijk. New York: Walter de Gruyter, 127–8. See also Michael Kligman and Charles M. Culver. 1992. "An Analysis of Interpersonal Manipulation," *The Journal of Medicine and Philosophy* 17: 173–97.

50. Lawrence R. Jacobs and Robert Y. Shapiro. 1994. "Issues, Candidate Image, and Priming: The Use of Private Polls in Kennedy's 1960 Presidential Campaign," *American Political Science Review* 88: 527–40.

51. See Stephen K. Medvic. 2006. "Understanding Campaign Strategy: 'Deliberate Priming' and the Role of Professional Political Consultants," *Journal of Political Marketing* 5 (1/2): 11–32.

52. See, for example, Alfred R. Mele and Piers Rawling, eds. 2004. *The Oxford Handbook of Rationality.* New York: Oxford University Press.

53. W. Russell Neuman, George E. Marcus, Ann N. Crigler, and Michael MacKuen. 2007. "Theorizing Affect's Effects," in *The Affect Effect: Dynamics of Emotion in Political Thinking and Behavior*, eds. W. Russel Neuman, George E. Marcus, Ann N. Crigler, and Michael MacKuen. Chicago: University of Chicago Press, 15. For a popular treatment of the interplay of emotion and reason, see Antonio Damasio. 1994. *Descartes' Error: Emotion, Reason, and the Human Brain.* New York: Penguin.

54. See Barry Richards. 2004. "The Emotional Deficit in Political Communication," *Political Communication* 21: 339–52.

55. For an attempt to measure the prevalence of emotional appeals in campaign advertising, see Lynda Lee Kaid and Anne Johnston. 2001. *Videostyle in Presidential Campaigns: Style and Content of Televised Political Advertising.* Westport: Praeger.

56. See Harvey Yunis. 1996. *Taming Democracy: Models of Political Rhetoric in Classical Athens*. Ithaca: Cornell University Press.
57. Stanley Wilcox. 1942. "The Scope of Early Rhetorical Instruction," *Harvard Studies in Classical Philology* 53: 121–55.
58. See Josiah Ober. 1989. *Mass and Elite in Democratic Athens: Rhetoric, Ideology, and the Power of the People*. Princeton: Princeton University Press, 165–77.
59. Yunis, *Taming Democracy*, Chapter II.
60. Michael Billig. 1996. *Arguing and Thinking: A Rhetorical Approach to Social Psychology*, new ed. New York: Cambridge University Press.
61. Hugo Mercier and Dan Sperber. 2011. "Why do Humans Reason? Arguments for an Argumentative Theory," *Behavioral and Brain Sciences* 34: 57.
62. Gil Troy. 1991. *See How They Ran: The Changing Role of the Presidential Candidate*. New York: The Free Press.
63. David Zarefsky. 1992. "Spectator Politics and the Revival of Public Argument," *Communication Monographs* 59: 414. See also David Zarefsky. 1990. *Lincoln, Douglas, and Slavery: In the Crucible of Public Debate*. Chicago: University of Chicago Press.
64. Russell Muirhead. 2006. "A Defense of Party Spirit," *Perspectives on Politics* 4: 719.
65. Jonathan White and Lea Ypi. 2011. "On Partisan Political Justification," *American Political Science Review* 105: 381–96. See also Rosenblum, *On the Side of the Angels*.

5 The 2011 Debt Ceiling Debate: A Case Study

1. Marketplace Morning Report. 2011. "America: One of Two Developed Nations with Debt Ceilings," July 26, www.marketplace.org/topics/world/raising-debt-ceiling/america-one-two-developed-nations-debt-ceilings (accessed February 2, 2012).
2. Jackie Calmes and Carl Hulse. 2011. "As the Federal Government Hits Its Debt Limit, Lawmakers Spar over Solution," *New York Times*, May 16, www.nytimes.com/2011/05/17/us/politics/17budget.html (accessed February 4, 2012).
3. Michael Cooper and Louise Story. 2011. "Q. and A. on the Debt Ceiling," *New York Times*, July 27, www.nytimes.com/2011/07/28/us/politics/28default.html?pagewanted=all (accessed February 2, 2012).
4. Naftali Bendavid. 2010. "Boehner Warns GOP on Debt Ceiling," Washington Wire blog, *The Wall Street Journal*, November 18, http://blogs.wsj.com/washwire/2010/11/18/boehner-warns-gop-on-debt-ceiling/ (accessed February 2, 2012).
5. This is precisely the analogy used by an advocacy group called Public Notice in an ad they produced in the summer of 2011, at the height of the battle over the debt ceiling, to argue for less government spending. See FactCheck.org. 2011. "Junkie Math," November 17, www.factcheck.org/2011/11/junkie-math/ (accessed February 2, 2012).
6. Carrie Budoff Brown. 2011. "Default Deniers: The New Skeptics," *Politico*, May 17, www.politico.com/news/stories/0511/55087.html (accessed February 2, 2012).

7. Pat Garofalo. 2011. "RNC Chairman Priebus: Americans Will Say 'Well Good' if the U.S. Defaults on Its Obligations," ThinkProgress.org, June 28, http://thinkprogress.org/economy/2011/06/28/255874/rnc-chaor-good-debt-ceiling/ (accessed February 2, 2012).
8. Dennis Jacobe. 2011. "Americans Oppose Raising Debt Ceiling, 47% to 19%," Gallup.com, May 13, www.gallup.com/poll/147524/Americans-Oppose-Raising-Debt-Ceiling.aspx (accessed February 2, 2012).
9. James Politi. 2011. "US Banks Warn Obama on Soaring Debt," *Financial Times*, April 27, www.cnbc.com/id/42775820/US_Banks_Warn_Obama_on_Soaring_Debt (accessed February 3, 2012); and Jim Puzzanghera. 2011. "Top Wall Street CEOs Warn Obama, Congress on Debt Ceiling," Money & Company blog, *Los Angeles Times*, July 28, http://latimesblogs.latimes.com/money_co/2011/07/top-wall-street-ceos-warn-obama-congress-on-debt-ceiling.html (accessed February 3, 2012).
10. Don Lee, Tom Hamburger, and Tom Petruno. 2011. "Surprise Warning on U.S. Debt Comes as Washington Inches Away from Gridlock," *Los Angeles Times*, April 19, http://articles.latimes.com/2011/apr/19/business/la-fi-us-credit-rating-20110419 (accesssed February 3, 2012).
11. Cheyenne Hopkins. 2011. "IMF Urges U.S. Debt-Ceiling Increase to Avoid a 'Severe Shock' to the Economy," Bloomberg, June 29, www.bloomberg.com/news/2011-06-29/imf-urges-u-s-debt-ceiling-increase-to-avoid-a-severe-shock-to-economy.html (accessed February 3, 2012).
12. Due to different rules in the House of Representatives, and to the so-called "Gephardt rule" specifically, the House has taken fewer votes on the debt ceiling than the Senate. Still, when they have taken those votes recently, the opposition party has voted almost unanimously against raising the ceiling in all instances.
13. Donald Marron. 2011. "Handicapping the Debt Ceiling Debate," Tax Policy Center, January 14, http://taxvox.taxpolicycenter.org/2011/01/14/handicapping-the-debt-ceiling-debate/ (accessed February 3, 2012). See also Donny Shaw. 2011. "The Republicans Haven't Always Been Against Raising the Debt Ceiling," OpenCongress Blog, OpenCongress.org, January 28, www.opencongress.org/articles/view/1500-The-Republicans-Haven-t-Always-Been-Against-Raising-the-Debt-Ceiling (accessed February 3, 2012); and Donny Shaw. 2011. "A Brief History of Debt Limit Votes in the House," OpenCongress Blog, OpenCongress.org, May 20, www.opencongress.org/articles/view/2295-A-Brief-History-of-Debt-Limit-Votes-in-the-House (accessed February 3, 2012).
14. Danny Yadron. 2011. "Tea Party Warns GOP Leaders on Debt Limit Vote," Washington Wire blog, *The Wall Street Journal*, May 9, http://blogs.wsj.com/washwire/2011/05/09/tea-party-warns-gop-leaders-on-debt-limit-vote/ (accessed February 3, 2012).
15. Jon Cohen. 2011. "Shifting Public Concerns in Debt Limit Debate," Behind the Numbers, *The Washington Post*, July 11, www.washingtonpost.com/blogs/behind-the-numbers/post/shifting-public-concerns-in-debt-limit-debate/2011/07/11/gIQAR4WL9H_blog.html (accessed February 3, 2012).
16. Pew Research Center for the People & the Press. 2011. "Public Wants Debt Ceiling Compromise, Expects a Deal Before Deadline," July 26, http://pewresearch.org/pubs/2071/debt-limit-ceiling-tea-party-compromise-deficit-reduction (accessed February 3, 2012).

17. Sean Sullivan. 2011. "Club Hitting Lugar, Hatch Over Debt Limit," Hotline on Call, *National Journal*, July 11, http://hotlineoncall.nationaljournal.com/ archives/2011/07/club-hitting-lu.php (accessed February 3, 2012).

18. Chris Cillizza. 2010. "Utah Sen. Bob Bennett Loses Convention Fight," The Fix, *The Washington Post*, May 8, http://voices.washingtonpost.com/thefix/ senate/utah-sen-bob-bennett-loses.html (accessed February 3, 2012).

19. Jonathan Allen and Jake Sherman. 2011. "How Grover Norquist Corners Congress,"*Politico*, November 8, www.politico.com/news/stories/1111/67906. html (accessed February 3, 2012); and Drake Bennett. 2011. "Grover Norquist, the Enforcer." *Businessweek*, May 26, www.businessweek.com/ magazine/content/11_23/b4231006685629.htm (accessed February 3, 2012).

20. Russell Berman. 2011. "House Republicans Mull Plan to Hike Debt Ceiling Every Two Months," *The Hill*, April 29, http://thehill.com/homenews/ house/158297-house-gop-considering-plan-to-increase-debt-limit-in-steps (accessed February 4, 2012).

21. See, for example, the Senate Democrats' proposal from early July 2011. Lori Montgomery. 2011. "Senate Democrats Draft Debt-Reduction Plan," *The Washington Post*, July 8, www.washingtonpost.com/business/economy/ senate-democrats-draft-debt-reduction-plan/2011/07/08/gIQAFQbS4H_ story.html (accessed February 4, 2012).

22. For a round-up of polls that indicate such support in the months leading up to, and during, the debt ceiling debate, see Bruce Bartlett. 2011. "Americans Support Higher Taxes. Really," *Capital Gains and Games*, June 29, www. capitalgainsandgames.com/blog/bruce-bartlett/2292/americans-support-higher-taxes-really (accessed February 4, 2012).

23. Jeffrey M. Jones. 2011. "On Deficit, Americans Prefer Spending Cuts; Open to Tax Hikes," Gallup, July 13, www.gallup.com/poll/148472/deficit-americans-prefer-spending-cuts-open-tax-hikes.aspx (accessed February 4, 2012).

24. Nate Silver. 2011. "G.O.P.'s No-Tax Stance Is Outside Political Mainstream," FiveThirtyEight, *The New York Times*, July 13, http://fivethirtyeight.blogs. nytimes.com/2011/07/13/house-republicans-no-tax-stance-far-outside-political-mainstream/ (accessed February 4, 2012).

25. Frank Newport and Lydia Saad. 2011. "American Oppose Cuts in Education, Social Security, Defense," Gallup, January 26, www.gallup.com/ poll/145790/americans-oppose-cuts-education-social-security-defense.aspx (accessed February 4, 2012).

26. Newport and Saad, "American Oppose Cuts in Education, Social Security, Defense."

27. Samuel Haass. 2011. "Debt Ceiling Medicaid Cuts: Union Lobbies Democratic Senators for Help." *Huffington Post*, July 13, www. huffingtonpost.com/2011/07/13/union-to-dem-senators-don_n_896581. html (accessed February 5, 2012).

28. As quoted in Alan Fram. 2011. "The Influence Game: Lobbying on Debt Limit Fight," Associated Press, July 28, http://abcnews.go.com/Politics/ wireStory?id=14174030 (accessed February 4, 2012).

29. Lori Montgomery and Paul Kane. 2011. "Debt-Limit Talks: As Obama, Boehner Rush to Strike Deal, Democrats are Left Fuming," *The Washington*

Post, July 21, www.washingtonpost.com/politics/obama-gop-leaders-said-to-discuss-new-debt-plan/2011/07/21/gIQAT81BSI_story.html?hpid=z1 (accessed June 21, 2012).

30. Felicia Sonmez. 2011. "Labor, Liberal Groups Mobilizing Against White House on Debt Deal." 2chambers, *The Washington Post*, July 22, www.washingtonpost.com/blogs/2chambers/post/labor-liberal-groups-mobilizing-against-white-house-on-debt-deal/2011/07/22/gIQAQ3D3TI_blog.html (accessed February 4, 2012).

31. Julian Pecquet. 2011. "Liberal Dem Lawmaker Vows to Reject GOP, White Debt Deal," *The Hill*, July 31, http://thehill.com/homenews/house/174593-liberal-dem-vows-to-reject-white-house-gop-deal- (accessed February 4, 2012).

32. Ezra Klein. 2011. "Wonkbook: A Deal that Found the Lowest-Common Denominator," Wonkblog, *The Washington Post*, July 31, www.washingtonpost.com/blogs/ezra-klein/post/a-deal-that-found-the-lowest-common-denominator/2011/07/11/gIQAde9TmI_blog.html (accessed February 4, 2012).

33. Shush Walshe. 2011. "Both the Left and Right Sour on Debt Deal," The Note, ABC News, August 1, http://abcnews.go.com/blogs/politics/2011/08/both-the-left-and-right-sour-on-debt-deal/ (accessed February 4, 2012).

34. A majority of Democrats (58 percent) supported the agreement. Jeffrey M. Jones. 2011. "More Americans Oppose Than Favor Debt Ceiling Agreement," Gallup, August 3, www.gallup.com/poll/148802/americans-oppose-favor-debt-ceiling-agreement.aspx (accessed February 4, 2012).

35. Pew Research Center for the People & the Press. 2011. "Public Sees Budget Negotiations as 'Ridiculous,' 'Disgusting,' 'Stupid,'" August 1, http://pewresearch.org/pubs/2078/debt-ceiling-limits-budget-deficit-tea-party-republicans-obama-democrats-republicans-ridiculous (accessed February 6, 2012).

36. One exception, which appeared eight months after the crisis ended, is Matt Bai's quite nuanced reporting on the efforts of President Obama and Speaker Boehner to reach a deal. Bai shows that both men took political risks in trying to find a compromise and that they were closer to a deal than anyone realized at the time. Matt Bai. 2012. "Obama vs. Boehner: Who Killed the Debt Deal?" *The New York Times*, March 28, www.nytimes.com/2012/04/01/magazine/obama-vs-boehner-who-killed-the-debt-deal.html?pagewanted=all (accessed June 21, 2012).

37. Elizabeth Drew. 2011. "What Were They Thinking?" *The New York Review of Books*, August 18, www.nybooks.com/articles/archives/2011/aug/18/what-were-they-thinking/?pagination=false (accessed August 25, 2012).

38. Thomas L. Friedman. 2011. "The Day Our Leaders Got Unstuck," *New York Times*, August 9, www.nytimes.com/2011/08/10/opinion/the-day-our-leaders-got-unstuck.html (accessed February 8, 2012).

39. Tim Newcomb. 2011. "QUOTE: NFL Teaches Washington How It's Done," NewsFeed, *Time*, July 27, http://newsfeed.time.com/2011/07/27/quote-nfl-teaches-washington-how-its-done/ (accessed February 8, 2012).

40. See minute 4:52 of the video clip from MSNBC's "Morning Joe" for July 22 at www.msnbc.msn.com/id/3036789//vp/43852506#43852506 (accessed February 8, 2012).

41. Drew, "What Were They Thinking?"
42. Ibid.
43. Ibid.
44. Ibid. (emphasis in original).
45. Arend Lijphart. 1999. *Patterns of Democracy: Government Forms and Performance in Thirty-Six Countries*. New Haven: Yale University Press, 2.
46. Ibid., 3–4.
47. Ibid., 3.
48. Ibid.
49. Ibid., 248.
50. See John T. Reed. 2011. "How the Tea Party Caucus Members Voted on Raising the Debt Ceiling," Johntreed.com, August 10, http://johntreed.com/headline/2011/08/10/how-the-tea-party-caucus-members-voted-on-raising-the-debt-ceiling/ (accessed February 8, 2012).
51. For the case for proportional representation in the United States, see Douglas J. Amy. 2002. *Real Choices/New Voices: How Proportional Representation Elections Could Revitalize American Democracy*, 2nd ed. New York: Columbia University Press. For information on electoral reform more generally, see FairVote.org.

6   The Private Lives of Politicians: Ambition and Hypocrisy

1. Daniel T. Gilbert and Patrick S. Malone. 1995. "The Correspondence Bias," *Psychological Bulletin* 117: 21.
2. Ibid.
3. Edward E. Jones and Victor A. Harris. 1967. "The Attribution of Attitudes," *Journal of Experimental Social Psychology* 3: 1–24.
4. For an examination of potential evolutionary explanations for the correspondence bias, see Paul W. Andrews. 2001. "The Psychology of Social Chess and the Evolution of Attribution Mechanisms: Explaining the Fundamental Attribution Error," *Evolution and Human Behavior* 22: 11–29.
5. Daniel Kahneman. 2011. *Thinking, Fast and Slow*. New York: Farrar, Straus and Giroux, 129.
6. Ibid., 81.
7. Karl Popper. 1959 [2002]. *The Logic of Scientific Discovery*. New York: Routledge.
8. Harold D. Lasswell. 1948. *Power and Personality*. New York: W. W. Norton & Company, 20.
9. Ibid., 39.
10. Paul M. Sniderman. 1975. *Personality and Democratic Politics*. Berkeley: University of California Press, 269.
11. Ibid., 272.
12. Ibid., 48.
13. Richard L. Fox and Jennifer L. Lawless. 2005. "To Run or Not to Run for Office: Explaining Nascent Political Ambition," *American Journal of Political Science* 49: 650.

14. One set of scholars has attempted, with some success, to administer a truncated personality questionnaire to legislators in several American states. See Bryce J. Dietrich, Scott Lasley, Jeffery J. Mundak, Megan L. Remmel, and Joel Turner. 2012. "Personality and Legislative Politics: The Big Five Trait Dimensions Among U.S. State Legislators," *Political Psychology*, 33: 195–210.

15. For a review of this approach, see David G. Winter. 2003. "Personality and Political Behavior," in *Oxford Handbook of Political Psychology*, eds. David O. Sears, Leonie Huddy, and Robert Jervis. New York: Oxford University Press.

16. One scholar has attempted to measure levels of right-wing authoritarianism among Canadian legislators and in the legislatures of several American states, but this particular focus is not of much relevance for my purposes in this book. See Bob Altemeyer. 1996. *The Authoritarian Specter*. Cambridge, MA: Harvard University Press.

17. Gian Vittorio Caprara, Claudio Barbaranelli, Chiara Consiglio, Laura Picconi, and Philip G. Zimbardo. 2003. "Personalities of Politicians and Voters: Unique and Synergistic Relationships," *Journal of Personality and Social Psychology* 84: 849–56.

18. See Oliver P. John, Laura P. Naumann, and Christopher J. Soto. 2008. "Paradigm Shift to the Integrative Big Five Trait Taxonomy: History, Measurement, and Conceptual Issues," in *Handbook of Personality: Theory and Research*, 3rd ed., eds. Oliver P. John, Richard W. Robins, and Lawrence A. Pervin. New York: The Guilford Press; and Robert R. McCrae and Paul T. Costa, Jr. 2008. "The Five-Factor Theory of Personality," in *Handbook of Personality: Theory and Research*, 3rd ed., eds. Oliver P. John, Richard W. Robins, and Lawrence A. Pervin. New York: The Guilford Press.

19. It would be interesting to see if candidates as a whole, including those who eventually lost their races, were also more agreeable than the general public. Perhaps, as suggested, disagreeable ones get weeded out. If so, personality inventories conducted with only those who hold office, and thus have won campaigns, overestimate the level of agreeableness in politicians generally.

20. Liad Uziel. 2010. "Rethinking Social Desirability Scales: From Impression Management to Interpersonally Oriented Self-Control," *Perspectives on Psychological Science* 5: 256.

21. Ibid.

22. Fox and Lawless, "To Run or Not to Run for Office," 650.

23. Connie Schultz. 2007. *. . . and His Lovely Wife: A Memoir from the Woman Beside the Man*. New York: Random House, 4–5.

24. There are plenty of examples. See *The Washington Post*. 2010. "Children of Politicians and Their Brushes with the Law," August 5, www.washingtonpost.com/wp-dyn/content/gallery/2010/08/05/GA2010080503952.html (accessed March 15, 2012).

25. Center for Responsive Politics. 2011. "Most Members of Congress Enjoy Robust Financial Status, Despite Nation's Sluggish Economic Recovery," November 15, www.opensecrets.org/news/2011/11/congress-enjoys-robust-financial-status.html (accessed March 15, 2012).

26. 2011 state legislative salaries can be found at National Conference of State Legislatures. n.d. "2011 NCSL Legislator Compensation Table," www.ncsl.org/legislatures-elections/legisdata/2011-ncsl-legislator-compensation-table.aspx (accessed March 16, 2012).

27. Illinois Policy Institute. 2010. "Pay Day! Illinois Legislators Among Highest Paid in Nation," July 22, www.illinoispolicy.org/uploads/files/Publications/payday%20(1).pdf (accessed March 16, 2012).
28. Joseph A. Schlesinger. 1966. *Ambition and Politics: Political Careers in the United States*. Chicago: Rand McNally & Company, 2.
29. Ibid., 8.
30. Ibid., 10.
31. Ibid.
32. Ibid.
33. Gordon S. Black. 1972. "A Theory of Political Ambition: Career Choices and the Role of Structural Incentives," *The American Political Science Review* 66: 159. See, more recently, Cherie D. Maestas, Sarah Fulton, L. Sandy Maisel, and Walter J. Stone. 2006. "When to Risk It? Institutions, Ambitions, and the Decision to Run for the U.S. House," *American Political Science Review* 100: 195–208.
34. Black, "A Theory of Political Ambition," 159.
35. See, for example, David T. Canon. 1990. *Actors, Athletes, and Astronauts: Political Amateurs in the United States Congress*. Chicago: University of Chicago Press.
36. See Cherie Maestas. 2003. "The Incentive to Listen: Progressive Ambition, Resources, and Opinion Monitoring among State Legislators," *The Journal of Politics*, 65: 439–56.
37. Frank R. Baumgartner, Jeffrey M. Berry, Marie Hojnacki, David C. Kimball, and Beth L. Leech. 2009. *Lobbying and Policy Change: Who Wins, Who Loses, and Why*. Chicago: University of Chicago Press, 239.
38. Ibid., 241.
39. Mark A. Smith. 2000. *American Business and Political Power: Public Opinion, Elections, and Democracy*. Chicago: University of Chicago Press.
40. Ibid., 140.
41. Schlesinger, *Ambition and Politics*, 2.
42. David Runciman. 2008. *Political Hypocrisy: The Mask of Power, From Hobbes to Orwell and Beyond*. Princeton: Princeton University Press, 9.
43. Erving Goffman. 1959. *The Presentation of Self in Everyday Life*. Garden City: Doubleday Anchor Books, 4.
44. Ibid., 9.
45. Ibid., 8.
46. Ibid., 8–9.
47. See, for example, Bruce Hood. 2012. *The Self Illusion: How the Social Brain Creates Identity*. New York: Oxford University Press; Thomas Metzinger. 2009. *The Ego Tunnel: The Science of the Mind and the Myth of the Self*. New York: Basic Books; and Robert Kurzban. 2010. *Why Everyone (Else) is a Hypocrite: Evolution and the Modular Mind*. Princeton: Princeton University Press.
48. Hood, *The Self Illusion*, xv.
49. Ibid., 218–19.
50. Kurzban, *Why Everyone (Else) is a Hypocrite*, 4.
51. Ibid., 6.
52. Ibid., 214.
53. Ibid., 217.

54. Joris Lammers, Diederik A. Stapel, and Adam D. Galinsky. 2010. "Power Increases Hypocrisy: Moralizing in Reasoning, Immorality in Behavior," *Psychological Science* 21: 737–44.

55. Ibid., 740.

56. Runciman, *Political Hypocrisy*, Conclusion.

57. Ibid., 44.

58. Ibid., 47.

59. Ibid., 53–4.

60. Ibid., 224.

61. Jeremy Waldron. 2011. "What to Tell the Axe-Man," *London Review of Books*, January 6, www.lrb.co.uk/v33/n01/jeremy-waldron/what-to-tell-the-axe-man (accessed May 23, 2012).

62. Runciman, *Political Hypocrisy*, 213.

7 The Private Lives of Politicians: Dishonesty

1. Aldert Vrij. 2008. *Detecting Lies and Deceit: Pitfalls and Opportunities*, 2nd ed. West Sussex: John Wiley and Sons, 22.

2. Ibid.

3. Bella M. DePaulo, Deborah A. Kashy, Susan E. Kirkendol, Melissa M. Wyer, and Jennifer Epstein. 1996. "Lying in Everyday Life," *Journal of Personality and Social Psychology* 70: 979–95.

4. See Timothy R. Levine, Rachel K. Kim, and Luaren M. Hamel. 2010. "People Lie for a Reason: Three Experiments Documenting the Principle of Veracity," *Communication Research Reports* 27: 271–85.

5. In what follows, I will not consider lies that national leaders tell in the realm of international politics. I avoid those because there is an element of statecraft in this type of lying. In other words, it is not about politicians telling lies as much as it is states lying to other states. Furthermore, I suspect that few would object to their country's leader lying to the leader of another country for the sake of national security. Having said that, leaders do sometimes lie to their own people about foreign policy. This is more problematic than lying as statecraft, though it is often justified. Of course, it is usually quite difficult to distinguish between lying that is necessary for national defense and lying that is purely in the leader's political self-interest. For a good recent treatment of lying in international affairs, see John Mearsheimer. 2011. *Why Leaders Lie: The Truth About Lying in International Politics*. New York: Oxford University Press.

6. Kathleen Hall Jamieson and Paul A. Waldman. 2000. "Watching the Adwatches," in *Campaign Reform: Insights and Evidence*, eds. Larry M. Bartels and Lynn Vavreck. Ann Arbor: The University of Michigan Press.

7. Ibid., 119.

8. See Craig Silverman. 2011. "Conferences Raise Unanswered Questions about Fact Checking," Poynter.org, December 28, www.poynter.org/latest-news/regret-the-error/157031/conferences-raise-unanswered-questions-about-fact-checking/ (accessed March 28, 2012).

9. For an early examination of this question, see Gerald Pomper. 1967. "'If Elected, I Promise': American Party Platforms," *Midwest Journal of Political Science* 11: 318–52.

10. Jeff Fishel. 1985. *Presidents & Promises: From Campaign Pledge to Presidential Performance*. Washington, DC: CQ Press, 38.
11. See, for instance, Glen Sussman and Byron W. Daynes. 2000. "Party Promises and Presidential Performance: Social Policies of the Modern Presidents, FDR-Clinton," *Southeastern Political Review* 28: 111–30.
12. Michele P. Claibourn. 2011. *Presidential Campaigns and Presidential Accountability*. Urbana: University of Illinois Press.
13. Ibid., 102.
14. Bill Clinton. 2004. *My Life*. New York: Alfred A. Knopf, 463.
15. Evan J. Ringquist and Carl Dasse. 2004. "Lies, Damned Lies, and Campaign Promises? Environmental Legislation in the 105th Congress," *Social Science Quarterly* 85: 414.
16. Tracy Sulkin. 2011. *The Legislative Legacy of Congressional Campaigns*. New York: Cambridge University Press. See also Tracy Sulkin. 2009. "Campaign Appeals and Legislative Action," *The Journal of Politics* 71: 1093–108; and Tracy Sulkin and Nathaniel Swigger. 2008. "Is There Truth in Advertising? Campaign Ad Images as Signals about Legislative Behavior," *The Journal of Politics* 70: 232–44.
17. Sulkin, *The Legislative Legacy of Congressional Campaigns*, 196.
18. Nina Mazar, On Amir, and Dan Ariely. 2008. "The Dishonesty of Honest People: A Theory of Self-Concept Maintenance," *The Journal of Marketing Research*, 45: 633–44. Available at SSRN: http://ssrn.com/abstract=979648, 32.
19. Ibid., 3.
20. Blaire Briody. 2012. "Cheat on Taxes 'As Much As Possible'? More Say Yes," *The Fiscal Times*, January 31, www.thefiscaltimes.com/Articles/2012/01/31/Cheat-on-Taxes-As-Much-As-Possible-More-Say-Yes.aspx#page1 (accessed April 1, 2012).
21. Several works suggest that such practices are widespread, but none offer a quantitative assessment. See Tracy Campbell. 2005. *Deliver the Vote: A History of Election Fraud, an American Political Tradition – 1742–2004*. New York: Carroll & Graf Publishers; and Larry J. Sabato and Glenn R. Simpson. 1996. *Dirty Little Secrets: The Persistence of Corruption in American Politics*. New York: Times Books.
22. See Delia Bailey. 2008. "Caught in the Act: Recent Federal Election Fraud Cases," in *Election Fraud: Detecting and Deterring Electoral Manipulation*, eds. R. Michael Alvarez, Thad E. Hall, and Susan D. Hyde. Washington, DC: Brookings Institution Press.
23. See Dale E. Miller and Stephen K. Medvic. 2002. "Civic Responsibility or Self-Interest?" in *Shades of Gray: Perspectives on Campaign Ethics*, eds. Candice J. Nelson, David A. Dulio, and Stephen K. Medvic. Washington, DC: Brookings Institution Press.
24. Dan Ariely. 2010. "Who Cheats More?" DanAriely.com, July 25, http://danariely.com/2010/07/25/who-cheats-more/ (accessed April 1, 2012). This experiment is described in Dan Ariely. 2012. *The (Honest) Truth about Dishonesty: How We Lie to Everyone – Especially Ourselves*. New York: Harper.
25. Allen Raymond with Ian Spiegelman. 2008. *How to Rig an Election: Confessions of a Republican Operative*. New York: Simon & Schuster, 17.

26. Here's a hint: The high profile cases involved Sen. John Ensign, Sen. John Edwards, Gov. Mark Sanford, Gov. Arnold Schwarzenegger, and Rep. Anthony Weiner.

27. See Sharon Jayson. 2008. "Getting Reliable Data on Infidelity isn't Easy," *USA Today*, November 17, www.usatoday.com/news/health/2008-11-16-infidelity-research_N.htm (accessed April 2, 2012).

28. See "Women in Congress: Historical Data – 112th Congress, 2011–2013," http://womenincongress.house.gov/historical-data/representatives-senators-by-congress.html?congress=112 (accessed April 3, 2012).

29. See "List of Federal Political Sex Scandals in the United States," http://en.wikipedia.org/wiki/List_of_federal_political_sex_scandals_in_the_United_States#cite_ref-42 (accessed April 3, 2012).

30. Each of these claims have been offered by scholars in the popular press. See, for example, Joe Hallett and Jonathan Riskind. 2008. "Egos to Blame for Political Sex Scandals," *The Columbus Dispatch*, May 12, www.dispatch.com/content/stories/local/2008/05/12/polisex.html (accessed April 22, 2012).

31. Joris Lammers, Janka I. Stoker, Jennifer Jordan, Monique Pollmann, and Diederik A. Stapel. 2011. "Power Increases Infidelity Among Men and Women," *Psychological Science* 22: 1191–7.

32. Monica Davey and Emma G. Fitzsimmons. 2011. "Jury Finds Blagojevich Guilty of Corruption," *New York Times*, June 27, www.nytimes.com/2011/06/28/us/28blagojevich.html (accessed April 28, 2012).

33. CNN. 2005. "Congressman Resigns After Bribery Plea," CNN.com, November 28, http://articles.cnn.com/2005-11-28/politics/cunningham_1_mzm-mitchell-wade-tax-evasion?_s=PM:POLITICS (accessed April 28, 2012).

34. Tim Morris. 2009. "William Jefferson Verdict: Guilty on 11 of 16 Counts," *The Times-Picayune*, August 5, www.nola.com/news/index.ssf/2009/08/william_jefferson_verdict_guil.html (accessed April 28, 2012).

35. Public Integrity Section. n.d. "Report to Congress on the Activities and Operations of the Public Integrity Section for 2010," U.S. Department of Justice, www.justice.gov/criminal/pin/docs/arpt-2010.pdf (accessed April 28, 2012).

36. In 1992, the last time the U.S. Census Bureau counted, there were 513,200 elected officials in 85,006 government units in the United States. The number of government units had grown to 87,576 by 2002, so there are even more than 513,200 elected officials in the United States today. For the 1992 numbers, see U.S. Census Bureau. 1995. *1992 Census of Governments, Volume 1: Government Organization, Number 2: Popularly Elected Officials.* GC92(1)-2. The number of government units in 2002 can be found in U.S. Census Bureau. 2002. *2002 Census of Governments, Volume 1, Number 1, Government Organization.* GC02(1)-1.

37. Transparency International. 2011. "Corruption Perceptions Index 2011," http://cpi.transparency.org/cpi2011/results/ (accessed May 1, 2012).

38. Ibid.

39. CBSNews.com. 2011. "Congress: Trading Stock on Inside Information?" *60 Minutes*, November 13, www.cbsnews.com/video/watch/?id=7388130n&tag=contentBody;storyMediaBox (accessed May 1, 2012).

40. See the comments by Robert Walker at 10:11:58 and 10:12:21 on the transcript of the December 21, 2011 *The Diane Rehm Show* on "Insider Trading

on Capitol Hill," http://thedianerehmshow.org/shows/2011-12-21/insider-trading-capitol-hill/transcript (accessed May 5, 2012).

41. Brody Mullins on ibid., at 10:15:01.
42. See Peter Schweizer. 2011. *Throw Them All Out: How Politicians and Their Friends Get Rich Off Insider Stock Tips, Land Deals, and Cronyism That Would Send the Rest of Us To Prison*. New York: Houghton Mifflin Harcourt.
43. Peter Schweizer on *The Diane Rehm Show*, "Insider Trading on Capitol Hill," at 10:09:49.
44. Ibid.
45. Schweizer, *Throw Them All Out*, xviii.
46. Members of the Senate do particularly well in the market, outperforming even the average corporate insider and the average hedge fund (ibid.). Schweizer speculates that this "is because they have relatively more power and therefore greater access to market-moving information" than House Members (ibid.). It could also be due to the fact that most Senators are extremely wealthy before entering the Senate and are therefore even more likely to get professional advice from the best financial planners.
47. See, for example, the following *Politico* article, which considers allegations Schweizer and *60 Minutes* make against both John Boehner and Nancy Pelosi; Keach Hagey and John Bresnahan. 2011. " '60 Minutes' Takes on John Boehner, Nancy Pelosi," *Politico*, November 3, www.politico.com/news/stories/1111/67593.html (accessed May 5, 2012).
48. Schweizer, *Throw Them All Out*, 73.
49. See, for instance, Gretchen Morgenson and Joshua Rosner. 2011. *Reckless Endangerment: How Outsized Ambition, Greed, and Corruption Led to Economic Armageddon*. New York: Times Books.
50. Robert Pear. 2012. "Insider Trading Ban for Lawmakers Clears Congress," *New York Times*, March 22, www.nytimes.com/2012/03/23/us/politics/insider-trading-ban-for-lawmakers-clears-congress.html (accessed May 16, 2012).
51. The campaign finance system presents an interesting, and unique, set of ethical considerations with respect to politicians and the concerns it elicits fall somewhere between the public lives of politicians and their dispositions. Their participation in the system is certainly part of their public activity and, thus, I have dealt with the pressures of fundraising and money's influence on elected officials in Chapter 4. But many believe that the pursuit of campaign cash reveals a character flaw in those who choose to enter politics. That is a different argument than the "power corrupts" contention and it is one that Lessig dismantles.
52. Lawrence Lessig. 2011. *Republic, Lost: How Money Corrupts Congress – and a Plan to Stop It*. New York: Twelve, 8.
53. Ibid., 17.
54. For a thorough review of Lessig's book that makes this case, see Ezra Klein. 2012. "Our Corrupt Politics: It's Not All Money," *The New York Review of Books*, March 22, www.nybooks.com/articles/archives/2012/mar/22/our-corrupt-politics-its-not-all-money/?pagination=false (accessed May 17, 2012).
55. Louis D. Brandeis. 1914. "What Publicity Can Do," in *Other People's Money*, www.law.louisville.edu/library/collections/brandeis/node/196 (accessed May 17, 2012).

8 Rebuilding Trust in Politicians

1. To be more accurate, the change in conservative rhetoric in the 1970s, as Mark Smith has shown, was not that it became anti-government; it had long been that. Instead, it is that conservative opposition to government solutions to problems was reframed in almost purely economic terms. Mark A. Smith. 2007. *The Right Talk: How Conservatives Transformed the Great Society into the Economic Society*. Princeton: Princeton University Press.
2. For a comparison of the rhetoric of Goldwater and Reagan, see ibid., 130–9.
3. Ronald Reagan. 1981. "Inaugural Address," The American Presidency Project, www.presidency.ucsb.edu/ws/index.php?pid=43130#axzz1wH1D7yhc (accessed May 29, 2012).
4. Indeed, political institutions themselves are likely to be altered by these arguments. See Walter Williams. 2003. *Reaganism and the Death of Representative Democracy*. Washington, DC: Georgetown University Press.
5. See Theda Skocpol and Vanessa Williamson. 2012. *The Tea Party and the Remaking of Republican Conservatism*. New York: Oxford University Press.
6. See Pippa Norris. 2011. *Democratic Deficit: Critical Citizens Revisited*. New York: Cambridge University Press, 4.
7. Ibid., 5.
8. Nadia Urbinati and Mark E. Warren. 2008. "The Concept of Representation in Contemporary Democratic Theory," *Annual Review of Political Science* 11: 402.
9. For such a discussion, see Sonia Alonso, John Keane, and Wolfgang Merkel, eds. 2011. *The Future of Representative Democracy*. New York: Cambridge University Press; and Nadia Urbinati. 2006. *Representative Democracy: Principles and Genealogy*. Chicago: University of Chicago Press.
10. Mark Warren makes a similar point in the introduction to his edited volume, *Democracy & Trust*. Mark E. Warren, ed. 1999. *Democracy & Trust*. New York: Cambridge University Press.
11. Mark E. Warren. 1999. "Democratic Theory and Trust," in *Democracy & Trust*, ed. Mark E. Warren. New York: Cambridge University Press, 311.
12. Robert D. Putnam. 2000. *Bowling Alone: The Collapse and Revival of American Community*. New York: Simon & Schuster.
13. On the correlation between both interpersonal trust and subjective well-being, on the one hand, and political stability, on the other, see Ronald Inglehart. 1999. "Trust, Well-being and Democracy," in *Democracy & Trust*, ed. Mark E. Warren. New York: Cambridge University Press.
14. Warren, "Democratic Theory and Trust," 317.
15. Russell Hardin. 1999. "Do We Want Trust in Government?" in *Democracy & Trust*, ed. Mark E. Warren. New York: Cambridge University Press, 24.
16. Ibid.
17. See Samuel L. Popkin. 1994. *The Reasoning Voter: Communication and Persuasion in Presidential Campaigns*, 2nd ed. Chicago: University of Chicago Press; Marion R. Just, Ann N. Crigler, Dean E. Alger, Timothy E. Cook, Montague Kern, and Darrell M. West. 1996. *Crosstalk: Citizens, Candidates, and the Media in a Presidential Campaign*. Chicago: University of Chicago Press; and Roderick P. Hart. 2000. *Campaign Talk: Why Elections Are Good for Us*. Princeton: Princeton University Press.

18. Hardin, "Do We Want Trust in Government?" 30.
19. Ibid., 26 (emphasis in original).
20. Ibid., 31.
21. Ibid., 38.
22. Admittedly, it may be in the Federal Deposit Insurance Corporation that we are actually placing our trust. But this takes us right back to trust in government.
23. Ibid., 30.
24. Ibid., 31.
25. Ibid., 30.
26. Bradley Dowden. 2010. "Fallacies," Internet Encyclopedia of Philosophy, www.iep.utm.edu/fallacy/#HastyGeneralization (accessed June 5, 2012).
27. Jeffrey C. Goldfarb. 1991. *The Cynical Society: The Culture of Politics and the Politics of Culture in American Life*. Chicago: University of Chicago Press, 22.
28. Ibid., 28.
29. Margaret Levi and Laura Stoker. 2000. "Political Trust and Trustworthiness," *Annual Review of Political Science* 3: 488.
30. Goldfarb, *The Cynical Society*, 16. On ancient Greek "kynicism," see Peter Sloterdijk. 1987. *Critique of Cynical Reason*. Minneapolis: University of Minnesota Press.
31. It should be said that partisanship offers a shortcut around much of this work and, yet, provides a way to avoid blanket distrust of all politicians. When one identifies closely with a party, he or she relies on that party (including its politicians) to behave in a trustworthy manner. The partisan must still keep tabs on his or her party to be sure that it doesn't violate his or her trust. But doing so is less burdensome than monitoring the machinations of everyday politics.
32. Steven Bilakovics. 2012. *Democracy without Politics*. Cambridge, MA: Harvard University Press, 3.
33. See ibid., for an intriguing account of how this is possible.
34. Seymour Martin Lipset. 1959. "Some Social Requisites of Democracy: Economic Development and Political Legitimacy," *The American Political Science Review* 53: 86.
35. Ibid.
36. William Chaloupka. 1999. *Everybody Knows: Cynicism in America*. Minneapolis: University of Minnesota Press, xiv.
37. David Easton. 1965. *A Systems Analysis of Political Life*. New York: John Wiley & Sons, 212. By "regime," Easton means "the general matrix of regularized expectations within the limits of which political actions are usually considered authoritative" (194). That is, a regime consists of the "values (goals and principles), norms, and structure of authority" (193) of a political system, which for Easton is a much broader concept. I use "system" here to mean, essentially, what Easton means by "regime."
38. Ibid., 216.
39. See Tom R. Tyler. 2006. *Why People Obey the Law*. Princeton: Princeton University Press.
40. Norris, *Democratic Deficit*, 227.
41. Sanford Levinson. 2012. "Our Imbecilic Constitution," *New York Times*, "Campaign Stops" blog, May 28, http://campaignstops.blogs.nytimes.

com/2012/05/28/our-imbecilic-constitution/ (accessed June 10, 2012). See also Sanford Levinson. 2012. *Framed: America's Fifty-One Constitutions and the Crisis of Governance*. New York: Oxford University Press.

42. Jodi Perlmuth Popofsky. 2012. "Is It Time to Rewrite the Constitution?" *New York Times*, Letters, June 4, www.nytimes.com/2012/06/05/opinion/is-it-time-to-rewrite-the-constitution.html (accessed June 10, 2012).

43. Sam Dillon. 2011. "Failing Grades on Civics Exam Called a 'Crisis,'" *New York Times*, May 4, www.nytimes.com/2011/05/05/education/05civics.html (accessed June 10, 2012).

44. Bernard Crick. 1972. *In Defense of Politics*, 2nd ed. Chicago: University of Chicago Press, 146.

45. Ibid.

46. Crick also sets politics against democracy. See n.47 in Chapter 2 of this book for a brief discussion of Crick's notion of democracy and how it can be juxtaposed with politics.

47. Ibid.

48. Emily Yoffe. 2012. "You Are Not the Speaker," *Slate.com*, March 20, www.slate.com/articles/news_and_politics/politics/2012/03/newt_gingrich_speaker_of_the_house_politicians_who_cling_to_their_old_titles_are_pretentious_incorrect_and_un_american_.html (accessed June 10, 2012).

49. Ibid.

50. Nadia Urbinati. 2006. *Representative Democracy: Principles and Genealogy*. Chicago: University of Chicago Press, 224.

51. Ibid.

52. Ibid.

References

Abramowitz, Alan I. 2010. *The Disappearing Center: Engaged Citizens, Polarization, and American Democracy*. New Haven: Yale University Press.

Abramowitz, Alan I. and Kyle L. Saunders. 2008. "Is Polarization a Myth?" *The Journal of Politics* 70: 542–55.

Aldrich, John H. 1995. *Why Parties? The Origin and Transformation of Political Parties in America*. Chicago: University of Chicago Press.

Allen, Jonathan and Jake Sherman. 2011. "How Grover Norquist Corners Congress." *Politico*, November 8, www.politico.com/news/stories/1111/67906. html.

Alonso, Sonia, John Keane, and Wolfgang Merkel, eds. 2011. *The Future of Representative Democracy*. New York: Cambridge University Press.

Altemeyer, Bob. 1996. *The Authoritarian Specter*. Cambridge, MA: Harvard University Press.

Altschuler, Glenn C. and Stuart M. Blumin. 2000. *Rude Republic: Americans and Their Politics in the Nineteenth Century*. Princeton: Princeton University Press.

Alvarez, Louis, Andrew Kolker, and Paul Stekler. 1996. *Vote For Me: Politics in America*. New York: The Center for New American Media.

American National Election Study. 1978. "Codebook Variable Documentation, 1978 Post-Election Study," VAR 780246, ftp://ftp.electionstudies.org/ftp/nes/ studypages/1978post/nes1978.txt.

American National Election Study. 2008. Variable 085150 – M1d, Survey Documentation and Analysis, University of California, Berkeley, http://sda. berkeley.edu/cgi-bin/hsda?harcsda+nes08new.

Amy, Douglas J. 2002. *Real Choices/New Voices: How Proportional Representation Elections Could Revitalize American Democracy*, 2nd ed. New York: Columbia University Press.

Andrews, Paul W. 2001. "The Psychology of Social Chess and the Evolution of Attribution Mechanisms: Explaining the Fundamental Attribution Error," *Evolution and Human Behavior* 22: 11–29.

Ansolabehere, Stephen, John M. de Figueiredo, and James M. Snyder, Jr. 2003. "Why Is There So Little Money in Politics?" *The Journal of Economic Perspectives* 17: 105–30.

Appleby, Joyce. 1992. "Recovering America's Historic Diversity: Beyond Exceptionalism," *The Journal of American History* 79: 419–31.

Ariely, Dan. 2010. "Who Cheats More?" DanAriely.com, July 25, http://danariely.com/2010/07/25/who-cheats-more/.

Ariely, Dan. 2012. *The (Honest) Truth about Dishonesty: How We Lie to Everyone – Especially Ourselves*. New York: Harper.

Bafumi, Joseph and Robert Y. Shapiro. 2009. "A New Partisan Voter," *The Journal of Politics* 71: 1–24.

Bai, Matt. 2012. "Obama vs. Boehner: Who Killed the Debt Deal?" *New York Times*, March 28, www.nytimes.com/2012/04/01/magazine/obama-vs-boehner-who-killed-the-debt-deal.html?pagewanted=all.

Bailey, Delia. 2008. "Caught in the Act: Recent Federal Election Fraud Cases," in *Election Fraud: Detecting and Deterring Electoral Manipulation*, eds. R. Michael Alvarez, Thad E. Hall, and Susan D. Hyde. Washington, DC: Brookings Institution Press, pp. 89–98.

Bartels, Larry M. 2002. "Beyond the Running Tally: Partisan Bias in Political Perceptions," *Political Behavior* 24: 117–50.

Bartlett, Bruce. 2011. "Americans Support Higher Taxes. Really," *Capital Gains and Games*, June 29, www.capitalgainsandgames.com/blog/bruce-bartlett/2292/americans-support-higher-taxes-really.

Baumgartner, Frank R., Jeffrey M. Berry, Marie Hojnacki, David C. Kimball, and Beth L. Leech. 2009. *Lobbying and Policy Change: Who Wins, Who Loses, and Why*. Chicago: University of Chicago Press.

Baumgartner, Jody and Jonathan S. Morris. 2006. "The Daily Show Effect: Candidates Evaluations, Efficacy, and American Youth," *American Politics Research* 34: 341–67.

Bendavid, Naftali. 2010. "Boehner Warns GOP on Debt Ceiling," Washington Wire blog, *The Wall Street Journal*, November 18, http://blogs.wsj.com/washwire/2010/11/18/boehner-warns-gop-on-debt-ceiling/.

Bennett, Drake. 2011. "Grover Norquist, the Enforcer," *Businessweek*, May 26, www.businessweek.com/magazine/content/11_23/b4231006685629.htm.

Bennett, Stephen Earl. 2001. "Were the Halcyon Days Really Golden? An Analysis of Americans' Attitudes about the Political System, 1945–1965," in *What is it About Government that Americans Dislike?*, eds. John R. Hibbing and Elizabeth Theiss-Morse. New York: Cambridge University Press, pp. 47–58.

Bennett, W. Lance. 2007. "Relief in Hard Times: A Defense of Jon Stewart's Comedy in an Age of Cynicism," *Critical Studies in Media Communication* 24: 278–83.

Berman, Russell. 2011. "House Republicans Mull Plan to Hike Debt Ceiling Every Two Months," *The Hill*, April 29, http://thehill.com/homenews/house/158297-house-gop-considering-plan-to-increase-debt-limit-in-steps.

Berry, Jeffrey M. and Clyde Wilcox. 2007. *The Interest Group Society*, 4th ed. New York: Pearson Longman.

Bilakovics, Steven. 2012. *Democracy without Politics*. Cambridge, MA: Harvard University Press.

Billig, Michael. 1996. *Arguing and Thinking: A Rhetorical Approach to Social Psychology*, new ed. New York: Cambridge University Press.

Black, Gordon S. 1972. "A Theory of Political Ambition: Career Choices and the Role of Structural Incentives," *The American Political Science Review* 66: 144–59.

Blair, Tony. 2007. Statement to the House of Commons, June 27. House of Commons Hansard Debates, column 334, www.publications.parliament.uk/pa/cm200607/cmhansrd/cm070627/debtext/70627-0003.htm#07062782003584.

Brady, David W. and Charles S. Bullock, III. 1980. "Is There a Conservative Coalition in the House?" *The Journal of Politics* 42: 549–59.

Brady, David W., Hahrie Han, and Jeremy C. Pope. 2007. "Primary Elections and Candidate Ideology: Out of Step with the Primary Electorate?" *Legislative Studies Quarterly* 32: 79–105.

Brandeis, Louis D. 1914. "What Publicity Can Do," in *Other People's Money*, www.law.louisville.edu/library/collections/brandeis/node/196.

Briody, Blaire. 2012. "Cheat on Taxes 'As Much As Possible'? More Say Yes," *The Fiscal Times*, January 31, www.thefiscaltimes.com/Articles/2012/01/31/Cheat-on-Taxes-As-Much-As-Possible-More-Say-Yes.aspx#page1.

Brown, Carrie Budoff. 2011. "Default Deniers: The New Skeptics," *Politico*, May 17, www.politico.com/news/stories/0511/55087.html.

Brutus. 1787. "No. 1," October 18, www.constitution.org/afp/brutus01.htm.

Burke, Edmund. 1774. "Speech to the Electors of Bristol," The Online Library of Liberty, http://oll.libertyfund.org/?option=com_staticxt&staticfile=show.php%3Ftitle=659&chapter=20392&layout=html&Itemid=27.

Calmes, Jackie and Carl Hulse. 2011. "As the Federal Government Hits Its Debt Limit, Lawmakers Spar over Solution," *New York Times*, May 16, www.nytimes.com/2011/05/17/us/politics/17budget.html.

Campaign Finance Institute. 2010. "Non-Party Spending Doubled in 2010 But Did Not Dictate Results," November 5, www.cfinst.org/Press/PReleases/10-11-05/Non-Party_Spending_Doubled_But_Did_Not_Dictate_Results.aspx, Table 3.

Campbell, Tracy. 2005. *Deliver the Vote: A History of Election Fraud, an American Political Tradition – 1742–2004*. New York: Carroll & Graf Publishers.

Canon, David T. 1990. *Actors, Athletes, and Astronauts: Political Amateurs in the United States Congress*. Chicago: University of Chicago Press.

Cantril, Hadley. 1951. *Public Opinion 1935–1946*. Princeton: Princeton University Press.

Cappella, Joseph N. and Kathleen Hall Jamieson. 1997. *The Spiral of Cynicism: The Press and the Public Good*. New York: Oxford.

Caprara, Gian Vittorio, Claudio Barbaranelli, Chiara Consiglio, Laura Picconi, and Philip G. Zimbardo. 2003. "Personalities of Politicians and Voters: Unique and Synergistic Relationships," *Journal of Personality and Social Psychology* 84: 849–56.

Carman, Christopher Jan. 2007. "Assessing Preferences for Political Representation in the US," *Journal of Elections, Public Opinion and Parties* 17: 1–19.

Carter, Charlene. 2011. "House Votes to End Presidential Campaign Fund," *Roll Call*, December 1, www.rollcall.com/news/house_votes_to_end_presidential_campaign_fund-210706-1.html.

Carwardine, Richard. 2007. *Lincoln: A Life of Purpose and Power*. New York: Vintage Books.

CBSNews.com. 2011. "Congress: Trading Stock on Inside Information?" *60 Minutes*, November 13, www.cbsnews.com/video/watch/?id=7388130n&tag =contentBody;storyMediaBox.

Center for Responsive Politics. 2011. "Most Members of Congress Enjoy Robust Financial Status, Despite Nation's Sluggish Economic Recovery," November 15, www.opensecrets.org/news/2011/11/congress-enjoys-robust-financial-status. html.

Chaloupka, William. 1999. *Everybody Knows: Cynicism in America*. Minneapolis: University of Minnesota Press.

Chambers, William Nisbet. 1963. *Political Parties in a New Nation: The American Experience, 1776–1809*. New York: Oxford University Press.

Cillizza, Chris. 2010. "Utah Sen. Bob Bennett Loses Convention Fight," The Fix, *The Washington Post*, May 8, http://voices.washingtonpost.com/thefix/senate/utah-sen-bob-bennett-loses.html.

Claibourn, Michele P. 2011. *Presidential Campaigns and Presidential Accountability*. Urbana: University of Illinois Press.

Clinton, Bill. 2004. *My Life*. New York: Alfred A. Knopf.

CNN. 2005. "Congressman Resigns After Bribery Plea." CNN.com, November 28,http://articles.cnn.com/2005-11-28/politics/cunningham_1_mzm-mitchell-wade-tax-evasion?_s=PM: POLITICS.

CNN. 2011. "Republican Debate." CNN.com, June 13, http://archives.cnn. com/TRANSCRIPTS/1106/13/se.02.html.

Cohen, Jon. 2011. "Shifting Public Concerns in Debt Limit Debate," Behind the Numbers, *The Washington Post*, July 11, www.washingtonpost.com/blogs/behind-the-numbers/post/shifting-public-concerns-in-debt-limit-debate/2011/07/11/gIQAR4WL9H_blog.html.

Cohen, Marty, David Karol, Hans Noel, and John Zaller. 2008. *The Party Decides: Presidential Nominations Before and After Reform*. Chicago: University of Chicago Press.

Committee on Political Parties. 1950. *Toward a More Responsible Two-Party System*. New York: Rinehart & Company.

Cooper, Michael and Louise Story. 2011. "Q. and A. on the Debt Ceiling," *New York Times*, July 27, www.nytimes.com/2011/07/28/us/politics/28default. html?pagewanted=all.

Cornwell, Elmer E., Jr. 1964. "Bosses, Machines, and Ethnic Groups," *Annals of the American Academy of Political and Social Science* 353: 27–39.

Crevecoeur, J. Hector St. John. 1782. *Letters from an American Farmer*, http://xroads.virginia.edu/~HYPER/CREV/letter03.html.

Crick, Bernard. 1972. *In Defense of Politics*, 2nd ed. Chicago: University of Chicago Press.

Crick, Bernard. 2005. *In Defense of Politics*, 5th ed. New York: Continuum.

Dahl, Robert A. 1998. *On Democracy*. New Haven: Yale University Press.

Dahl, Robert A. 2006. *On Political Equality*. New Haven: Yale University Press.

Dalton, Russell J. 2004. *Democratic Challenges, Democratic Choices: The Erosion of Political Support in Advanced Industrial Democracies*. New York: Oxford University Press.

Damasio, Antonio. 1994. *Descartes' Error: Emotion, Reason, and the Human Brain*. New York: Penguin.

Davey, Monica and Emma G. Fitzsimmons. 2011. "Jury Finds Blagojevich Guilty of Corruption," *New York Times*, June 27, www.nytimes.com/2011/06/28/us/28blagojevich.html.

Davidson, Roger H. 1970. "Public Prescriptions for the Job of Congressman," *Midwest Journal of Political Science* 14: 648–66.

Davies, Christie. 2011. Personal e-mail correspondence, March 5.

Dawkins, Richard and John R. Krebs. 1978. "Animal Signals: Information or Manipulation?" in *Behavioural Ecology*, eds. John R. Krebs and Nicholas B. Davies. Oxford: Blackwell Scientific, pp. 282–309.

DePaulo, Bella M., Deborah A. Kashy, Susan E. Kirkendol, Melissa M. Wyer, and Jennifer Epstein. 1996. "Lying in Everyday Life," *Journal of Personality and Social Psychology* 70: 979–95.

The Diane Rehm Show. 2011. "Insider Trading on Capitol Hill," December 21, http://thedianerehmshow.org/shows/2011-12-21/insider-trading-capitol-hill/transcript.

Dietrich, Bryce J., Scott Lasley, Jeffery M. Mundak, Megan L. Remmel, and Joel Turner. 2012. "Personality and Legislative Politics: The Big Five Trait Dimensions Among U.S. State Legislators," *Political Psychology* 33:195–210.

Dillon, Sam. 2011. "Failing Grades on Civics Exam Called a 'Crisis,' " *New York Times*, May 4, www.nytimes.com/2011/05/05/education/05civics.html.

Dionne, E. J., Jr. 1991. *Why Americans Hate Politics*. New York: Simon & Schuster.

Dowden, Bradley. 2010. "Fallacies," Internet Encyclopedia of Philosophy, www.iep.utm.edu/fallacy/#HastyGeneralization.

Drew, Elizabeth. 2011. "What Were They Thinking?" *The New York Review of Books*, August 18, www.nybooks.com/articles/archives/2011/aug/18/what-were-they-thinking/?pagination=false.

Druckman, Daniel, Benjamin J. Broome, and Susan H. Korper. 1988. "Value Differences and Conflict Resolution: Facilitation or Delinking?" *The Journal of Conflict Resolution* 32: 489–510.

Easton, David. 1965. *A Systems Analysis of Political Life*. New York: John Wiley & Sons.

Eigen, Lewis D. and Jonathan P. Siegel. 1993. *The Macmillan Dictionary of Political Quotations*. New York: Macmillan Publishing Company.

Eliasoph, Nina. 1998. *Avoiding Politics: How Americans Produce Apathy in Everyday Life*. New York: Cambridge University Press.

Evans, Murray. 2008. "Retired General Says Politicians Need to Provide Leadership," Associated Press, June 3.

FactCheck.org. 2011. "Junkie Math," November 17, www.factcheck.org/2011/11/junkie-math/.

Fifield, Anna. 2010. "Everyman Charm Delivers Republican Triumph," FT.com, January 20, www.ft.com/cms/s/0/b6b0842a-05d1-11df-88ee-00144feabdc0.html#axzz1R95p5QeL.

Fiorina, Morris P. with Samuel J. Abrams and Jeremy C. Pope. 2011. *Culture War? The Myth of a Polarized America*, 3rd ed. Boston: Longman.

Fishel, Jeff. 1985. *Presidents & Promises: From Campaign Pledge to Presidential Performance*. Washington, DC: CQ Press.

Fox, Richard L. and Jennifer L. Lawless. 2005. "To Run or Not to Run for Office: Explaining Nascent Political Ambition," *American Journal of Political Science* 49: 642–59.

Fram, Alan. 2011. "The Influence Game: Lobbying on Debt Limit Fight," Associated Press, July 28, http://abcnews.go.com/Politics/wireStory?id=14174030.

Franklin, Mark N. 2004. *Voter Turnout and the Dynamics of Electoral Competition in Established Democracies Since 1945*. New York: Cambridge University Press.

Fridkin, Kim L. and Patrick J. Kenney. 2011. "The Role of Candidate Traits in Campaigns," *The Journal of Politics* 73: 61–73.

Friedman, Thomas L. 2011. "The Day Our Leaders Got Unstuck," *New York Times*, August 9, www.nytimes.com/2011/08/10/opinion/the-day-our-leaders-got-unstuck.html.

Funk, Carolyn L. 1996. "Understanding Trait Inferences in Candidate Images," in *Research in Micropolitics: Rethinking Rationality*, Vol. 5, eds. Michael X. Delli Carpini, Leonie Huddy, and Robert Y. Shapiro. Greenwich: JAI, pp. 97–123.

Funk, Carolyn L. 1999. "Bringing the Candidate into Models of Candidate Evaluation," *The Journal of Politics* 61: 700–20.

Funk, Carolyn L. 2001. "Process Performance: Public Reaction to Legislative Policy Debate," in *What is it About Government that Americans Dislike?*, eds. John R. Hibbing and Elizabeth Theiss-Morse. New York: Cambridge University Press, pp. 193–204.

Gallup. 2008. "Honesty/Ethics in Professions: Selected Trend," November 7–9, www.gallup.com/poll/1654/honesty-ethics-professions.aspx.

Gallup. 2008. "Blagojevich Scandal Feeds Into Public Skepticism," December 12, www.gallup.com/poll/113308/blagojevich-scandal-feeds-into-public-skepticism.aspx.

Garofalo, Pat. 2011. "RNC Chairman Priebus: Americans Will Say 'Well Good' if the U.S. Defaults on Its Obligations," ThinkProgress.org, June 28, http://thinkprogress.org/economy/2011/06/28/255874/rnc-chaor-good-debt-ceiling/.

Gibb, Cecil A. 1969. "Leadership," in *The Handbook of Social Psychology*, 2nd ed., Vol. 4, eds. Gardner Lindzey and Elliot Aronson. Reading, MA: Addison-Wesley Publishing Company, pp. 205–82.

Gilbert, Daniel T. and Patrick S. Malone. 1995. "The Correspondence Bias," *Psychological Bulletin* 117: 21–38.

Gillon, Steven M. 1987. *Politics and Vision: The ADA and American Liberalism, 1947–1985.* New York: Oxford University Press.

Goffman, Erving. 1959. *The Presentation of Self in Everyday Life.* Garden City: Doubleday Anchor Books.

Goldfarb, Jeffrey C. 1991. *The Cynical Society: The Culture of Politics and the Politics of Culture in American Life.* Chicago: University of Chicago Press.

Guttman, Robert. 2010. "Lack of Leadership Is the Problem: Not the System," *Huffington Post,* March 3, www.huffingtonpost.com/robert-guttman/lack-of-leadership-is-the_b_483660.html.

Haass, Samuel. 2011. "Debt Ceiling Medicaid Cuts: Union Lobbies Democratic Senators for Help," *Huffington Post,* July 13, www.huffingtonpost.com/2011/07/13/union-to-dem-senators-don_n_896581.html.

Hagey, Keach and John Bresnahan. 2011. "'60 Minutes' Takes on John Boehner, Nancy Pelosi," *Politico,* November 3, www.politico.com/news/stories/1111/67593.html.

Hallett, Joe and Jonathan Riskind. 2008. "Egos to Blame for Political Sex Scandals," *The Columbus Dispatch,* May 12, www.dispatch.com/content/stories/local/2008/05/12/polisex.html.

Hardin, Russell. 1999. "Do We Want Trust in Government?" in *Democracy & Trust,* ed. Mark E. Warren. New York: Cambridge University Press, pp. 22–41.

Hariman, Robert. 2007. "In Defense of Jon Stewart," *Critical Studies in Media Communication* 24: 273–7.

Harré, Rom. 1985. "Persuasion and Manipulation," in *Discourse and Communication: New Approaches to the Analysis of Mass Media Discourse and Communication,* ed. Teun A. van Dijk. New York: Walter de Gruyter, pp. 126–42.

Hart, Roderick P. 2000. *Campaign Talk: Why Elections Are Good for Us.* Princeton: Princeton University Press.

Hart, Roderick P. and E. Johanna Hartelius. 2007. "The Political Sins of Jon Stewart," *Critical Studies in Media Communication* 24: 263–72.

Hayes, Danny. 2009. "Has Television Personalized Voting Behavior?" *Political Behavior* 31: 231–60.

Herbst, Susan. 1993. *Numbered Voices: How Opinion Polling Has Shaped American Politics.* Chicago: University of Chicago Press.

Hetherington, Marc J. and Jonathan D. Weiler. 2009. *Authoritarianism & Polarization in American Politics.* New York: Cambridge University Press.

Hibbing, John R. and Elizabeth Theiss-Morse. 1995. *Congress as Public Enemy: Public Attitudes Toward American Political Institutions.* New York: Cambridge University Press.

Hibbing, John R. and Elizabeth Theiss-Morse. 2002. *Stealth Democracy: American's Beliefs about How Government Should Work.* New York: Cambridge University Press.

Hitchens, Christopher. 2010. "In Search of the Washington Novel: A Colorful Genre Awaits its Masterpiece," *City Journal* 20 (4), www.city-journal.org/2010/20_4_urb-the-washington-novel.html.

Hollis, Paul. 2008. "Second 'Great Malaise' Gripping U.S. as Lack of Leadership Continues to Prevail," *Southeast Farm Press*, May 7, http://southeastfarmpress.com/second-great-malaise-gripping-us-lack-leadership-continues-prevail.

Hood, Bruce. 2012. *The Self Illusion: How the Social Brain Creates Identity*. New York: Oxford University Press.

Hopkins, Cheyenne. 2011. "IMF Urges U.S. Debt-Ceiling Increase to Avoid a 'Severe Shock' to the Economy," Bloomberg, June 29, www.bloomberg.com/news/2011-06-29/imf-urges-u-s-debt-ceiling-increase-to-avoid-a-severe-shock-to-economy.html.

Hurley, Patricia A. 2001. "David Mayhew's *Congress: The Electoral Connection* after 25 Years," *PS: Political Science and Politics* 34: 259–61.

Huus, Kari. 2008. "Pro or Con, Readers Decry Lack of Leadership," MSNBC.com, September 30, www.msnbc.msn.com/id/26948830/ns/us_news-gut_check/t/pro-or-con-readers-decry-lack-leadership/.

Illinois Policy Institute. 2010. "Pay Day! Illinois Legislators Among Highest Paid in Nation," July 22, www.illinoispolicy.org/uploads/files/Publications/payday%20(1).pdf.

Inglehart, Ronald. 1999. "Trust, Well-being and Democracy," in *Democracy & Trust*, ed. Mark E. Warren. New York: Cambridge University Press, pp. 88–120.

Ingersoll, Thomas N. 1999. "'Riches and Honour Were Rejected by Them as Loathsome Vomit': The Fear of Leveling in New England," in *Inequality in Early America*, eds. Carla Gardina Pestana and Sharon V. Salinger. Hanover: University Press of New England, pp. 46–66.

Jacobe, Dennis. 2011. "Americans Oppose Raising Debt Ceiling, 47% to 19%," Gallup.com, May 13, www.gallup.com/poll/147524/Americans-Oppose-Raising-Debt-Ceiling.aspx.

Jacobs, Lawrence R. and Robert Y. Shapiro. 1994. "Issues, Candidate Image, and Priming: The Use of Private Polls in Kennedy's 1960 Presidential Campaign," *American Political Science Review* 88: 527–40.

Jacobs, Lawrence R. and Robert Y. Shapiro. 2000. *Politicians Don't Pander: Political Manipulation and the Loss of Democratic Responsiveness*. Chicago: University of Chicago Press.

Jacobson, Gary C. 2007. *A Divider, Not a Uniter: George W. Bush and the American People*. New York: Pearson Longman.

Jamieson, Kathleen Hall. 1992. *Dirty Politics: Deception, Distraction, and Democracy*. New York: Oxford University Press.

Jamieson, Kathleen Hall and Paul A. Waldman. 2000. "Watching the Adwatches," in *Campaign Reform: Insights and Evidence*, eds. Larry M. Bartels and Lynn Vavreck. Ann Arbor: The University of Michigan Press, pp. 106–21.

Jayson, Sharon. 2008. "Getting Reliable Data on Infidelity isn't Easy," *USA Today*, November 17, www.usatoday.com/news/health/2008-11-16-infidelity-research_N.htm.

John, Oliver P., Laura P. Naumann, and Christopher J. Soto. 2008. "Paradigm Shift to the Integrative Big Five Trait Taxonomy: History, Measurement, and

Conceptual Issues," in *Handbook of Personality: Theory and Research*, 3rd ed., eds. Oliver P. John, Richard W. Robins, and Lawrence A. Pervin. New York: The Guilford Press, pp. 114–58.

Jones, Edward E. and Victor A. Harris. 1967. "The Attribution of Attitudes," *Journal of Experimental Social Psychology* 3: 1–24.

Jones, Jeffrey M. 2011. "On Deficit, Americans Prefer Spending Cuts; Open to Tax Hikes," Gallup, July 13, www.gallup.com/poll/148472/deficit-americans-prefer-spending-cuts-open-tax-hikes.aspx.

Jones, Jeffrey M. 2011. "More Americans Oppose Than Favor Debt Ceiling Agreement," Gallup, August 3, www.gallup.com/poll/148802/americans-oppose-favor-debt-ceiling-agreement.aspx.

Just, Marion R., Ann N. Crigler, Dean E. Alger, Timothy E. Cook, Montague Kern, and Darrell M. West. 1996. *Crosstalk: Citizens, Candidates, and the Media in a Presidential Campaign*. Chicago: University of Chicago Press.

Kahneman, Daniel. 2011. *Thinking, Fast and Slow*. New York: Farrar, Straus and Giroux.

Kaid, Lynda Lee and Anne Johnston. 2001. *Videostyle in Presidential Campaigns: Style and Content of Televised Political Advertising*. Westport: Praeger.

Keyssar, Alexander. 2000. *The Right to Vote: The Contested History of Democracy in the United States*. New York: Basic Books.

King, Anthony. 2000. "Distrust of Government: Explaining American Exceptionalism," in *Disaffected Democracies: What's Troubling the Trilateral Countries?*, eds. Susan J. Pharr and Robert D. Putnam. Princeton: Princeton University Press, pp. 74–98.

Kingdon, John W. 1993. "Politicians, Self-Interest, and Ideas," in *Reconsidering the Democratic Public*, eds. George E. Marcus and Russell L. Hanson. University Park: Pennsylvania State University Press, pp. 73–89.

Klein, Ezra. 2011. "Wonkbook: A Deal that Found the Lowest-Common Denominator," Wonkblog, *The Washington Post*, July 31, www.washingtonpost.com/blogs/ezra-klein/post/a-deal-that-found-the-lowest-common-denominator/2011/07/11/gIQAde9TmI_blog.html.

Klein, Ezra. 2012. "Our Corrupt Politics: It's Not All Money," *The New York Review of Books*, March 22, www.nybooks.com/articles/archives/2012/mar/22/our-corrupt-politics-its-not-all-money/?pagination=false.

Klemp, Nathaniel J. 2012. *The Morality of Spin: Virtue and Vice in Political Rhetoric and the Christian Right*. Lanham: Rowman & Littlefield.

Kligman, Michael and Charles M. Culver. 1992. "An Analysis of Interpersonal Manipulation," *The Journal of Medicine and Philosophy* 17: 173–97.

Knight, Kathleen. 2006. "Transformations of the Concept of Ideology in the Twentieth Century," *American Political Science Review* 100: 619–26.

Koger, Gregory, Seth Masket, and Hans Noel. 2009. "Partisan Webs: Information Exchange and Party Networks," *British Journal of Political Science* 39: 633–53.

Kollman, Ken. 1998. *Outside Lobbying: Public Opinion & Interest Group Strategies*. Princeton: Princeton University Press.

Koole, Sander L., Wander Jager, Agnes E. van den Berg, Charles A. J. Vlek, and Willem K. B. Hofstee. 2001. "On the Social Nature of Personality: Effects of Extraversion, Agreeableness, and Feedback About Collective Resource Use on Cooperation in a Resource Dilemma," *Personality and Social Psychology Bulletin* 27: 289–301.

Krasny, Ros. 2010. "New U.S. Senator Drives Pick-up Truck to Victory," Reuters.com, January 20, www.reuters.com/article/2010/01/20/usa-politics-brown-idUSN1911214820100120.

Kurzban, Robert. 2010. *Why Everyone (Else) is a Hypocrite: Evolution and the Modular Mind.* Princeton: Princeton University Press.

Lammers, Joris, Diederik A. Stapel, and Adam D. Galinsky. 2010. "Power Increases Hypocrisy: Moralizing in Reasoning, Immorality in Behavior," *Psychological Science* 21: 737–44.

Lammers, Joris, Janka I. Stoker, Jennifer Jordan, Monique Pollmann, and Diederik A. Stapel. 2011. "Power Increases Infidelity Among Men and Women," *Psychological Science* 22: 1191–7.

Lasswell, Harold D. 1948. *Power and Personality.* New York: W. W. Norton & Company.

Lawrence, Regina G. 2000. "Game-Framing the Issues: Tracking the Strategy Frame in Public Policy News," *Political Communication* 17: 93–114.

Layman, Geoffrey C., Thomas M. Carsey, and Juliana Menasce Horowitz. 2006. "Party Polarization in American Politics: Characteristics, Causes, and Consequences," *Annual Review of Political Science* 9: 83–110.

Le Cheminant, Wayne and John Parrish, eds. 2011. *Manipulating Democracy: Democratic Theory, Political Psychology, and Mass Media.* New York: Routledge.

Lee, Don, Tom Hamburger, and Tom Petruno. 2011. "Surprise Warning on U.S. Debt Comes as Washington Inches Away from Gridlock," *Los Angeles Times,* April 19, http://articles.latimes.com/2011/apr/19/business/la-fi-us-credit-rating -20110419.

Lee, Frances E. 2009. *Beyond Ideology: Politics, Principles, and Partisanship in the U.S. Senate.* Chicago: University of Chicago Press.

Lessig, Lawrence. 2011. *Republic, Lost: How Money Corrupts Congress – and a Plan to Stop It.* New York: Twelve.

Levendusky, Matthew. 2009. *The Partisan Sort: How Liberals Became Democrats and Conservatives Became Republicans.* Chicago: University of Chicago Press.

Levi, Margaret and Laura Stoker. 2000. "Political Trust and Trustworthiness," *Annual Review of Political Science* 3: 475–507.

Levine, Timothy R., Rachel K. Kim, and Luaren M. Hamel. 2010. "People Lie for a Reason: Three Experiments Documenting the Principle of Veracity," *Communication Research Reports* 27: 271–85.

Levinson, Sanford. 2012. *Framed: America's Fifty-One Constitutions and the Crisis of Governance.* New York: Oxford University Press.

Levinson, Sanford. 2012. "Our Imbecilic Constitution," *New York Times,* "Campaign Stops" blog, May 28, http://campaignstops.blogs.nytimes.com/2012/05/28/our-imbecilic-constitution/.

Lijphart, Arend. 1999. *Patterns of Democracy: Government Forms and Performance in Thirty-Six Countries*. New Haven: Yale University Press.

Lipset, Seymour Martin. 1959. "Some Social Requisites of Democracy: Economic Development and Political Legitimacy," *The American Political Science Review* 53: 69–105.

Lipset, Seymour Martin. 1963. "The Value Patterns of Democracy: A Case Study in Comparative Analysis," *American Sociological Review* 28: 515–31.

Lipset, Seymour Martin. 1979. *The First New Nation: The United States in Historical and Comparative Perspective*. New York: W. W. Norton and Company.

Lipset, Seymour Martin and Gary Marks. 2000. *It Didn't Happen Here: Why Socialism Failed in the United States*. New York: W. W. Norton and Company.

Madariaga, S. de. 1937. *Anarchy or Hierarchy*. New York: The Macmillan Company.

Madison, James. 1787 [1987]. *Notes of Debates in the Federal Convention of 1787, Reported by James Madison*. New York: W. W. Norton & Company.

Madison, James. 1787. "The Federalist No. 10," November 22, www.constitution. org/fed/federa10.htm.

Maestas, Cherie. 2003. "The Incentive to Listen: Progressive Ambition, Resources, and Opinion Monitoring among State Legislators," *The Journal of Politics*, 65: 439–56.

Maestas, Cherie D., Sarah Fulton, L. Sandy Maisel, and Walter J. Stone. 2006. "When to Risk It? Institutions, Ambitions, and the Decision to Run for the U.S. House," *American Political Science Review* 100: 195–208.

Mansbridge, Jane. 1983. *Beyond Adversary Democracy*. Chicago: University of Chicago Press.

Marketplace Morning Report. 2011. "America: One of Two Developed Nations with Debt Ceilings," July 26, www.marketplace.org/topics/world/raising-debt-ceiling/america-one-two-developed-nations-debt-ceilings.

Marron, Donald. 2011. "Handicapping the Debt Ceiling Debate," Tax Policy Center, January 14, http://taxvox.taxpolicycenter.org/2011/01/14/handicapping-the-debt-ceiling-debate/.

Maxey, Chester. 1948. "A Plea for the Politician," *The Western Political Quarterly* 1: 271–9.

Mazar, Nina, On Amir, and Dan Ariely. 2008. "The Dishonesty of Honest People: A Theory of Self-Concept Maintenance," *The Journal of Marketing Research* 45: 633–44.

McAllister, Ian. 2007. "The Personalization of Politics," in *The Oxford Handbook of Political Behavior*, eds. Russell J. Dalton and Hans-Dieter Klingemann. New York: Oxford University Press, pp. 571–88.

McAvoy, Gregory E. and Peter K. Enns. 2010. "Using Approval of the President's Handling of the Economy to Understand Who Polarizes and Why," *Presidential Studies Quarterly* 40: 545–58.

McCarty, Nolan, Keith T. Poole, and Howard Rosenthal. 2006. *Polarized America: The Dance of Ideology and Unequal Riches*. Cambridge, MA: The MIT Press.

McClosky, Herbert. 1964. "Consensus and Ideology in American Politics," *American Political Science Review* 58: 361–82.

McCrae, Robert R. and Paul T. Costa, Jr. 2008. "The Five-Factor Theory of Personality," in *Handbook of Personality: Theory and Research*, 3rd ed., eds. Oliver P. John, Richard W. Robins, and Lawrence A. Pervin. New York: The Guilford Press, pp. 159–81.

McGerr, Michael E. 1986. *The Decline of Popular Politics: The American North, 1865–1928*. New York: Oxford University Press.

McGerr, Michael. 2003. *A Fierce Discontent: The Rise and Fall of the Progressive Movement in America, 1870–1920*. New York: Free Press.

McMurray, Carl D. and Malcolm B. Parsons. 1965. "Public Attitudes Toward the Representational Roles of Legislators and Judges," *Midwest Journal of Political Science* 9: 167–85.

Mearsheimer, John. 2011. *Why Leaders Lie: The Truth About Lying in International Politics*. New York: Oxford University Press.

Medvic, Stephen K. 2001. *Political Consultants in U.S. Congressional Elections*. Columbus: Ohio State University Press.

Medvic, Stephen K. 2006. "Understanding Campaign Strategy: 'Deliberate Priming' and the Role of Professional Political Consultants," *Journal of Political Marketing* 5 (1/2): 11–32.

Mele, Alfred R. and Piers Rawling, eds. 2004. *The Oxford Handbook of Rationality*. New York: Oxford University Press.

Mercier, Hugo and Dan Sperber. 2011. "Why do Humans Reason? Arguments for an Argumentative Theory," *Behavioral and Brain Sciences* 34: 57–74.

Metzinger, Thomas. 2009. *The Ego Tunnel: The Science of the Mind and the Myth of the Self*. New York: Basic Books.

Miller, Arthur H., Martin P. Wattenberg, and Oksana Malanchuk. 1986. "Schematic Assessments of Presidential Candidates," *American Political Science Review* 80: 521–40.

Miller, Dale E. and Stephen K. Medvic. 2002. "Civic Responsibility or Self-Interest?" in *Shades of Gray: Perspectives on Campaign Ethics*, eds. Candice J. Nelson, David A. Dulio, and Stephen K. Medvic. Washington, DC: Brookings Institution Press, pp. 18–38.

Mitchell, William C. 1959. "The Ambivalent Social Status of the American Politician," *The Western Political Quarterly* 12: 683–98.

Montgomery, Lori. 2011. "Senate Democrats Draft Debt-Reduction Plan," *The Washington Post*, July 8, www.washingtonpost.com/business/economy/senate-democrats-draft-debt-reduction-plan/2011/07/08/gIQAFQbS4H_story.html.

Montgomery, Lori and Paul Kane. 2011. "Debt-Limit Talks: As Obama, Boehner Rush to Strike Deal, Democrats are Left Fuming," *The Washington Post*, July 21,www.washingtonpost.com/politics/obama-gop-leaders-said-to-discuss-new-debt-plan/2011/07/21/gIQAT81BSI_story.html?hpid=z1.

Morgenson, Gretchen and Joshua Rosner. 2011. *Reckless Endangerment: How Outsized Ambition, Greed, and Corruption Led to Economic Armageddon*. New York: Times Books.

Morone, James A. 1990. *The Democratic Wish: Popular Participation and the Limits of American Government*. New York: Basic Books.

Morris, Tim. 2009. "William Jefferson Verdict: Guilty on 11 of 16 Counts," *The Times-Picayune*, August 5, www.nola.com/news/index.ssf/2009/08/william_jefferson_verdict_guil.html.

MSNBC. 2011. "Morning Joe," July 22, www.msnbc.msn.com/id/3036789//vp/43852506#43852506.

Muirhead, Russell. 2006. "A Defense of Party Spirit," *Perspectives on Politics* 4: 713–27.

National Conference of State Legislatures. n.d. "2011 NCSL Legislator CompensationTable,"www.ncsl.org/legislatures-elections/legisdata/2011-ncsl-legislator-compensation-table.aspx.

Neely, Mark E., Jr. 2002. *The Union Divided: Party Conflict in the Civil War North*. Cambridge, MA: Harvard University Press.

Neuman, W. Russell, George E. Marcus, Ann N. Crigler, and Michael MacKuen. 2007. "Theorizing Affect's Effects," in *The Affect Effect: Dynamics of Emotion in Political Thinking and Behavior*, eds. W. Russel Neuman, George E. Marcus, Ann N. Crigler, and Michael MacKuen. Chicago: University of Chicago Press, pp. 1–20.

Newcomb, Tim. 2011. "QUOTE: NFL Teaches Washington How It's Done," NewsFeed, *Time*, July 27, http://newsfeed.time.com/2011/07/27/quote-nfl-teaches-washington-how-its-done/.

Newport, Frank. 2005. "Americans Want Leaders to Pay Attention to Public Opinion," Gallup.com, October 12, www.gallup.com/poll/19138/americans-want-leaders-pay-attention-public-opinion.aspx.

Newport, Frank and Lydia Saad. 2011. "American Oppose Cuts in Education, Social Security, Defense," Gallup, January 26, www.gallup.com/poll/145790/americans-oppose-cuts-education-social-security-defense.aspx.

Norris, Pippa, ed. 1999. *Critical Citizens: Global Support for Democratic Governance*. New York: Oxford University Press.

Norris, Pippa. 2011. *Democratic Deficit: Critical Citizens Revisited*. New York: Cambridge University Press.

Obama, Barack. 2004. "Keynote Address to the Democratic National Convention," July 27, www.washingtonpost.com/wp-dyn/articles/A19751-2004Jul27.html.

Ober, Josiah. 1989. *Mass and Elite in Democratic Athens: Rhetoric, Ideology, and the Power of the People*. Princeton: Princeton University Press.

Office of the Clerk. n.d. "Women in Congress: Historical Data – 112th Congress, 2011–2013," U.S. House of Representatives, http://womenincongress.house.gov/historical-data/representatives-senators-by-congress.html?congress=112.

Page, Benjamin I. and Robert Y. Shapiro. 1992. *The Rational Public: Fifty Years of Trends in Americans' Policy Preferences*. Chicago: University of Chicago Press.

Parker, Glenn R. 1974. *Political Beliefs about the Structure of Government: Congress and the Presidency*. Beverly Hills: Sage.

Patterson, Samuel C., Ronald D. Hedlund, and G. Robert Boynton. 1975. *Representatives and Represented: Bases of Public Support for the American Legislatures*. New York: John Wiley & Sons.

Patterson, Thomas E. 1993. *Out of Order*. New York: Knopf.

Patterson, Thomas E. 2000. "Doing Well and Doing Good: How Soft News and Critical Journalism Are Shrinking the News Audience and Weakening Democracy – And What News Outlets Can Do About It," The Joan Shorenstein Center on the Press, Politics and Public Policy, Harvard Kennedy School, www.hks.harvard.edu/presspol/publications/reports/soft_news_and_ critical_journalism_2000.pdf.

Pear, Robert. 2012. "Insider Trading Ban for Lawmakers Clears Congress," *New York Times*, March 22, www.nytimes.com/2012/03/23/us/politics/insider-trading-ban-for-lawmakers-clears-congress.html.

Pecquet, Julian. 2011. "Liberal Dem Lawmaker Vows to Reject GOP, White Debt Deal," *The Hill*, July 31, http://thehill.com/homenews/house/ 174593-liberal-dem-vows-to-reject-white-house-gop-deal-.

Pestana, Carla Gardina and Sharon V. Salinger, eds. 1999. *Inequality in Early America*. Hanover: University Press of New England.

Peterson, Russell L. 2008. *Strange Bedfellows: How Late-Night Comedy Turns Democracy into a Joke*. New Brunswick: Rutgers University Press.

Pew Research Center. 2010. "Millennials: Confident. Connected. Open to Change," February, http://pewsocialtrends.org/files/2010/10/millennials-confident-connected-open-to-change.pdf.

Pew Research Center for the People & the Press. 2007. "Broad Support for Political Compromise in Washington; But Many Are Hesitant to Yield on Contentious Issues," January 22, http://people-press.org/2007/01/22/broad-support-for-political-compromise-in-washington/.

Pew Research Center for the People & the Press. 2010. "Little Compromise on Compromising," September 20, http://pewresearch.org/pubs/1735/ political-compromise-unpopular-neither-party-favored-on-economy-four-in-ten-say-cutting-tax-cuts-for-wealthy-hurts-economy.

Pew Research Center for the People & the Press. 2011. "Public Wants Debt Ceiling Compromise, Expects a Deal Before Deadline," July 26, http:// pewresearch.org/pubs/2071/debt-limit-ceiling-tea-party-compromise-deficit-reduction.

Pew Research Center for the People & the Press. 2011. "Public Sees Budget Negotiations as 'Ridiculous,' 'Disgusting,' 'Stupid,'" August 1, http:// pewresearch.org/pubs/2078/debt-ceiling-limits-budget-deficit-tea-party-republicans-obama-democrats-republicans-ridiculous.

Pharr, Susan J. and Robert D. Putnam, eds. 2000. *Disaffected Democracies: What's Troubling the Trilateral Countries?* Princeton: Princeton University Press.

Pitkin, Hanna Fenichel. 1967. *The Concept of Representation*. Berkeley: University of California Press.

Politi, James. 2011. "US Banks Warn Obama on Soaring Debt," *Financial Times*, April 27, www.cnbc.com/id/42775820/US_Banks_Warn_Obama_on_ Soaring_Debt.

Pollingreport.com. 2010. "Congress: Misc. Questions," McClatchy-Marist Poll, November 15–18, www.pollingreport.com/congress.htm.

Pomper, Gerald. 1967. " 'If Elected, I Promise': American Party Platforms," *Midwest Journal of Political Science* 11: 318–52.

Popkin, Samuel L. 1994. *The Reasoning Voter: Communication and Persuasion in Presidential Campaigns*, 2nd ed. Chicago: University of Chicago Press.

Popofsky, Jodi Perlmuth. 2012. "Is It Time to Rewrite the Constitution?" *New York Times*, Letters, June 4, www.nytimes.com/2012/06/05/opinion/is-it-time-to-rewrite-the-constitution.html.

Popper, Karl. 1959 [2002]. *The Logic of Scientific Discovery*. New York: Routledge.

Posner, Richard A. 2001. *Breaking the Deadlock: The 2000 Election, the Constitution, and the Courts*. Princeton: Princeton University Press.

Prior, Markus. 2003. "Any Good News in Soft News? The Impact of Soft News Preference on Political Knowledge," *Political Communication* 20: 149–71.

Prothro, James W. and Charles M. Grigg. 1960. "Fundamental Principles of Democracy: Bases of Agreement and Disagreement," *The Journal of Politics* 22: 276–94.

Public Integrity Section. n.d. "Report to Congress on the Activities and Operations of the Public Integrity Section for 2010," U.S. Department of Justice, www.justice.gov/criminal/pin/docs/arpt-2010.pdf.

Putnam, Robert D. 2000. *Bowling Alone: The Collapse and Revival of American Community*. New York: Simon & Schuster.

Putnam, Robert D., Susan J. Pharr, and Russell J. Dalton. 2000. "Introduction: What's Troubling the Trilateral Democracies," in *Disaffected Democracies: What's Troubling the Trilateral Countries?*, eds. Susan J. Pharr and Robert D. Putnam. Princeton: Princeton University Press, pp. 3–27.

Puzzanghera, Jim. 2011. "Top Wall Street CEOs Warn Obama, Congress on Debt Ceiling," Money & Company blog, *Los Angeles Times*, July 28, http://latimesblogs.latimes.com/money_co/2011/07/top-wall-street-ceos-warn-obama-congress-on-debt-ceiling.html.

Quirk, Paul J. 2009. "Politicians Do Pander: Mass Opinion, Polarization, and Law Making," *The Forum* 7 (1), www.bepress.com/forum/vol7/iss4/art10.

Quirk, Paul J. 2011. "Polarized Populism: Masses, Elites, and Partisan Conflict," *The Forum* 9 (5), www.bepress.com/forum/vol9/iss1/art5.

Rae, Nicol C. 2007. "Be Careful What You Wish For: The Rise of Responsible Parties in American National Politics," *Annual Review of Political Science* 10: 169–91.

Raymond, Allen with Ian Spiegelman. 2008. *How to Rig an Election: Confessions of a Republican Operative*. New York: Simon & Schuster.

Reagan, Ronald. 1981. "Inaugural Address," The American Presidency Project, www.presidency.ucsb.edu/ws/index.php?pid=43130#axzz1wH1D7yhc.

Reed, John T. 2011. "How the Tea Party Caucus Members Voted on Raising the Debt Ceiling," Johntreed.com, August 10, http://johntreed.com/headline/2011/08/10/how-the-tea-party-caucus-members-voted-on-raising-the-debt-ceiling/.

Richards, Barry. 2004. "The Emotional Deficit in Political Communication," *Political Communication* 21: 339–52.

Ringquist, Evan J. and Carl Dasse. 2004. "Lies, Damned Lies, and Campaign Promises? Environmental Legislation in the 105th Congress," *Social Science Quarterly* 85: 400–19.

Riordon, William L. 1905 [1963]. *Plunkitt of Tammany Hall*. New York: E. P. Dutton & Co.

Roscoe, Douglas D. and Shannon Jenkins. 2005. "A Meta-Analysis of Campaign Contributions' Impact on Roll Call Voting," *Social Science Quarterly* 86: 52–68.

Rosenblum, Nancy L. 2008. *On the Side of the Angels: An Appreciation of Parties and Partisanship*. Princeton: Princeton University Press.

Runciman, David. 2008. *Political Hypocrisy: The Mask of Power, From Hobbes to Orwell and Beyond*. Princeton: Princeton University Press.

Sabato, Larry J. and Glenn R. Simpson. 1996. *Dirty Little Secrets: The Persistence of Corruption in American Politics*. New York: Times Books.

Safire, William. 2008. *Safire's Political Dictionary*, updated and expanded ed. New York: Oxford University Press.

Schattschneider, E. E. 1942. *Party Government*. New York: Rinehart & Company.

Schlesinger, Arthur M. 1955. "Political Mobs and the American Revolution, 1765–1776," *Proceedings of the American Philosophical Society* 99: 244–50.

Schlesinger, Joseph A. 1966. *Ambition and Politics: Political Careers in the United States*. Chicago: Rand McNally & Company.

Schudson, Michael. 1998. *The Good Citizen: A History of American Civic Life*. New York: Martin Kessler Books.

Schultz, Connie. 2007. *. . . and His Lovely Wife: A Memoir from the Woman Beside the Man*. New York: Random House.

Schweizer, Peter. 2011. *Throw Them All Out: How Politicians and Their Friends Get Rich Off Insider Stock Tips, Land Deals, and Cronyism That Would Send the Rest of Us To Prison*. New York: Houghton Mifflin Harcourt.

Shapiro, Robert Y. and Lawrence Jacobs. 2010. "Simulating Representation: Elite Mobilization and Political Power in Health Care Reform," *The Forum* 8 (9), www.bepress.com/forum/vol8/iss1/art4.

Shaw, Donny. 2011. "The Republicans Haven't Always Been Against Raising the Debt Ceiling," OpenCongress Blog, OpenCongress.org, January 28, www.opencongress.org/articles/view/1500-The-Republicans-Haven-t-Always-Been-Against-Raising-the-Debt-Ceiling.

Shaw, Donny. 2011. "A Brief History of Debt Limit Votes in the House," OpenCongress Blog, OpenCongress.org, May 20, www.opencongress.org/articles/view/2295-A-Brief-History-of-Debt-Limit-Votes-in-the-House.

Sheingate, Adam. 2009. "Why Can't Americans See the State?" *The Forum* 7 (4), Article 1, www.bepress.com/forum/vol7/iss4/art1.

Sigelman, Lee, Carol K. Sigelman, and Barbara J. Walkosz. 1992. "The Public and the Paradox of Leadership: An Experimental Analysis," *American Journal of Political Science* 36: 366–85.

Silver, Nate. 2011. "G.O.P.'s No-Tax Stance Is Outside Political Mainstream," FiveThirtyEight, *New York Times*, July 13, http://fivethirtyeight.blogs.nytimes.com/2011/07/13/house-republicans-no-tax-stance-far-outside-political-mainstream/.

Silverman, Craig. 2011. "Conferences Raise Unanswered Questions about Fact Checking," Poynter.org, December 28, www.poynter.org/latest-news/regret-the-error/157031/conferences-raise-unanswered-questions-about-fact-checking/.

Simonton, Dean Keith. 1993. "Putting the Best Leaders in the White House: Personality, Policy, and Performance," *Political Psychology* 14: 537–48.

Skocpol, Theda and Vanessa Williamson. 2012. *The Tea Party and the Remaking of Republican Conservatism.* New York: Oxford University Press.

Sloterdijk, Peter. 1987. *Critique of Cynical Reason.* Minneapolis: University of Minnesota Press.

Smith, Mark A. 2000. *American Business and Political Power: Public Opinion, Elections, and Democracy.* Chicago: University of Chicago Press.

Smith, Mark A. 2007. *The Right Talk: How Conservatives Transformed the Great Society into the Economic Society.* Princeton: Princeton University Press.

Smith, Paul H. 1968. "The American Loyalists: Notes on Their Organization and Numerical Strength," *The William and Mary Quarterly* 25: 259–77.

Smith, Rogers M. 1993. "Beyond Tocqueville, Myrdal, and Hartz: The Multiple Traditions in America," *American Political Science Review* 87: 549–66.

Smith, Steven S. 2007. *Party Influence in Congress.* New York: Cambridge University Press.

Sniderman, Paul M. 1975. *Personality and Democratic Politics.* Berkeley: University of California Press.

Sonmez, Felicia. 2011. "Labor, Liberal Groups Mobilizing Against White House on Debt Deal," 2chambers, *The Washington Post*, July 22, www.washingtonpost.com/blogs/2chambers/post/labor-liberal-groups-mobilizing-against-white-house-on-debt-deal/2011/07/22/gIQAQ3D3TI_blog.html.

Stanley, Harold W. and Richard G. Niemi. 2009. *Vital Statistics on American Politics 2009–2010.* Washington, DC: CQ Press, http://library.cqpress.com/vsap/vsap09_tab5-9.

Stoloff, David M. 1999. "'Boxers or Briefs' Girl Recalls Fleeting Fame; Question to President Now Seems Tame," *The Washington Times*, January 17.

Stromquist, Shelton. 2006. *Reinventing "The People": The Progressive Movement, The Class Problem, and the Origins of Modern Liberalism.* Urbana: University of Illinois Press.

Sulkin, Tracy. 2009. "Campaign Appeals and Legislative Action," *The Journal of Politics* 71: 1093–108.

Sulkin, Tracy. 2011. *The Legislative Legacy of Congressional Campaigns.* New York: Cambridge University Press.

Sulkin, Tracy and Nathaniel Swigger. 2008. "Is There Truth in Advertising? Campaign Ad Images as Signals about Legislative Behavior," *The Journal of Politics* 70: 232–44.

Sullivan, John L., John H. Aldrich, Eugene Borgida, and Wendy Rahn. 1990. "Candidate Appraisal and Human Nature: Man and Superman in the 1984 Election," *Political Psychology* 11: 459–84.

Sullivan, Sean. 2011. "Club Hitting Lugar, Hatch Over Debt Limit," Hotline on Call, *National Journal*, July 11, http://hotlineoncall.nationaljournal.com/archives/2011/07/club-hitting-lu.php.

Sunstein, Cass R. 2007. "Ideological Amplification," *Constellations* 14: 273–9.

Sunstein, Cass R. 2009. *Republic.com 2.0.* Princeton: Princeton University Press.

Sunstein, Cass R. 2009. *Going to Extremes: How Like Minds Unite and Divide.* New York: Oxford University Press.

Surowiecki, James. 2004. *The Wisdom of Crowds: Why the Many Are Smarter than the Few and How Collective Wisdom Shapes Business, Economies, Societies, and Nations.* New York: Doubleday.

Sussman, Glen and Byron W. Daynes. 2000. "Party Promises and Presidential Performance: Social Policies of the Modern Presidents, FDR-Clinton," *Southeastern Political Review* 28: 111–30.

Taber, Charles S. and Milton Lodge. 2006. "Motivated Skepticism in the Evaluation of Political Beliefs," *American Journal of Political Science* 50: 755–69.

Tetlock, Philip E. 1981. "Pre- to Postelection Shifts in Presidential Rhetoric: Impression Management or Cognitive Adjustment?" *Journal of Personality and Social Psychology* 41: 207–12.

Tocqueville, Alexis de. 1835 [2000]. *Democracy in America.* Translated and edited by Harvey C. Mansfield and Delba Winthrop. Chicago: University of Chicago Press.

Transparency International. 2011. "Corruption Perceptions Index 2011," http://cpi.transparency.org/cpi2011/results/.

Troy, Gil. 1991. *See How They Ran: The Changing Role of the Presidential Candidate.* New York: The Free Press.

Tyler, Tom R. 2006. *Why People Obey the Law.* Princeton: Princeton University Press.

Urbinati, Nadia. 2006. *Representative Democracy: Principles and Genealogy.* Chicago: University of Chicago Press.

Urbinati, Nadia and Mark E. Warren. 2008. "The Concept of Representation in Contemporary Democratic Theory," *Annual Review of Political Science* 11: 387–412.

U.S. Census Bureau. 1995. *1992 Census of Governments, Volume 1: Government Organization, Number 2: Popularly Elected Officials.* GC92(1)-2.

U.S. Census Bureau. 2002. *2002 Census of Governments, Volume 1, Number 1, Government Organization.* GC02(1)-1.

Uziel, Liad. 2010. "Rethinking Social Desirability Scales: From Impression Management to Interpersonally Oriented Self-Control," *Perspectives on Psychological Science* 5: 243–62.

Valentino, Nicholas A., Thomas A. Buhr, and Matthew N. Beckmann. 2001. "When the Frame is the Game: Revisiting the Impact of 'Strategic' Campaign Coverage on Citizens' Information Retention," *Journalism & Mass Communication Quarterly* 78: 93–112.

VoteView.com. 2011. "Party Polarization: 1879–2010," http://voteview.com/Polarized_America.htm.

Vreese, Clause H. de and Matthijs Elenbaas. 2008. "Media in the Game of Politics: Effects of Strategic Metacoverage on Political Cynicism," *The International Journal of Press/Politics* 13: 285–309.

Vrij, Aldert. 2008. *Detecting Lies and Deceit: Pitfalls and Opportunities*, 2nd ed. West Sussex: John Wiley and Sons.

Waldron, Jeremy. 2011. "What to Tell the Axe-Man," *London Review of Books*, January 6, www.lrb.co.uk/v33/n01/jeremy-waldron/what-to-tell-the-axe-man.

Walshe, Shush. 2011. "Both the Left and Right Sour on Debt Deal," The Note, ABC News, August 1, http://abcnews.go.com/blogs/politics/2011/08/both-the-left-and-right-sour-on-debt-deal/.

Ware, Alan. 2002. *The American Direct Primary: Party Institutionalization and Transformation in the North*. New York: Cambridge University Press.

Warren, Mark E., ed. 1999. *Democracy & Trust*. New York: Cambridge University Press.

Warren, Mark E. 1999. "Democratic Theory and Trust," in *Democracy & Trust*, ed. Mark E. Warren. New York: Cambridge University Press, pp. 310–45.

Washington, George. 1796. "Farewell Address," The Avalon Project, http://avalon.law.yale.edu/18th_century/washing.asp.

The Washington Post. 2010. "Children of Politicians and Their Brushes with the Law," August 5, www.washingtonpost.com/wp-dyn/content/gallery/2010/08/05/GA2010080503952.html.

White, Jonathan and Lea Ypi. 2011. "On Partisan Political Justification," *American Political Science Review* 105: 381–96.

White, Joseph B.. 2010. "Pickup Truck Politics in Massachusetts Senate Race," Washington Wire, *The Wall Street Journal*, January 19, http://blogs.wsj.com/washwire/2010/01/19/pickup-truck-politics-in-massachusetts-senate-race/.

Wikipedia. n.d. "List of Federal Political Sex Scandals in the United States," http://en.wikipedia.org/wiki/List_of_federal_political_sex_scandals_in_the_United_States#cite_ref-42.

Wikiquote. n.d. "Talk:Otto von Bismarck," http://en.wikiquote.org/wiki/Talk:Otto_von_Bismarck.

Wilcox, Stanley. 1942. "The Scope of Early Rhetorical Instruction," *Harvard Studies in Classical Philology* 53: 121–55.

Wilentz, Sean. 2011. "The Mirage: The Long and Tragical History of Post-Partisanship, from Washington to Obama," *The New Republic*, November 17.

Williams, Walter. 2003. *Reaganism and the Death of Representative Democracy.* Washington, DC: Georgetown University Press.

Wilson, James Q. 1966. *The Amateur Democrat: Club Politics in Three Cities.* Chicago: University of Chicago Press.

Winter, David G. 2003. "Personality and Political Behavior," in *Oxford Handbook of Political Psychology,* eds. David O. Sears, Leonie Huddy, and Robert Jervis. New York: Oxford University Press, pp. 110–45.

Witcover, Jules. 2003. *Party of the People: A History of the Democrats.* New York: Random House.

Wood, Gordon S. 1993. *The Radicalism of the American Revolution.* New York: Vintage Books.

Woodruff, Paul. 2005. *First Democracy: The Challenge of an Ancient Idea.* New York: Oxford University Press.

Yadron, Danny. 2011. "Tea Party Warns GOP Leaders on Debt Limit Vote," Washington Wire blog, *The Wall Street Journal,* May 9, http://blogs.wsj.com/washwire/2011/05/09/tea-party-warns-gop-leaders-on-debt-limit-vote/.

Yoffe, Emily. 2012. "You Are Not the Speaker," *Slate.com,* March 20, www.slate.com/articles/news_and_politics/politics/2012/03/newt_gingrich_speaker_of_the_house_politicians_who_cling_to_their_old_titles_are_pretentious_incorrect_and_un_american_.html.

Yunis, Harvey. 1996. *Taming Democracy: Models of Political Rhetoric in Classical Athens.* Ithaca: Cornell University Press.

Zarefsky, David. 1990. *Lincoln, Douglas, and Slavery: In the Crucible of Public Debate.* Chicago: University of Chicago Press.

Zarefsky, David. 1992. "Spectator Politics and the Revival of Public Argument," *Communication Monographs* 59: 411–14.

Index

Note: Page numbers in *italics* are for tables, those in **bold** are for figures.